D0920113

The Snail Darter Case

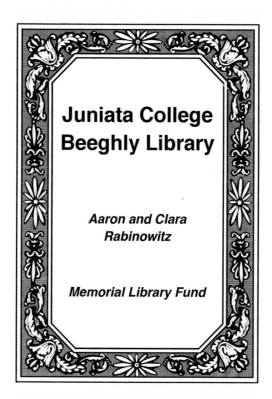

LANDMARK LAW CASES

AMERICAN SOCIETY

Peter Charles Hoffer

N. E. H. Hull

Series Editors

For a complete list of titles in the series go to www.kansaspress.ku.edu

KENNETH M. MURCHISON

The Snail Darter Case

TVA versus the Endangered Species Act

UNIVERSITY PRESS OF KANSAS

Published by the University Press of Kansas (Lawrence, Kansas 66045), which was
organized by the Kansas Board of Regents and is operated and funded by Emporia
State University, Fort Hays State University, Kansas State University, Pittsburg State
University, the University of Kansas, and Wichita State University

Library of Congress Cataloging-in-Publication Data

Murchison, Kenneth M.

The Snail Darter case : TVA versus the Endangered Species Act /
Kenneth M. Murchison.

p. cm. — (Landmark law cases & American society)

Includes bibliographical references and index.

ISBN-13: 978-0-7006-1504-9 (cloth : alk. paper)

ISBN-13: 978-0-7006-1505-6 (pbk. : alk. paper)

1. Endangered species — Law and legislation — United States — Cases.   2.
Wildlife conservation — Law and legislation — United States — Cases.   3.
Endangered species — Government policy — United States.   4. Environmental
law — United States.   5. United States. Endangered Species Act of 1973.
6. United States. National Environmental Policy Act of 1969.   7.
Tennessee Valley Authority.   8. Tellico Dam (Tenn.)   1. Title.

KF5640.A7M87   2007

346.7304'69522 — DC22

2006034360

British Library Cataloguing-in-Publication Data is available.

Printed in the United States of America

10 9 8 7 6 5 4 3 2 1

The paper used in this publication meets the minimum requirements of the
American National Standard for Permanence of Paper for Printed Library Materials
Z39.48-1992.

CONTENTS

In 1978, a very small endangered species of fish found itself swimming in a pond filled with very big fish. The snail darter's fate in the Little Tennessee River had become the center of a decade of litigation. There were very big fish in the same waters. A huge and unregulated Tennessee Valley Authority, accustomed to its place at the top of the waterway's food chain, demanded that it be permitted to place the fifteenth dam on the Little Tennessee River system. Set up forty years earlier by the federal government to provide rural electrification, clean water, and flood protection, it had long since become privatized and now looked for new prey — gobbling up farmland and Indian sites to promote recreational facilities for developers.

The farmers and the Native Americans swam in the pond long before the TVA arrived. They filed lawsuits to save their homes and ancestral burial places. On the verge of losing, they found a new ally. A zoologist serving as an expert witness for the opponents of the dam went snorkeling in the waters one day and identified in them a new and rare species of perch that he named the snail darter. Environmentalists well schooled in American politics as well as law had pushed the Endangered Species Act through Congress, and with that came hope for all the little fish.

The struggle still seemed uneven. The TVA was a giant in the public relations field and had many friends in the business community and in Congress. Local historical groups and individual farmers were swallowed whole by the TVA. Congress would authorize $100 million to pay off the local owners and construct the dam. A challenge in the courts looked hopeless, given the precedents. The TVA had long since vindicated its power to take by eminent domain from private owners, paying them the market price, whether or not they wanted to move.

But the courts and Congress were rethinking the nonmarket values of land, including the impact on the environment of damming rivers and draining marshes. Ecologists' studies changed how governments thought about natural resources and microenvironments, about the benefit and loss of any government program, including the TVA's dam building. By the 1970s, federal law required environmental impact studies prior to new construction and gave to federal judges the authority to enjoin projects that might lead to the extinction of endangered species. The waters of this pond were becoming cloudier, and the TVA was having trouble seeking out its prey. If the snail darter's waters constituted a "critical habitat," they, and their fellow Little Tennessee dwellers, would be safe.

Kenneth Murchison has told this story far better than we can, with a sensitivity to all its nuances. With clarity and fair-mindedness, he explains how the TVA grew, how the environmental legislation works, and how administrative agencies, courts, and committees of Congress have done their parts. Step by step he translates very technical legal and scientific arguments into easy-to-understand texts and adds anecdotal touches to humanize the account. He lays out the injunctive power of judges and how judges try to balance interests, costs, and anticipated gains in framing their commands to the parties, and how one federal district court judge struggled with the case. He does not neglect the parallel story in Congress, for while the courts heard testimony, Congress was holding hearings of its own. Indeed, the story of the snail darter and the Tellico Dam provides a superb example of the interconnection of legislation and judicial action.

There is a hero, too, an academic one, Zygmunt Plater, a law professor whose wisdom and doggedness grace the middle portions of the book. So often law professors seem to be part of the system, teaching tactics in clinical courses or advocacy or dry rules, that one forgets how much a law professor can do to change law. Plater, like Murchison, understood that the litigation was about more than a rare species of fish. It was about how we govern ourselves, about who speaks for the powerless, and what law can do to save us from our own worst instincts. Plater would lose in the district court, win in the circuit court of appeals, and argue the case before the U.S. Supreme Court.

Murchison takes us through the briefs and oral argument, into the conference of the Court, then to the justices' chambers using newly available primary sources. He allows us to think along with the members of the Court, seeing the politics behind the law and the way that law spurred political responses outside the courtroom. To Chief Justice Warren Burger, the language of the Endangered Species Act was plain as day. The U.S. Fish and Wildlife Service played a key role, placing the new species on the endangered list and reporting that the Little Tennessee was their only habitat. Though members of the High

Court would find some wiggle room in the statute, and one justice would find no grounds for injunctive relief at all, the Court gave a temporary reprieve to the tiny perch. But this was not the end of its tale.

In Congress, supporters of the dam faced the General Accounting Office's review of the TVA's expenditures and continued environmental pressure. Murchison's narrative gains speed as it covers these concluding maneuvers. Again, judicial decisions and legislative enactments crisscrossed, as the story wound to its close. The result was a combination of administrative, judicial, and legislative oversight — in short, the separation of powers working in characteristic American fashion.

In the end, the Indians lost their burial sites, the farmers lost their holdings, the fishermen lost their trout streams, and the TVA never realized the economic gains it promised. Only the upscale developers won. They bought the lakeside properties and resold plots to wealthy buyers. In effect, the TVA had transferred the land from its poor owners to rich buyers.

This is a cautionary tale told by a master of its detail and its implications.

ACKNOWLEDGMENTS

Colleagues at the Paul M. Hebert Law Center of Louisiana State University helped with this project in various ways. Chancellor John C. Costonis offered research support in each of the summers when I was working on the manuscript. An invitation from Jim Bowers to share my research at a faculty workshop prompted me to begin articulating the ideas that now form the concluding chapter. During and after the presentation, a number of colleagues provided helpful critiques of my analysis. The comments of Paul Baier, Bill Corbett, Glenn Morris, Chris Pietruszkiewicz, and Catherine Rogers were particularly useful as I refined my initial thoughts.

The library staff at the LSU Law Center was always helpful in locating documents and books not available in the law center collection. The aid of Charlene Cain, initially the government services librarian and later the head of access services, was particularly valuable. Both my research assistants and I were repeatedly amazed with how quickly she could locate the most obscure government documents.

My research assistants and secretary also provided support without which the project would never have been completed. Jennifer Jaubert was my research assistant for most of the time I was working on the manuscript, and she was extremely helpful in locating and reviewing sources. When Jennifer graduated, Nicole Viscomi took her place and assisted me in bringing the project to completion. In addition to typing the manuscript, my secretary, Susan Sarnataro, provided me with a very careful final review of the text.

Government employees at the Department of the Interior and the National Archives also aided me in locating materials in government files. James Willack, a fisheries biologist in the Cookeville, Tennessee, office of the Fish and Wildlife Service, and Arlene Rogers, an archives specialist at the National Archives facility in Morrow, Georgia, were especially helpful.

Extended discussions with several individuals who were involved in the Tellico Dam litigation and its aftermath enriched my research. Hank Hill, David Etnier, Peter Alliman, William R. Willis, and Kenneth Penegar all provided valuable insights in interviews during 2004 and 2005. Zygmunt Plater was particularly gracious. Even though he is writing his own book on the snail darter case, he provided me with numerous documents from his personal files, and he regularly answered my questions via telephone or e-mail.

Various friends who teach environmental law and natural resources law at other law schools agreed to read portions of the manuscript. Michael Blumm, Oliver Houck, Dale Goble, and J. B. Ruhl all provided helpful suggestions and corrections.

I am also grateful to the University Press of Kansas and to the series editors, Peter Charles Hoffer and N. E. H. Hull, for supporting this project. Michael Briggs, the Editor in Chief at the Press, was supportive of my proposal from the beginning and patient when completion of the manuscript took several months longer than I originally projected.

Ultimately, however, I owe my greatest debt to my family. My son, Julian, my daughter, Kathryn, and my daughter-in-law, Sandra, continued to listen even when I said more about my research than they wanted to hear. My greatest thanks for this project, however, goes to Eloise, my partner for nearly thirty-seven years. Her support has made it possible for me to complete this project and all the work of my adult life.

The Snail Darter Case

The Supreme Court Decision

On June 18, 1978, the U.S. Supreme Court announced its decision in *TVA v. Hill.* The case was the Supreme Court's first interpretation of the Endangered Species Act of 1973, and it produced sharp divisions on and off the Court. By a 6-to-3 vote, the Court affirmed an injunction issued by the Sixth Circuit. The injunction forbade the Tennessee Valley Authority (TVA) from completing and operating the Tellico Dam on the Little Tennessee River because the dam would eliminate the only known habitat of the snail darter, a three-inch member of the perch family.

The Supreme Court divided three ways in the snail darter case. Writing for the majority, Chief Justice Burger concluded that completion of the dam would violate the Endangered Species Act and that an injunction was required to prevent the violation. Dissenters challenged the chief justice on both grounds. Writing for himself and Justice Blackmun, Justice Powell argued that completing the dam would not violate the Endangered Species Act. Justice Rehnquist contended that the district court had discretion regarding whether it should issue an injunction.

According to Chief Justice Burger's majority opinion, the case was a simple one: The Court had to follow the text of the statute even when the law produced results that the judges might regard as unwise. Completing the Tellico Dam would violate the Endangered Species Act, and continued congressional appropriations for the dam after passage of the act did not create an implied exception to the substantive statute. Section 7 of the Endangered Species Act prohibited the TVA from taking any action that would jeopardize the existence of an endangered species or destroy its critical habitat, and the evidence supported the trial court's findings that completing the Tellico Dam would jeopardize the snail darter and destroy its critical habitat. Moreover, respect for the separation of powers established by the Constitution required an injunction prohibiting completion of the dam. Congress had established an absolute prohibition on federal action that jeopardized an endangered species or threatened its critical habitat, and the courts lacked the authority to create an exception to the statutory provision.

Justice Powell insisted that a rule of reasonableness should guide statutory interpretation. He found the text of the statute less clear than did the majority. The "actions" covered by the act, he argued, did not encompass "all actions that an agency can ever take, but rather actions that the agency is *deciding whether* to authorize, to fund, or to carry out." In his view, this language did not compel the absolute prohibition embraced by the majority; he thought a more reasonable interpretation of the statutory text was to limit the act's coverage to "prospective actions; i.e., actions with respect to which the agency has reasonable decisionmaking alternatives still available."

Justice Rehnquist's dissent focused on the remedy granted by the district court. Although he was "far less convinced than is the Court that the Endangered Species Act . . . was intended to prohibit completion of the dam," he found it unnecessary to resolve that issue. As he interpreted the act, it did not require an injunction even if Section 7 applied to the Tellico Dam. The Endangered Species Act, he argued, only authorized injunctive relief; it did not mandate an injunction for every violation of its provisions. Instead, the act committed the decision of whether an injunction should be granted to the discretion of the district court, and the district judge had not abused his discretion in refusing to grant an injunction in the Tellico Dam case.

Legal analyses of the Supreme Court decision have generally characterized it as a conflict of techniques of interpretation. They suggest that the case required a choice between literalism and purposive interpretation when the Court faced a decision that produced undesirable results. Should a court follow the words of the statute even if it forced the government to waste $100 million to save a small fish with no known economic value? Or should the court create an exception to avoid an undesirable result while preserving the underlying statutory purposes? A leading casebook introducing law students to the Anglo-American legal system presents the case as an illustration of this dilemma of statutory construction and concludes its description with a sentence noting: "After the [Supreme Court] decision was handed down, Congress overturned it and ordered completion of the dam." The legal philosopher Ronald Dworkin offers an extended analysis of the case in which he implicitly criticizes the literalism of Chief Justice Burger's majority opinion and praises Justice Powell's dissent as the best construction of the statute.

The Supreme Court decision inspired more than professional debate. The snail darter decision was politically divisive because it quickly became an important symbol in an increasingly polarized debate over federal environmental law. Environmental activists lauded the decision and the statute on which it was based, while their ideological opponents criticized the Supreme Court decision and the failure to close the dam as prime examples of environmental extremism.

Environmental activists praised the Supreme Court decision in part because they liked the result it produced. By delaying the closing of the Tellico Dam, it stopped (at least temporarily) the flooding of the last thirty-three miles of the Little Tennessee River. Equally important for the environmentalists was the Court's willingness to follow the literal wording of one of the most stringent federal environmental statutes. Advocates of increased protection for natural resources regularly praised the decision because it established Section 7 as one of the few legal weapons that can actually stop governmental destruction of the environment. In an Internet survey in 2001, environmental law professors rated the snail darter decision as one of the Supreme Court's most important environmental law decisions.

Environmentalists were pleased with each of the major legal principles that guided the Supreme Court in *TVA v. Hill.* First, the Court confirmed that Section 7 of the Endangered Species Act was a strong substantive provision that could halt major federal projects and that its prohibitions would be applied without exceptions. Second, the case required that the Court issue an injunction to halt violations regardless of the stage of the project. Third, the Court ruled that the subsequent appropriation acts could not amend the substantive provisions of the Endangered Species Act by implication.

Conservative critics lambasted the Supreme Court decision. At one level, the conservative criticism of the Supreme Court decision and the completion of the dam is surprising because the dam opponents were attempting to protect rights of private property and to prevent a wasteful government expenditure. On the other hand, the conservative opposition is more understandable when seen as part of the growing conservative opposition to increasingly strict federal environmental laws.

The conservative critics viewed both the outcome of the litigation and the Supreme Court's approach as the triumph of environmental ideology over common sense. The Supreme Court decision, they claimed, required abandonment of a project on which the federal government had already spent $100 million; and it would cost the area much-needed economic development. The critics also charged that the Court's interpretation of the statute was overly legalistic. In their view, the Court compounded its unreasonable construction of the statutory text by limiting the district court's discretion regarding when an injunction was needed and by ignoring the appropriation acts in which Congress had indicated its desire that the projects be completed.

One of the most outspoken critics of the decisions protecting the snail darter was Ronald Reagan, who was a radio commentator and aspiring presidential candidate as the snail darter litigation was winding its way through the federal courts. In radio addresses between 1977 and 1979, Reagan made several unfavorable references to the decisions of the Sixth Circuit and the Supreme Court in the snail darter litigation. For example, a July 1977 address described the Tellico Dam as designed "to produce electricity for about 200,000 homes and I [don't] know how many industries providing jobs for people in those homes." A federal court had, Reagan noted, stopped the project for the snail darter "even though it differs only slightly from the 77 other Darters found in the rivers of Tennessee."

In fact, the snail darter case is more complicated than either the conventional legal analysis or the political debate would suggest. The Supreme Court decision was merely one part of a long struggle; it did not begin or end the fight over the Tellico Dam.

The modern battle over the Tellico Dam project began in the mid-1960s, a decade before the snail darter was discovered or Congress enacted the Endangered Species Act. Moreover, the Endangered Species Act lawsuit followed both earlier litigation under the National Environmental Policy Act and the refusal of the TVA to accept the administrative interpretation of the Endangered Species Act by the

Department of the Interior. Perhaps most important, the Supreme Court decision did not produce the final word on the Tellico Dam. Following the Supreme Court decision, Congress created a new committee authorized to grant exemptions to Section 7. The committee decided an exemption was inappropriate for the Tellico project, but supporters of the dam persuaded Congress to amend an appropriation act to include an express provision allowing the dam to be completed. In November 1979, the TVA closed the dam, and the last thirty-three miles of the Little Tennessee River became the Tellico Reservoir.

The significance of the snail darter litigation extends beyond the Tellico Dam. The case helped to define the modern role of the TVA, and it was an important chapter in the development of federal environmental law.

The dispute over the mission of the TVA began in the 1930s. Arthur E. Morgan, the first chairman of the TVA, envisioned a regional planning function for the agency, but David E. Lilienthal's competing vision to emphasize the production of electricity eventually prevailed. Until the 1950s, Congress appropriated funds to support power generation projects, but the Eisenhower administration opposed new projects. A compromise of 1959 allowed the TVA to initiate new power projects but required that they be funded with bonds guaranteed by TVA revenues, not the full faith and credit of the federal government. In the 1960s, Chairman Aubrey Wagner encouraged the TVA staff to develop a "new mission" to secure federal appropriations from the Kennedy administration. The new mission focused on projects designed to stimulate economic development, and the Tellico Dam was to be the demonstration project for the new mission. Although the TVA did complete the Tellico project, the legal and political problems the Authority encountered ultimately doomed the new mission and returned the TVA to its role as a federally owned utility.

TVA v. Hill is also an important part of the story of the emergence of federal environmental law in the 1960s and 1970s. It confirmed that the prohibitions of Section 7 of the Endangered Species Act were substantive and absolute and that those prohibitions established significant limits for government development projects. Nonetheless, the impact of the decision has not been as profound as environmental activists would have hoped. The Supreme Court has not mandated injunctions to halt all violations of other environmental statutes, and the Court has allowed express provisions in appropriation acts to amend substantive legislation.

This book tells the story of the legal challenges to the Tellico Dam. Chapter 1 describes the creation of the TVA in 1933 and the Authority's revival of the Tellico Dam in the 1960s. Chapter 2 explains how new environmental decisions and statutes changed the legal background in the 1960s and 1970s and made possible judicial challenges to the Tellico project. Chapter 3 details the first of the judicial challenges: the attempt to use the National Environmental Policy Act to stop the dam. Chapter 4 chronicles the discovery of the snail darter and the lower court proceedings under the Endangered Species Act of 1973. Chapter 5 analyzes the Supreme Court battle that produced the decision in *TVA v. Hill*, and chapter 6 explains the subsequent administrative proceedings and congressional actions that allowed the dam to be completed. Finally, chapter 7 evaluates the complicated legacy of the case and the broader effort to stop the dam.

CHAPTER I

The TVA and the Tellico Dam

Rising from sources in the mountains of southern Virginia and western North Carolina, the Holston and French Broad rivers join to form the Tennessee River just east of Knoxville. From that point, the Tennessee River winds a circuitous 650-mile route to Paducah, Kentucky. Initially, it flows in a southwesterly direction out of Tennessee and toward the Gulf of Mexico. After reaching Guntersville, Alabama, the river turns west and then north, heading back through northern Alabama and the extreme northeastern tip of Mississippi and into western Tennessee. It then enters Kentucky and joins the Ohio River at Paducah.

The biggest obstacle to navigation on the Tennessee River came near Muscle Shoals, Alabama, where the river falls 100 feet in sixteen miles. As early as 1825, Congress granted 400,000 acres to the state of Alabama to aid the state with developments on this portion of the river. On several occasions over the course of the nineteenth century, the federal government offered aid for locks and canals that would allow shallow-draft navigation of the river.

As the twentieth century dawned, the potential for hydroelectric development spawned new interest in the Muscle Shoals portion of the Tennessee River. In 1899 and 1906, Congress authorized private franchises for power generation, but neither of these efforts came to fruition. As the United States prepared to enter World War I, supporters of southern agriculture joined the War Department to support construction of a hydroelectric dam to produce electricity for nitrate plants at Muscle Shoals. The National Defense Act of 1916 authorized the president to identify sites to produce hydroelectric power for use with plants that would produce nitrates. President Woodrow Wilson selected the Muscle Shoals site, and Congress authorized construction of both the nitrate plants and the dam, which was later named the Wilson Dam.

The construction of both the dam and the nitrate plants began in 1918, but neither was completed before the war ended in November of that year. The plants first produced nitrates approximately two weeks after the armistice was signed, but the U.S. Army Corps of Engineers did not complete the Wilson Dam until 1924.

The end of World War I eliminated the national defense justification for governmental production of electricity at the Wilson Dam and led to demands that the dam be sold to private interests. The proposals for privatization began even before the dam was completed. In 1921, Henry Ford offered to pay $5 million for the dam, nitrate plants, and related properties in which the federal government had invested approximately $90 million. Later in the decade, the Alabama Power Company and others offered to purchase the facilities on terms that were similarly favorable for the private investors. However, Senator George Norris of Nebraska — a progressive Republican and an enthusiastic supporter of public ownership of electricity generation — successfully stalled the plans for privatization throughout the 1920s.

The 1920s also saw proposals for federal operation of the plants and dam. Secretary of War Newton Baker — later the attorney for private utilities who challenged the constitutionality of the TVA power generation program — made the initial proposal in 1921, and Senator Norris introduced his first bill in 1922. In 1928, the House of Representatives broadened the Norris bill passed by the Senate to establish the Muscle Shoals Corporation with authority to sell power at the highest price obtainable and fertilizer at the lowest reasonable price. President Calvin Coolidge, however, pocket vetoed the bill, and President Herbert Hoover vetoed a similar bill two years later.

The election of Franklin D. Roosevelt in 1932 gave a new boost to Senator Norris's fight to have the federal government operate the nitrate plants and electric generating facilities at Muscle Shoals. The Tennessee Valley Authority Act of 1933 created the TVA but expanded its purposes beyond operating the Wilson Dam and nitrate plants. New Deal supporters of the TVA expected it to build additional dams to provide flood control, to improve navigation, to generate electricity, and to stimulate economic development. The new law explicitly authorized the Authority to sell electric power, and it gave the TVA broad authority to construct new projects on the Tennessee River and its tributaries to generate power, improve navigation, and provide flood control. Finally, President Roosevelt insisted on adding broad economic development and regional planning goals to the TVA mission, envisioning the Authority as a mechanism to stimulate growth in an economically deprived area of the country.

Section 1 of the TVA Act created the Tennessee Valley Authority "for the purpose of maintaining and operating properties now owned by the United States in the vicinity of Muscle Shoals, Alabama." The interests to be served by the new Authority included "national defense and . . . agricultural and industrial development," as well as improving "navigation in the Tennessee River and . . . [controlling] the destructive flood waters in the Tennessee River and Mississippi River Basins." A 1935 amendment clarified that the primary purposes of all dams and reservoirs were "promoting navigation and controlling floods," but explicitly authorized the TVA to generate electricity at any of the dams it constructed.

Section 4 expanded the powers of the TVA beyond the existing properties at Muscle Shoals. Subsection l explicitly authorized the TVA to "produce, distribute, and sell electric power." Subsection j gave the Authority broad power to "construct dams, reservoirs, power houses, power structures, transmission lines, navigation projects, and incidental works in the Tennessee River and its tributaries," as well as the power "to unite the various power installations into one or more systems by transmission lines." A 1935 amendment expanded Subsection j to authorize the TVA to provide "a nine-foot channel" in the Tennessee River from Knoxville to its mouth. In using these powers, the TVA could acquire real estate by purchase or eminent domain.

The TVA Act vested the powers it conferred on the Authority in a three-member board of directors. A unique aspect of the powers given to the TVA was the board's broad power to authorize its own projects. Normally, securing federal support for a public works project is a two-step process. Congress must first authorize a project that the agency has proposed. In both the House of Representatives and the Senate, the committees with substantive jurisdiction over the agency seeking approval for the project are responsible for reviewing the authorization request. After a project has been authorized, Congress must then appropriate funds to support it. The appropriation committees in each house are responsible for reviewing requests for appropriations. Because the TVA Act authorizes the Authority to build dams and other projects anywhere on the Tennessee River or its tributaries, only the appropriation step applies to the TVA. Once the TVA Board of Directors approves a project, the Authority can begin construction if Congress appropriates funds for the project or if the TVA has another source of funding.

The TVA Act of 1933 primarily focused on the Authority's specific powers regarding power generation, navigation, flood control, and agricultural assistance. However, two provisions — Sections 22 and 23 — hinted at broader goals for regional economic development. Section 22 authorized presidential action to promote two very general purposes: "the proper use, conservation, and development of the natural resources of the Tennessee River drainage basin and of . . . adjoining territory" and the "general welfare of the citizens" of the Tennessee River basin. To accomplish these purposes, the president could "make such surveys of and general plans for [the] Tennessee basin and adjoining territory" as would assist Congress and the states in guiding and controlling development, "all for the general purpose of fostering an orderly and proper physical, economic, and social development of the area" the TVA was to serve. Section 23 directed the president to recommend legislation to Congress. It instructed the president to recommend such legislation as he deemed proper to carry out the general purposes stated in Section 22. Moreover, the recommendations were to go beyond improving flood control, navigation, power generation, proper use of marginal lands, and reforestation to serve the "especial purpose" of bringing about "the economic and social well-being of the people living in [the] river basin."

The ambiguity of the statute, especially Sections 22 and 23, contributed to conflict among the initial members of the TVA Board of Directors. Arthur E. Morgan, the first chairman of the TVA board, wanted the Authority to embrace broad goals of regional planning and economic development. The other two board members, David Lilienthal and Harcourt Morgan, favored concentrating on the more narrowly defined goals of power generation, navigation, flood control, and agricultural assistance. The board majority frustrated Arthur Morgan, who publicly charged Lilienthal and Harcourt Morgan with moral neglect and possibly criminal misconduct. In 1938, President Roosevelt resolved the conflict among the board members by removing Arthur Morgan. He then named Harcourt Morgan as the new chairman and James P. Pope as the third member of the board. Thereafter, the board focused its efforts on the more specific goals of the act, with power generation as the TVA's dominant activity.

The TVA did attempt to incorporate broader planning into one of its early dam projects. Construction on the Norris Dam on the Clinch River, a Tennessee River tributary, began in 1933; the TVA completed the project in 1936. The project displaced more than 3,000 people and included more ambitious goals than its primary purposes of power generation and flood control. For the Norris Dam, the TVA employed a "large take" policy to enable the Authority to control shoreline access and development. The policy required the TVA to purchase and condemn not only the property that would be flooded by the reservoir but adjacent property as well. Furthermore, the project included creation of a model city, Norris, Tennessee, north of Knoxville. The TVA planned to operate the new city as an example of how rural areas in the Tennessee Valley could transition to industrial life in the twentieth century.

The residents displaced by the dam were farmers, not urban workers, and they had to relocate before the new city was completed. As a result, the first residents were workers on the dam itself. After those workers left, Norris primarily served as a residence for middle-class employees of the TVA. Before long, the residents tired of corporate ownership, and the TVA tired of the expenses of maintaining the city. Ultimately, the Authority sold the property to a private corporation that sold the land in individual parcels to residents. As a result, Norris became a middle-class, suburban community northwest of Knoxville.

After Arthur Morgan left the board in 1938, the TVA concentrated on power generation, navigation, flood control, and agricultural demonstrations. The power generation program prompted legal opposition from private utility companies, but the legal challenges had largely failed by the end of the 1930s. World War II accelerated the need for electric power in the area, especially to support the nuclear research facility at Oak Ridge. To meet that need, the TVA completed several major dams during the war years. Before the war ended, the Authority had constructed dams on most locations with significant potential for generation of electrical power. Moreover, the dams and locks built by the TVA on the Tennessee River had completed the nine-foot navigation channel from Knoxville to Paducah. During the war years, the TVA also began an ambitious program to construct steam generators fueled by coal. By the end of World War II, steam generation produced the bulk of TVA power; and the shift to steam generation continued after the end of the war.

Except for plants designed to meet defense needs associated with the Korean War, Congress was unwilling to fund new power facilities during the 1950s. The Eisenhower administration would not support new appropriations for projects to generate electricity, and revenues from the power plants were insufficient to fund the construction needed for future demand. As a result, the TVA began to search for an alternate funding mechanism, and in 1959 President Eisenhower signed legislation that authorized the Authority to issue bonds secured only by TVA revenues to finance power generation facilities. Thereafter, the Authority received no congressional appropriations for its power generation projects.

By the 1960s, the TVA was a huge, unregulated utility. Only a fraction of TVA power still came from hydroelectric dams. Most came from coal-fired plants, but during the 1960s the TVA adopted an aggressive plan to build nuclear plants. The TVA board could initiate these power projects without congressional authorization and fund them without congressional appropriations. The board also established the rates for the power it generated, and its contracts even controlled the rates that public utilities could charge when they resold the electricity to consumers.

The TVA could still seek congressional appropriations to fund public works projects for other purposes such as navigation improvements and flood control. Moreover, the election of President John Kennedy and a Democratic Congress in 1960 gave the TVA board and its employees hope that the political system might now be more sympathetic to new appeals for appropriations to support TVA projects. The Kennedy administration, however, emphasized the need for benefit-cost analyses to demonstrate the wisdom of public works projects and developed written guidelines to assist federal agencies in calculating benefit-cost ratios for projects. In 1962, the Senate published these guidelines as Senate Document 97.

The new guidelines made it difficult for the TVA to justify water resource projects. Traditionally, the TVA had relied on power generation, navigation, and flood control as the benefits to support its projects, but the new rules made it impossible to justify new projects relying solely on these factors. The Authority had long since completed construction of dams on the sites on the Tennessee River with significant potential for hydroelectric power, and — in any event — Congress would no longer consider appropriations for such projects. Furthermore, the TVA had also completed the nine-foot navigation channel on the entire Tennessee River, thus vastly reducing the potential for claiming that class of benefits. Floods still occurred, principally in the Chattanooga area, but flood benefits alone would rarely, if ever, justify construction of a significant dam.

Aubrey "Red" Wagner was the general manager of the TVA from 1954 to 1961, a board member from 1961 to 1978, and board chairman from 1962 to 1978. Recognizing the inability of TVA projects to generate positive benefit-cost ratios relying on power generation, navigation, and flood control alone, he exhorted TVA employees to search for new benefits to include in the calculus. More broadly, he encouraged the Authority to search for a "new mission" for which the TVA could seek congressional appropriations. The Tellico Dam was the project chosen to develop the new mission.

The basic goal of the new mission was economic development, and it was the benefit that the TVA touted to obtain local support for the Tellico Dam project. Access to the navigation channel of the Tennessee River as well as excellent rail and highway connections would, the TVA claimed, stimulate industrial development along the reservoir and increase job opportunities in the area.

During the early 1960s, the TVA also settled on two new "direct" benefits to support the Tellico project. Recreational use, a benefit recognized by Senate Document 97 and previously claimed by the Army Corps of Engineers for its projects, was an obvious choice, albeit one with arguably limited potential given the large number of reservoirs the TVA had already constructed on the Tennessee River and its tributaries. The other benefit that the TVA embraced was land enhancement. The Authority proposed to return to the "large take" policy abandoned after the Norris Dam and to condemn property that would not be inundated by the reservoir. It would then sell the property for a profit after the project was complete.

The TVA chose the Little Tennessee River as the site for the Tellico Dam. Just above the point where that river joins the Tennessee River, the TVA proposed to build a dam and reservoir that it claimed would dramatically improve the quality of life in an economically depressed area.

The Little Tennessee River originates in northeastern Georgia and flows 135 miles through southwestern North Carolina and eastern Tennessee until it becomes part of the Tennessee River, south of Knoxville. By the 1960s, the TVA and others had built fourteen dams on the Little Tennessee River. The largest was the Fontana Dam in western North Carolina; it was part of the expansion of hydroelectric power in World War II and has the largest vertical drop of any dam built by the TVA. The existing dam closest to the proposed Tellico Dam site was the Chilhowee Dam, which the Aluminum Company of America (ALCOA) had built about thirty-three miles upstream in the 1950s.

Unlike most of the typography of the Little Tennessee River, the last thirty-three miles flowed through a fairly shallow valley. Moreover, this section of the river and its valley had important agricultural, recreational, historical, and archaeological values. The rich land in the valley included some of the most valuable farmlands in east Tennessee; some owners in the mid-twentieth century traced their families' ownership back to the first white settlers who came after Andrew Jackson removed the Cherokees in the 1830s. Below the Chilhowee Dam, the Little Tennessee River was a popular fishery that the Tennessee Game and Fish Commission regularly stocked with trout to take advantage of the cold water released by the dam. Finally, the valley was home to significant historical and archaeological sites. During the French and Indian War, the British army built Fort Loudoun, the westernmost British fort, on the spot where the Tellico River merges with the Little Tennessee. In addition, the Little Tennessee Valley also contained the sites of important Cherokee villages.

The Tellico project was an old idea given new life in the 1960s. A 1936 map identifying potential dam sites in the Tennessee River watershed included the mouth of the Little Tennessee River as one potential site. When the TVA was planning the Fort Loudon Dam on the Tennessee River, it tried to locate the dam below the point where the Little Tennessee River and the Tennessee River joined. Such a dam would have created reservoirs in both rivers, but the TVA could not identify a suitable dam site below the mouth of the Little Tennessee River.

Unable to locate the Fort Loudon Dam site below the junction of the two rivers, the TVA proposed an auxiliary dam on the Little Tennessee. Originally known as the Fort Loudon Extension Project, it included a canal to divert water into the reservoir of the Fort Loudon Dam. This diversion would allow the Fort Loudon Dam to run a fourth turbine generator. Anticipating that a dam on the Little Tennessee would eventually be built, the TVA added a fourth spillway to the Fort Loudon Dam. In 1942, the TVA board approved the Fort Loudon Extension Project but withdrew the approval when the War Production Board refused to grant the preference rating needed to add more generators at the Fort Loudon Dam. By the end of World War II, the Fort Loudon Extension Project had dropped to near the bottom of the TVA's construction priorities. Although the Authority never abandoned the project, it took no formal steps to reactivate the project for nearly two decades.

The Fort Loudon Extension Project resurfaced in 1959 as the proposed Tellico Dam project. That name is somewhat misleading, however, because the concrete portion of the Tellico Dam was a relatively modest part of the proposed project. The river was only about a few hundred feet wide where the dam was built, and the structure is about 129 feet high. The dam itself contains no turbines to generate electricity. However, an earthen dam extends approximately a mile north of the Little Tennessee River, and the TVA had to reroute several roads and bridges in the area. The earthen dam stopped the flow of a narrow second channel of the river and allowed the Tellico Reservoir to be connected to the existing reservoir of the Fort Loudon Dam. This connection created a navigation canal that would allow barge traffic to move from the Tellico Reservoir into the Tennessee River and from there to travel the entire length of the Tennessee River. The canal also allowed the TVA to use waters from the Tellico Reservoir as a supplemental source to run the hydroelectric turbines associated with the Fort Loudon Dam.

From the beginning of the project, one of the chief problems that the Authority faced with respect to the Tellico Dam was to prepare an economic justification for the project. As noted earlier, the TVA had traditionally relied on power generation, navigation improvements, and flood control as the benefits to justify its projects, but not even the TVA could produce a positive benefit-cost ratio using only those benefits. Moreover, no congressional appropriations would have been available had the Tellico project been justified as a power generation project alone. In some early comments, Aubrey Wagner — the TVA chairman — even referred to the power generation and flood control benefits as insignificant. Later he dropped that phrasing, perhaps at the suggestion of the public information office.

Using the traditional factors of power generation, navigation, and flood control, the TVA estimates of the benefits of the Tellico project totaled between 50 and 60 percent of costs, giving the project a benefit-cost ratio between .5 to 1 and .6 to 1. This ratio was, however, the best one that the traditional factors could produce from more than twenty projects that the Authority considered. As a result, the TVA chose Tellico as the model for identifying new benefits to justify projects economically. The TVA focused on economic development as its primary reason for the Tellico project, but it relied on the direct benefits of recreation and shoreline development to give the Tellico project a positive benefit-cost ratio in its presentation to Congress.

Economic development was the benefit that the TVA emphasized in the local area. The Authority promised numerous water-based, industrial firms that would offer 6,000 new jobs and stimulate the development of 9,000 new jobs in service industries in the area. The TVA also claimed that the new jobs would stimulate population growth and provide homes for 25,000 people. By 1968, the Authority was even proposing to include a model city named Timberlake. The Authority eventually raised its projection of the size of the new city to 50,000 and its prediction of the total number of jobs that would be added to 25,000.

The economic development benefits depended on the assumption that the Tellico project would stimulate industrialization of the region. The TVA projected that industrial development would eventually occupy 5,000 acres of the shore lands that were being condemned. Its analysts reasoned that the Tellico Reservoir would give the area all the prerequisites for industrial development: a good industrial location, a navigation channel to the Tennessee River, good rail and highway access, cheap electricity, and a good labor supply.

During the late 1960s, the TVA expanded its plans for development in the Tellico area to include the related proposal for development of the model city of Timberlake. The Authority had difficulty in locating a private development partner for the proposed city, but the Boeing Corporation eventually expressed interest in the project in the early 1970s. The model city project was, however, really never more than a dream of some TVA officials and employees, and it never progressed beyond the concept step. In March 1975, Boeing formally withdrew from the project, and not even TVA officials were seriously pushing the proposal by the time of the snail darter litigation.

The TVA frequently cited the indirect economic development benefits of the Tellico project when testifying before Congress. However, adding the new benefits of recreation and shoreline enhancement to power generation, navigation, and flood control enabled the Authority to produce a positive benefit-cost ratio using direct benefits of the project.

From a conceptual standpoint, the least innovative of the new benefits was recreation. Although the TVA had not previously considered recreational use as a benefit in economic analyses of its projects, the Army Corps of Engineers had calculated recreational opportunities as benefits for its public works projects. Calculation of recreational benefits is always difficult and subjective because it involves estimating the number of recreational users as well as the value of each use. Moreover, determining the incremental value of recreation was particularly problematic as applied to the Tellico project. Long before the 1960s, the TVA had completed its major dams. As a result, the Tennessee River was a river of dams and reservoirs, with many nearby recreational opportunities similar to those that the Tellico project would offer. Indeed, a canal connected the Tellico Reservoir itself to the Fort Loudon Reservoir, which offered similar lake-based recreational alternatives.

The most innovative way that the TVA sought to improve the benefit side of the benefit-cost ratio was the proposal to capture the enhancement of land values associated with the project. The TVA plan was to condemn land that was adjacent to the Tellico Dam reservoir and to include the projected increase in the value of that property as a project benefit to be returned to the U.S. Treasury when the land was later sold to developers. Essentially, this approach made the positive benefit-cost ratio dependent on a real estate speculation supported by the use of the TVA's power of eminent domain.

The land enhancement benefit was essential to achieving a positive benefit-cost ratio for the Tellico project, but it contributed significantly to the growth of local opposition. To reap the benefit of the increased value of the land above the reservoir, the TVA had to condemn far more land than would actually be flooded by the Tellico Reservoir. Basically, the Authority reverted to the "large take" policy that it had abandoned after the Norris Dam. The TVA initially decided to acquire 30,000 acres — 13,500 for the reservoir and 16,500 for shoreline development; it later expanded the total to 38,000 acres. This "large take" policy changed the TVA practice of the previous twenty-five years and committed the TVA to acquire whole farms when only a small section of the farm would actually be flooded as the result of the construction of the dam. The "large take" policy particularly angered property owners in the Tellico area because the TVA had followed a far more conservative land acquisition policy when it built the Fort Loudon Dam in the 1940s.

With the addition of these new benefits, the TVA claimed a positive benefit-cost ratio of 1.4 to 1 for the Tellico project. No one other than the TVA verified these claims, and critics offered a variety of objections to the Authority's figures. Over the years, various reviewers — an economics class at the University of Tennessee, the Army Corps of Engineers, the comptroller general, and the Endangered Species Committee — raised questions about the accuracy of the TVA calculations. However, all these reviews came after the TVA board had authorized the project and Congress had made initial appropriations for it. None of the reviews was ever sufficient to stop congressional funding for the project.

The TVA worked hard to develop local support for the project, and the local political establishment consistently supported it. Most observers have concluded that a majority of people in the counties directly affected by the project — Blount, Loudon, and Monroe — probably supported it. The TVA, however, rejected an early proposal from opponents for a referendum on the project, and significant local opposition emerged from at least three groups: landowners, trout fishers, and individuals concerned with historic preservation. The opponents formed a citizen group, The Association for the Preservation of the Little Tennessee River, to fight the project, but they were unable to deter the TVA from its plans. In the later stages of the legal battle over the dam, a fourth group — the Eastern Band of the Cherokee Indians — also joined the opposition.

Some landowners supported the Tellico project, but others objected to the condemnation of their property, especially when the land would not be inundated by the reservoir. The families of some landowners had farmed their property for generations, and the TVA was now condemning it to sell to private developers. The sense of injustice was especially great in cases where the TVA's "large take" policy required condemnation of an entire farm even though only a small portion of a landowner's property would be flooded. One egregious example involved the farm of Jean Ritchey and her husband. Although the Tellico Reservoir covered only a few acres of their farm, the TVA insisted on taking almost 100 acres.

The Little Tennessee River had a reputation as an excellent trout fishery. Some enthusiasts rated it as the best trout stream east of the Rocky Mountains. Interestingly, the Little Tennessee River had become an outstanding trout fishery as a result of previous dams on the river. ALCOA's Chilhowee Dam stopped the flow of the river thirty-three miles upstream from the place where the Little Tennessee joined the Tennessee River. Cold-water releases from that dam made the lower portion of the Little Tennessee an excellent habitat for trout. Although the species did not spawn on the Little Tennessee, the Tennessee Game and Fish Commission stocked the river annually. The trout thrived, making the stream a favorite of trout fishers in the East.

The fishing enthusiasts helped to attract national support for the dam opponents. Perhaps the most visible opponent was Supreme Court Justice William O. Douglas, who visited the area to fish in 1965 and again in 1969. On both visits, his opposition to the dam received widespread coverage in the media; he blasted the dam verbally and in an article eventually published in *True Magazine* in May 1969. In addition, the local chapter of Trout Unlimited persuaded its parent organization to join the opposition. In the 1970s, the national organization was one of the plaintiffs in the lawsuit filed under the National Environmental Policy Act.

Most of the dam opponents who were concerned about historic preservation were members of the Fort Loudoun Association. When the Tellico Dam was proposed in the 1960s, the president of the association, Judge Sue Hicks, was a leader of the early opponents. The original plans would have flooded the fort, but the TVA later agreed to raise the entire structure with seventeen feet of fill dirt. Even after the plans were revised, the project changed the location of the fort from the intersection of two rivers to the edge of a large reservoir.

First established in 1756, Fort Loudoun was the westernmost outpost established by the British in the French and Indian War. The British located the fort at the point where the Tellico River, one of the tributaries of the Little Tennessee River, merged with the Little Tennessee. On the other bank of the Tellico River were the ruins of the Tellico Blockhouse, which had been established by the U.S. Army in 1794.

The Little Tennessee River valley was also the home of numerous abandoned villages and other archaeological sites of the Cherokees. These villages included Chota, the historic capital of the Cherokees; Tanasi, the village from which the name Tennessee is derived; and Tuskegee, the birthplace of Sequoyah, who produced the written language for the Cherokees. The loss of the Cherokee sites provided a substantial argument against the Tellico Dam, but the Cherokees failed to provide an early or unified opposition. The Eastern Band of the Cherokee Indians, the descendants of the remnant that had remained in the mountains when Andrew Jackson drove the Cherokees from their lands in the 1830s, eventually opposed the Tellico project. Unfortunately, they did not actively join the opposition until after the TVA Board of Directors had approved the project and Congress had made substantial appropriations to support it. The Cherokee Nation of Oklahoma, the descendants of the Cherokees who had been removed to Oklahoma, were satisfied by TVA funding for excavation of some sites before the dam was completed.

The dam opponents battled the TVA in newspapers and public hearings, and they appeared before Congress to oppose appropriations for the Tellico project. They were, however, no match for the political clout of the TVA or the Authority's skillful public relations.

By the 1960s, the TVA had the unified support of congressional delegations from Tennessee and other states through which the Tennessee River flowed. Senator Allen Ellender of Louisiana tried to assist the opponents by requesting the Army Corps of Engineers to review the benefit-cost analysis prepared by the TVA. Despite a critical assessment from the corps, Senator Ellender was unable to kill the project.

Approval for the project came, and initial funding began, in the 1960s. On April 15, 1963, the TVA board voted to endorse the project and to seek congressional funding. The budget that President Lyndon Johnson proposed in January 1965 included $5,775,000 to begin the project in fiscal year 1966. Representative Joe Evins, a TVA ally and chairman of the Public Works Subcommittee of the House Appropriations Committee, temporarily derailed the schedule by diverting the funds requested for the Tellico project in 1966 to the Tims Ford Dam in his district. When the TVA renewed its request the following year, Representative Evins supported the Tellico project, and the coalition of the TVA and local politicians and developers supporting the dam prevailed. The 1967 Public Works Appropriation Act included $3.2 million to begin work on the Tellico Dam, and the TVA began construction in March 1967. Two years later, the Authority had completed the concrete portion of the dam, and its early presentations to the Public Works Subcommittee of the House Appropriation Committee estimated that the project would be completed in 1970 or 1971.

Opponents of the dam continued to fight the project, but the TVA appeared to have won in the legislative arena. In 1967, 1968, and 1969, Congress made additional appropriations for the Tellico project even though the projected cost had increased to $69 million and the estimated completion date had slipped to 1973. To stop the project, opponents would have to turn to the courts, but the opponents had few — if any — viable theories for challenging the dam judicially.

Of course, landowners could refuse to sell their property, but the TVA Act gave the Authority broad condemnation power for its projects. Moreover, Congress had also designed the procedures the TVA had to follow in condemning property to preclude high compensation awards that would inflate the cost of the project. Prior to 1968, a property owner had no right to a jury trial in condemnation proceedings under Section 25 of the TVA Act, and the Federal District Court for the Eastern District of Tennessee apparently applied these pre-1968 rules to all the Tellico condemnations. The procedures of Section 25 required the district court to appoint three commissioners to assess the value of the property being condemned by the TVA. Either the owner or the TVA could appeal the award to the district court and then to the court of appeals.

Despite the legal rules favoring the government, a few individuals who owned property in the area affected by the Tellico project refused to sell their land to the TVA. Their refusal forced the TVA to institute condemnation proceedings and slowed the land acquisition process. The U.S. District Court for the Eastern District of Tennessee resolved most of these cases in unreported judgments, but the court did issue one reported opinion in 1974. The result in all the cases was the same. The court upheld the TVA condemnation and referred the case to commissioners to establish the value of the property.

During the 1970s, changes in the legal environment occurred. The opponents acquired new legal claims when Congress enacted new environmental laws. The chapters that follow describe these new statutes and the lawsuits they produced.

New Environmental Protections

Opponents had no substantial basis for a judicial challenge to the Tellico Dam when the TVA first approved the Tellico project in 1963 or when Congress initially appropriated funds for it in 1966. The legal landscape was gradually changing, however. Beginning in the 1960s, a number of judicial opinions indicated that the federal courts were becoming more receptive to environmental challenges to development projects. Unfortunately for dam opponents, none of the early judicial decisions involved the TVA Act. In the 1970s, however, two new federal statutes — the National Environmental Policy Act of 1970 (NEPA) and the Endangered Species Act of 1973 — imposed additional environmental constraints on the decisions of all federal agencies, including the TVA.

The power companies for which the TVA provided government-supported competition led the opposition to the TVA during the 1930s and 1940s. They filed a series of judicial actions seeking to limit the authority of the TVA to generate electricity for sale to governments and private parties. Although those actions ultimately failed, they did delay implementation of the TVA power plan for several years. However, the TVA's eventual victory gave the Authority largely unreviewable discretion regarding its public works projects.

The private utilities vigorously challenged the constitutionality of the TVA power program. The companies conceded that Congress had the power to authorize a federal agency to generate electricity for defense operations and to dam a river to improve navigability. They claimed, however, that Congress could not authorize a federal agency to sell electricity to local governments and private individuals in competition with private companies.

The issue was a critical one for the TVA. When the agency assumed responsibility for the Wilson Dam at Muscle Shoals in 1933, the nitrate plants near the dam consumed only a fraction of the power generated by the dam. The Alabama Power Company had the only distribution line to the Muscle Shoals facility, but that company had purchased less than half of the available electricity in the preceding seven years. Furthermore, the TVA Act directed the Authority to give preference to governments and nonprofit cooperatives when it distributed electricity, and the Wilson Dam was just the beginning. Congress had also appropriated funds to begin construction of the Norris Dam and the Wheeler Dam, thus beginning the development of the TVA as a major supplier of electricity in the Southeast.

The presence of the TVA as a competitor presented a major dilemma for power companies in the region. The TVA and the municipalities that wanted to purchase TVA power needed distribution lines. If the power companies sold their distribution systems, they would concede the markets to the TVA. If the power companies refused to sell the distribution lines, the facilities might become worthless if the TVA built competing lines. Faced with this prospect, the Alabama Power Company and its affiliated power companies signed a contract in which they agreed to sell their distribution lines and rural distribution systems to the TVA, and the TVA agreed to sell the companies a large block of power.

A group of preferred shareholders filed a lawsuit challenging the validity of the contract between the TVA and the Alabama Power Company. The contract was invalid, they argued, because the TVA lacked the power to purchase the distribution lines or to sell electricity to private parties or to governments other than federal agencies. After the suit was filed, the Edison Electric Institute circulated a legal opinion provided by two prominent attorneys — James M. Beck and Newton D. Baker, who as secretary of war had proposed continuing public ownership of the Wilson Dam. The opinion concluded that the TVA power program was unconstitutional. The district court agreed, but the Fifth Circuit reversed the lower court.

In 1936, *Ashwander v. TVA* gave the TVA an equivocal victory in the Supreme Court. Only Justice McReynolds voted to declare the statute unconstitutional. However, the majority opinion applied only to electricity generated at the Wilson Dam, and four members of the eight-justice majority favored deciding the case without reaching the substantive constitutional issue at all.

{ *Chapter 2* }

Chief Justice Hughes wrote the majority opinion in *Ashwander*. He simplified the constitutional issues by declining to address the broad question of the constitutionality of the TVA power program. The transmission line involved in *Ashwander* originated at the Wilson Dam at Muscle Shoals, Alabama, and the electricity generated at the dam was more than sufficient to satisfy the TVA obligation to supply power to the Alabama Power Company and its affiliated companies. Thus, the chief justice concluded, the only questions before the court involved distribution and sale of electric power generated at the Wilson Dam.

According to Chief Justice Hughes, two separate powers allowed Congress to enact the 1916 statute that authorized construction of the Wilson Dam. The war power applied because the dam was designed to ensure sufficient electricity for plants that manufactured nitrate for munitions. The commerce power also applied because the dam improved the navigability of the river.

When the dam was constructed "in the exercise of [these] constitutional purposes," the federal government "acquired full title to the dam site." This ownership included the "exclusive control" of the water power that was convertible into electric energy. The electric power thus produced became the property of the United States, and the property clause granted Congress broad authority to dispose of property owned by the federal government. In exercising the power to dispose of the electric power, the TVA could purchase transmission lines so it could seek a wider market for the power it wished to sell.

At the conclusion of his opinion, Chief Justice Hughes reiterated the narrow scope of the Court's ruling. The case did not raise, the chief justice noted, the issues of whether the TVA might use the electric power generated at the Wilson Dam for manufacturing purposes unrelated to the purposes for which the dam was constructed or whether the TVA could operate a local or urban distribution system for electricity. Finally, the chief justice emphasized, the case did not involve the constitutionality or status of any other dam or power development project.

Justice Brandeis wrote a concurring opinion that Justices Stone, Roberts, and Cardozo joined. Although he did "not disagree" with the majority's "conclusion on the constitutional question," he thought that the Court should have dismissed the case without deciding the constitutional issue, even in the narrow formulation adopted by the chief justice. Ruling on the underlying constitutional question, Justice Brandeis argued, violated several principles of constitutional adjudication, including the general rule that the Supreme Court should "not pass upon the validity of a statute upon complaint of one who fails to show that he is injured by its operation."

The majority opinion in *Ashwander* left the power companies a ray of hope. Although the Supreme Court validated the sale of electricity produced at the Wilson Dam, one could plausibly argue that the dam was exceptional in two respects. First, the connection of the Wilson Dam to the war power was significant. When Congress authorized construction of the dam in 1916, the United States was getting ready to enter World War I, and the electricity from the dam would provide power for the Muscle Shoals plants that were producing nitrate for use by the military. Second, the Wilson Dam made it possible to navigate the Tennessee River at the point of its greatest fall in water level, and the Supreme Court had long recognized navigation improvements as an appropriate use of congressional power under the commerce clause. By contrast, the TVA constructed the other Tennessee River dams during peacetime, without any specific connection to military power needs. Although the TVA dams did improve the navigability of the Tennessee River, a 1930 report by the Army Corps of Engineers had concluded that the cheapest method for opening a nine-foot navigation channel from Knoxville, Tennessee, to Paducah, Kentucky, was a series of "low" dams that did not generate hydroelectric power.

On May 29, 1936, a group of eighteen utility companies filed a new challenge to the TVA power generation program. After a lengthy trial, the district court ruled in favor of the TVA. Some of the power companies then appealed. By the time *Tennessee Electric Power Company v. TVA* reached the Supreme Court in 1939, however, the prospects for a successful challenge to the TVA power program had diminished significantly.

In 1937, the Supreme Court decided a series of cases sustaining a variety of important New Deal statutes, including the National Labor Relations Act, the Agricultural Adjustment Act, the unemployment compensation statute, and the welfare provisions of the Social Security Act. Shortly thereafter, significant changes began to occur in the Court's personnel as well. President Roosevelt appointed four new justices — Hugo Black, Stanley Reed, Felix Frankfurter, and William

Douglas — between 1937 and 1939. By 1941, Roosevelt had promoted Harlan Fiske Stone to chief justice and appointed seven of the eight associate justices on the Court. Not surprisingly, he consistently appointed supporters of his New Deal programs, including the TVA.

In 1938, the Supreme Court ruled that a power company could not challenge the constitutionality of federal loans and grants to assist municipalities in constructing electricity distribution systems. The power company argued that the loans and grants would harm it by funding competition from the municipalities, but the Court unanimously concluded that the competitive threat did not authorize the power company to challenge the loans and grants. Following the approach advocated by Justice Brandeis in *Ashwander*, *Alabama Power Co. v. Ickes* held that the "mere consummation of the loans and grants" would not invade any "legal right" of the power company because the municipalities had "the right under state law to engage in the business in competition" with the power company. Thus, if the business of the power company were "curtailed or destroyed," the damage would occur as the result of "lawful competition from which no legal wrong results."

The 1939 decision in the *Tennessee Electric Power Company* case resembled *Ashwander* in that the Supreme Court decided in favor of the TVA, but the victory was an equivocal one. Once again, the Court decided the case without resolving the underlying constitutional issue, and the number of justices in the majority temporarily fell from eight to six. Justice Butler joined Justice McReynolds in dissent, and Justice Reed — who had been the solicitor general representing the United States in *Ashwander* — did not participate.

Writing for the majority, Justice Roberts followed the approach that Justice Brandeis had urged in *Ashwander* and the Court had unanimously embraced in *Alabama Power Co.* The power companies, he concluded, lacked "standing" to bring the action to restrain the TVA from generating electric power. The TVA had not interfered with any property right of the power companies, and competition from a federal agency was not an injury that would allow the companies to challenge the constitutionality of the government's action.

A few years after the *Tennessee Electric Power Company* decision, the Supreme Court did affirm a broad federal power to control the electricity generated on navigable waterways, albeit in decisions that did not involve the TVA. In two separate cases, states challenged congressional power to license a private company to construct a hydroelectric dam on a navigable stream and to build a hydroelectric dam on the tributary of a navigable river. The Supreme Court decided both cases in favor of the federal government. Federal power over navigable waters was not, the Court ruled, limited to controls to improve navigation. Instead, Congress's power over navigable waters also extended to "flood protection, watershed development, [and] recovery of the cost of improvements through utilization of power." Nor was Congress precluded from authorizing hydroelectric projects on tributaries of navigable waters. If the project would aid in the control of floods on the navigable waterway, the project was not an unconstitutional exercise of congressional power merely because it would also make possible the generation of large quantities of electric power.

As a practical matter, the cases from the 1930s and early 1940s established the constitutionality of the TVA power program. In fact, the Supreme Court never ruled on the constitutionality of the accelerated construction program that the TVA began during World War II and continued after the war, even though this program emphasized coal-generated power rather than the hydroelectric power that had been the subject of the earlier cases. Several factors combine to explain the lack of a judicial challenge. First, the courts would almost certainly have sustained the early coal plants under the war power since construction was begun during World War II. Second, the New Deal decisions enlarging the scope of congressional power under the commerce clause were probably broad enough to encompass a federally owned utility and to allow the plants constructed after the war was over. Third, the power companies would still have had to overcome the standing hurdle. Fourth — and most important — the private power companies no long had any strong incentive to litigate the constitutional issues. They had retreated from competing with the TVA when they sold their distribution lines to the Authority in the 1930s.

The Supreme Court did, however, decide another important case involving the TVA after World War II. In 1946, *United States ex rel. TVA v. Welch* broadly construed the TVA Act to give the Authority virtually unreviewable discretion as to whether land was needed for a hydroelectric dam project.

The particular problem before the Court in the *Welch* case arose out of the construction of the Fontana Dam on the Little Tennessee River. The reservoir created by the dam had flooded most of North Carolina Highway 28. Although the road was "narrow, dangerous, [and] far below modern standards for useful highways," it provided the only access to 44,000 acres of private property situated between the Fontana Reservoir and the Great Smoky Mountains National Park. None of the governmental entitles involved—the TVA, the National Park Service, the state of North Carolina, or the county where the property was located—wanted to bear the costs of building an "improved highway" for private access to the property isolated by the flooding of Highway 28. Instead, the TVA negotiated a four-party agreement that satisfied all the governmental entities. Aided by a $100,000 contribution from the state, the TVA agreed to purchase the entire 44,000 acres and to transfer the land to the National Park Service for inclusion in the national park. The TVA also agreed to pay the county $400,000 to help the local government retire outstanding road bonds that had been issued to finance construction of the flooded highway.

Six landowners in the area isolated by the flooding of Highway 28 refused to sell their property, and the TVA initiated condemnation procedures. The lower courts both ruled in favor of the landowners, holding that the agency "had no power under the [TVA] Act to condemn the [property]."

The author of the Supreme Court opinion was Associate Justice Hugo Black, one of the justices appointed by Franklin Roosevelt. When the TVA was created in 1933, Justice Black was a Democratic senator from Alabama. He was one of Roosevelt's floor leaders in the Senate and had voted for the TVA Act. His opinion in the *Welch* case reversed the decision of the court of appeals and broadly defined the TVA's power to acquire property by eminent domain.

Justice Black quickly dismissed the decision of the district court, which had concluded that the TVA could only condemn lands "needed for the dam and reservoir proper." To reach that conclusion, the district judge had relied on "the common law rule of construction requir[ing] that statutory power to condemn be given a restrictive interpretation." That reliance was erroneous, Justice Black declared, in light of Section 31 of the TVA Act. Section 31 "expressly" directed "that the Act shall be 'liberally construed to carry out the purposes of

Congress to provide . . . for the national defense, improve navigation, control destructive floods and promote interstate commerce and the general welfare."

"Without expressly relying on a rule of strict construction," the Fourth Circuit had "also interpreted the statute narrowly." After "segregating the total problem into distinct parts," the appellate court concluded "that T.V.A.'s purpose in condemning the land in question was only one to reduce its liability arising from the destruction of the highway." According to the court of appeals, "use of the lands for that purpose [was] a 'private' and not a 'public use' or, at best, a 'public use' not authorized by the statute."

Rejecting the "reasoning and conclusion" of the Fourth Circuit, Justice Black emphasized the legislative character of the power of eminent domain and defined the scope of the congressional power in extremely broad terms: "It is the function of Congress to decide what type of taking is for a public use," and an "agency authorized to do the taking may do so to the full extent of its statutory authority." Justice Black acknowledged that some prior decisions had indicated that "the question of what is a public use is a judicial one" when state laws were challenged. He insisted, however, that the judicial role was more limited when a federal law was involved. "When Congress has spoken" on the issue of what constitutes a public use, the Court's opinions had established that the congressional "decision is entitled to deference until it is shown to involve an impossibility." In light of this rule of deference, "the T.V.A. took the tracts here involved for a public purpose if . . . Congress authorized the Authority to acquire, hold, and use the lands to carry out the purposes of the T.V.A. Act."

According to Justice Black, "the entire transaction [was] a single integrated effort on the part of the T.V.A. to carry out its congressionally authorized function." The act, he declared, "does far more than authorize the T.V.A. to build isolated dams." It placed "broad responsibilities" on the TVA relative "to navigability, flood control, reforestation, marginal lands, and agricultural and industrial development of the whole Tennessee Valley." To carry out these broad responsibilities, the act empowered the TVA "to make contracts, purchase and sell property, deemed necessary or convenient in the transaction of its business, and to build dams, reservoirs, transmission lines, power houses, and other structures." Furthermore, the statute "particularly admonished" the TVA "to cooperate with other governmental agencies — federal, state, and local — specifically in relation to the problem of 'readjustment of the population displaced by the construction of dams, the acquisition of reservoir areas, the protection of watersheds, the acquisition of rights-of-way, and other necessary acquisitions of land.' " To enable the TVA to discharge these responsibilities, the act generally granted the agency "such powers as may be necessary or appropriate" to fulfill the statutory mandate. With respect to eminent domain, Section 4 of the TVA Act specifically granted the substantive power, and Section 25 authorized the TVA to "file proceedings, such as the one before us."

"All of these provisions," Justice Black insisted, "show a clear congressional purpose" to authorize the TVA "to acquire lands by purchase or condemnation" if it deems them "necessary for carrying out the Act's purpose." Neither the aim of the TVA "to prevent a waste of government funds" nor its intention "to cooperate with the National Park Service detracted from its power to condemn." The federal government was "not required to proceed oblivious to elements of cost," nor was the government "barred from making a common sense adjustment in the interest of all the public."

Justice Black closed his opinion with a reaffirmation of the government's power of eminent domain. "An individual's unwillingness to sell" could not, he emphasized, frustrate the "public need" for property. The government could require individuals "to relinquish control of property so long as [the owners] are given just compensation."

The Supreme Court decision in *Welch* was unanimous, but the breadth of Justice Black's opinion prompted two brief concurring opinions. Justice Reed agreed that the TVA had the "authority to condemn the tracts of land" involved in *Welch*. Nonetheless, he declined to join Justice Black's opinion because it implied "that there is no judicial review of the Authority's determination that acquisition of these isolated pieces of private property is within the purposes of the TVA Act." Justice Reed's opinion prompted an even briefer concurring opinion from Justice Frankfurter. Justice Frankfurter did "join in the opinion of the Court" because he read it as recognizing "judicial competence" to determine "whether a taking is for a public purpose."

The decisions summarized in the foregoing paragraphs left opponents of the Tellico Dam little hope of stopping the project by challenging it in court. Moreover, the procedures Congress had designed for the TVA to follow in condemning property made it unlikely that high compensation awards would inflate the cost of the project beyond Congress's willingness to appropriate funds. As explained in chapter 1, Section 25 of the TVA Act of 1933 did not authorize a jury trial for a property owner whose land was being condemned. Instead, the district court appointed three commissioners to assess the value of the property being condemned by the TVA. Either the owner or the TVA could appeal the award to the district court and then to the court of appeals.

During the 1960s and the early years of the 1970s, the legal protections for the environment changed significantly. Federal courts, including the Supreme Court, were increasingly receptive to arguments that promoted environmental preservation, and Congress enacted important new environmental protections. Environmental groups won several important victories in lawsuits challenging public works projects by persuading federal courts to interpret federal statutes to require federal agencies to consider environmental values in their decisions regarding development projects. They also persuaded the courts to modify the rules regarding standing to make it easier for plaintiffs to assert environmental claims challenging development projects. When Congress reinforced these decisions with new statutory protections for the environment during the 1970s, opponents of the Tellico Dam had new legal arguments for stopping the dam.

One of the earliest environmental victories came in a 1965 decision of the U.S. Court of Appeals for the Second Circuit. Preservationists unsuccessfully tried to persuade the Federal Power Commission to deny Consolidated Edison a license to construct a pumped-storage plant at Storm King Mountain on the Hudson River. In granting the license, the commission claimed that it lacked the authority to consider aesthetic and environmental aspects of the project. The court of appeals rejected that position. It held that the commission's duty to consider "recreational purposes" in deciding whether to issue the license required it to consider the "unique beauty and major historical significance" of Storm King Mountain.

Two years later, the Supreme Court overturned a Federal Power Commission license to construct a dam in Idaho. According to Justice Douglas's majority opinion, the act did not allow the commission to simply choose between competing license applications of private power companies and a municipality to build a dam at High Mountain Sheep on the Snake River. Instead, the Federal Power Act affirmatively required the commission to decide whether federal development would be superior to development by private individuals or a state and whether the public interest would be better served by deferring construction of any dam.

In 1971, the Supreme Court issued another important opinion requiring a federal agency to give greater consideration to environmental values. This one halted the proposed extension of an interstate highway through Overton Park in Memphis, Tennessee. Section 4(f) of the Transportation Act prohibited the construction of any federal highway through a park, unless the secretary of transportation found that no "feasible and prudent alternative" existed. That standard, the Supreme Court ruled, was an exacting one. It did not give the secretary discretion "to engage in a wide-ranging balancing of interests." Instead, it allowed the secretary to approve highway construction through a park "only when truly unusual factors [were] present in a particular case or the cost or community disruption resulting from alternative routes reached extraordinary magnitude."

In addition to construing federal statutes to mandate consideration of environmental values, the federal courts also made it easier for plaintiffs with environmental claims to challenge development projects. This modification of the standing rules for judicial challenges to governmental decisions was a broad development that was not limited to environmental cases. Federal courts, however, applied the new standing rules to plaintiffs seeking to protect the environment. Those decisions made it possible for plaintiffs with environmental claims to obtain judicial review of development projects.

Since 1946, the primary federal statute authorizing judicial review of administrative action has been the Administrative Procedure Act. That statute allows a person to file suit if the person suffers "legal wrong because of an agency action" or if the person is "adversely affected or aggrieved by agency action." Until the 1960s, federal courts basically followed the approach of Justice Brandeis's concurring opinion in *Ashwander* and the majority opinion in the 1936 *Tennessee Electric Power Company* case. They generally limited review of administrative decisions to persons who were the direct subjects of the agency action or whose property rights were impacted by the decision.

Two Supreme Court decisions in 1970 significantly expanded the class of plaintiffs who could challenge governmental decisions. They specifically overruled decisions that denied standing to those whose competitive positions were harmed by governmental actions. More important, they broadly defined those who were entitled to judicial review under the Administrative Procedure Act because they were "aggrieved by agency action." Under the new definition, anyone who suffered "injury in fact" from an agency action was "aggrieved" under the Administrative Procedure Act.

Lower federal courts increasingly applied the expanded rules to grant standing to individuals who were seeking to protect environmental values, and the Supreme Court endorsed this trend in 1972. The Sierra Club had filed a lawsuit seeking to overturn a decision by the Forest Service to grant a franchise to build a ski resort on Mineral King Mountain in California. The Supreme Court refused to recognize a blanket rule that would grant the Sierra Club standing in all environmental cases. It did, however, expand the definition of injuries that would allow individuals to bring suit to include damages to "aesthetic or environmental well-being." So long as the person challenging the governmental decision actually used the aesthetic or environmental amenity that would be harmed by the government's action, that person had standing. Moreover, an organization like the Sierra Club could bring suit on behalf of its members so long as at least one of its members would be injured by the challenged governmental action and the action being challenged was related to the purposes of the organization.

None of these decisions directly applied to the TVA's decision to build the Tellico Dam. The TVA did not disavow its ability to consider scenic and environmental issues, nor did the TVA Act contain any limitation comparable to Section 4(f) of the Transportation Act. Moreover, the expansion of standing to include aesthetic and environmental interests was not essential to obtaining judicial review of the Tellico project. The dam opponents had always included some individuals who owned land in the area affected by the project, and loss of that ownership interest would satisfy the traditional requirement for a property interest.

An aggressive attorney might have suggested some creative arguments to the Tellico Dam opponents. As explained later, however, the federal courts had already rejected most of those arguments in cases decided before the increased environmental sensitivity of the 1960s.

Congress had begun in the 1930s to require federal agencies to prepare benefit-cost analyses for public works projects before they could obtain authorizations for the projects. For two reasons, however, the Flood Control Act of 1936 provided no basis for a legal challenge to the Tellico project. First, the act applied to projects of the Corps of Engineers; it did not apply to the TVA, presumably because the Authority did not have to seek congressional authorization for specific projects. Second, at least two courts of appeals had ruled that the determination of whether the benefits of a project exceeded its costs was not subject to judicial review because it involved a legislative rather than a judicial determination. Unfortunately, this second rationale also applied to the rules for benefit-cost analysis in Senate Document 97 of 1962, which did apply to the TVA.

One study of the TVA decision to build the Tellico Dam suggests that some of the TVA legal staff feared a lawsuit challenging the "large take" policy used in Tellico to condemn land for shoreline development. The probability of success for such a lawsuit was small, however. Justice Black's majority opinion in the *Welch* case indicated that the TVA decision regarding what land was needed for a project was unreviewable, and the Supreme Court had adhered to a broad definition of what constitutes a public use in a 1954 decision upholding a condemnation by a local government for urban renewal. A few landowners who owned property in the Tellico project area did try to fight the condemnation of their property, but both the district court and the Sixth Circuit upheld the TVA condemnation decisions.

One condemnation argument might have had potential for delaying the Tellico project and increasing its costs significantly, but the issue was never raised in a reported decision. As explained earlier, Section 25 of the 1933 TVA Act created a special valuation procedure for condemnations by the TVA. It referred all contested cases to a panel of three commissioners appointed by the district court and did not offer the right to demand a jury trial. Jury trials were available in condemnations by other federal agencies, and a 1968 act amended Section 25 to delete the special procedures for property valuation in TVA condemnations. The 1968 statute provided that it applied to all condemnations initiated more than thirty days after the statute was enacted into law. This effective-date rule seemed to give anyone whose property condemnation was initiated after October 28, 1968, the right to demand a jury trial. In the only reported decision involving condemnations for the Tellico project, the U.S. District Court for the Eastern District of Tennessee used a panel of commissioners to value the property, and neither the district court nor the Sixth Circuit addressed the jury trial issue. The plaintiff did not assign the jury trial question as a ground for appeal, and the judicial opinions do not indicate when the condemnation was initiated.

Even though none of the early environmental decisions applied directly to the Tellico project, the trend of the decisions did signal an increased judicial sensitivity to environmental claims. The decisions thus encouraged new legal claims once Congress began enacting environmental statutes in the 1970s.

One group of statutes from the 1970s established the modern framework for environmental regulation. The first modern regulatory statute was the Clean Air Act of 1970, but others followed in quick succession: amendments to the Federal Water Pollution Control Act and the federal pesticide statute in 1972, as well as the Safe Drinking Water Act in 1974 and the Toxic Substances Control Act and the Resource Conservation and Recovery Act in 1976. Although the Environmental Defense Fund asserted a Clean Water Act claim in its 1972 suit against the Tellico Dam, none of the regulatory statutes provided a strong argument for stopping the project. Nonetheless, the new statutes were further evidence of changing attitudes toward environmental values.

In addition to the new regulatory statutes, Congress also passed other statutes designed to force federal agencies to give greater weight to environmental issues in their decisions. Two of these laws provided new grounds for challenging the Tellico project. When NEPA became effective on January 1, 1970, it required every federal agency to prepare an environmental impact statement for any proposal for legislation or major federal action significantly affecting the environment. Almost four years later, Congress amended the Endangered Species Act to forbid federal agencies from taking any action that would jeopardize the continued existence of an endangered species or destroy or modify its critical habitat. Litigation under these two statutes delayed completion of the Tellico Dam until Congress finally granted the project a special statutory exemption.

NEPA is a brief statute that attempts to integrate environmental values into the decision making of all federal agencies. It announces a broad "national policy" to "encourage productive and enjoyable harmony" between humans and the environment. In addition, it established the Council on Environmental Quality in the Executive Office of the President.

Sections 101 and 102 are the heart of NEPA. Section 101 defines the substantive obligations of federal agencies. Section 102 describes how the agencies are to perform those obligations.

Section 101 articulates a broad vision of federal support for environmental values, but it qualifies the commitment with considerations of practicality. "Recognizing . . . the critical importance of restoring and maintaining environmental quality to the overall welfare and development of" humans, Subsection a declares "the continuing policy of the Federal Government." Federal agencies are "to use all practicable means . . . to create and maintain conditions under which man and nature can exist in productive harmony, and fulfill the social, economic and other requirements of present and future generations of Americans." To carry out this policy, Subsection b acknowledges "the continuing responsibility of the Federal Government to use all practicable means, consistent with other essential considerations of national policy, to improve and coordinate" federal activities to serve environmental values. Subsection c recognizes that "each person should enjoy a healthful environment and that each person has a responsibility to contribute to the preservation and enhancement of the environment."

Section 102 prescribes how federal agencies are to implement the policy articulated in Section 101. "To the fullest extent possible," Congress directed, "the policies, regulations, and public laws of the United States shall be interpreted and administered in accordance with the public policies set forth" in NEPA. Congress also required federal agencies to take certain actions to implement the policies.

Most of the requirements of Section 102 are vague and abstract. Agencies are to use "a systematic, interdisciplinary approach . . . in planning and decisionmaking." They are to "identify and develop methods and procedures . . . which will insure that presently unquantified environmental values may be given appropriate consideration in decisionmaking." They are also to "lend appropriate support to initiatives . . . designed to maximize international cooperation"; to "make available . . . advice and information useful in restoring, maintaining, and enhancing the quality of the environment"; to "initiate and utilize ecological information in the planning and development of resource-oriented projects"; and to assist the Council on Environmental Quality.

Two of the requirements are more specific. Section 102(2)(C) requires "the responsible federal official" to include a "detailed statement" with "every recommendation or report on proposals for legislation or other major federal action significantly affecting the quality of the human environment." Section 102(2)(D) in the 1970 act—subsequently renumbered as 102(2)(E)—adds an obligation for federal agencies to "study, develop, and describe appropriate alternatives to recommended courses of action in any proposal which involves unresolved conflicts concerning alternative uses of available resources."

The "detailed statement" mandate of Section 102(2)(C) has become the most significant NEPA requirement. The statute requires the statement, which has come to be known as the environmental impact statement, to cover five specific areas:

(i) the environmental impact of the proposed action,
(ii) any adverse environmental impacts which cannot be avoided should the proposal be implemented,
(iii) alternatives to the proposed action,
(iv) the relationship between local short-term uses of [the human] environment and the maintenance and enhancement of long-term productivity, and
(v) any irreversible and irretrievable commitments of resources which would be involved in the proposed action should it be implemented.

Before preparing the statement, the "responsible Federal official" has to obtain "the comments of any Federal agency which has jurisdiction by law or special expertise with respect to any environmental impact involved." Once the statement is prepared, the agency must also make the statement "available to the President, the Council on Environmental Quality, and . . . the public." The agency must also seek "the comments and views of the appropriate Federal, State, and local agencies, which are authorized to develop and enforce environmental standards."

To many observers, NEPA appeared innocuous when it was enacted. Although the statute imposed some new obligations on federal agencies, it contained no express provision authorizing administrative or judicial enforcement of its provisions. Moreover, many of the specific obligations of the statute had been modified to make them less onerous on federal agencies by the time NEPA became law. The duty for federal agencies to prepare a detailed statement analyzing the impact of "any proposal for . . . major federal action significantly affecting the quality of the human environment" had been weakened from an initial version that directed the responsible official to make a finding that the benefits of the proposal exceeded its environmental costs. Even the congressional recognition that every citizen "should" enjoy a healthful environment and has a duty to help protect the environment was a watered-down version of a proposal recognizing that every citizen has a "right" to a healthful environment.

The Council on Environmental Quality took the lead in advising agencies how to satisfy the NEPA requirements. On May 12, 1970— just over four months after NEPA became law — the council proposed interim "guidelines" to help other agencies comply with NEPA. Approximately a year later, the council issued final guidelines on April 23, 1971. Both the interim and the final guidelines generally gave a broad interpretation to the duty to prepare environmental impact statements. Of particular relevance to the Tellico project, both sets of guidelines said the impact statement requirement could apply to projects initiated prior to NEPA if the agency's decisions after NEPA's effective date would have significant environmental consequences. According to the final guidelines, the NEPA procedures should be applied "to the maximum extent practicable" when "further major Federal action" on projects initiated prior to NEPA would have "a significant effect on the environment."

Although NEPA contains no express provision for judicial review, the federal courts uniformly ruled that they could enforce the new statutory provisions. A series of early decisions in the lower federal courts gave some teeth to NEPA, especially to the requirement to prepare an environmental impact statement for every proposal for major federal action significantly affecting the quality of the environment.

The seminal case was *Calvert Cliffs' Coordinating Committee v. Atomic Energy Commission.* This 1971 decision by the Court of Appeals for the District of Columbia Circuit found that the rules the Atomic Energy Commission had adopted to comply with NEPA were insufficient in several respects. The federal courts were responsible, Judge Skelly Wright's opinion declared, for making certain that "important legislative purposes, heralded in the halls of Congress," were "not lost or misdirected in the vast hallways of the federal bureaucracy."

According to Judge Wright, NEPA made "environmental protection a part of the mandate of every federal agency and department." The statute did not, however, eliminate agency discretion with respect to decisions that significantly affected the environment. Recognizing that Section 101 only required agencies to use "all practicable means" to achieve its substantive policies, Judge Wright concluded that a "reviewing court probably cannot reverse a substantive decision on the merits . . . unless it be shown that the actual balance struck was arbitrary or clearly gave insufficient weight to environmental values."

By contrast, Section 102 set a more demanding standard. Federal agencies had to comply with "the procedural duties" of this section "to the fullest extent possible." Only "a clear conflict of statutory authority" would excuse noncompliance with the procedural requirements of Section 102, including the duty to prepare an environmental impact statement for actions significantly affecting the quality of the human environment. If an agency reached its decision "procedurally without individualized consideration and balancing of environmental factors — conducted fully and in good faith — it is the responsibility of the courts to reverse."

Calvert Cliffs involved an attack on agency rules for implementing NEPA, but Judge Wright's opinion provided the framework that other courts used in resolving challenges to specific public works projects. Development agencies frequently resisted the Council on Environmental Quality position that the environmental impact statement requirement could apply to projects initiated prior to NEPA's effective date. As a result, environmental organizations filed numerous actions across the country challenging the failure to prepare impact statements for ongoing projects. The Environmental Defense Fund filed a number of such lawsuits. The ongoing projects they challenged included the Cross-Florida Barge Canal, the Gilham Dam in Arkansas, the Tennessee-Tombigbee Waterway, and the Tellico Dam. Environmental organizations fared well in many of these early cases involving projects begun before NEPA's effective date. Federal courts uniformly ruled that the duty to prepare an environmental impact statement was mandatory, and they routinely enjoined the completion of development projects until the agency prepared the impact statement.

One issue was particularly important for the Tellico Dam litigation. Agencies that had begun their projects prior to the date NEPA was enacted frequently argued that the environmental impact statement requirement did not apply to them. Following the Council on Environmental Quality Guidelines, the federal courts took a pragmatic approach to the problem. A few early decisions held that NEPA was not retroactive and refused to require the preparation of impact statements when projects were substantially complete or when the remaining agency actions were ministerial. However, most courts refused to allow the project to be completed until an impact statement was prepared when the agency still had discretion with respect to decisions with significant environmental consequences.

The early cases gave environmentalists hope that NEPA litigation might actually stop environmentally harmful projects. In the pre-NEPA cases involving Storm King Mountain, the Snake River, Overton Park, and Mineral King Mountain, federal courts had not issued decisions overturning the projects on the merits; instead, they had required the federal agencies to give further consideration to environmental factors and expanded standing rules to allow more judicial challenges to agency decisions. Significantly, however, the federal agencies never completed any of those projects. In all four of these pre-NEPA cases, opponents of the projects subsequently succeeded in stopping them administratively or politically, and a similar result occurred with respect to the Cross-Florida Barge Canal, one of the first NEPA challenges to an ongoing project. After a federal district court granted a preliminary injunction against further construction activities, President Nixon issued an executive order suspending further work on the project. Many years later, the federal government and the state formally abandoned it. The halting of the Cross-Florida

Barge Canal project encouraged opponents of other projects to hope they would also be canceled once objective impact statements demonstrated their harmful environmental consequences.

The Cross-Florida Barge Canal dispute was, however, an exception among the NEPA cases. In most cases, politicians and bureaucrats failed to halt environmentally harmful projects after an impact statement was prepared. Those failures stimulated a new set of lawsuits arguing that the impact statement was inadequate and that NEPA allowed substantive review of the merits of a project, including the agency's calculation of the benefit-cost ratio. If that review demonstrated that the agency's decision to proceed with the project was arbitrary or capricious, the environmentalists contended, federal courts could permanently enjoin the project.

The ultimate outcome in the second group of NEPA cases did not fulfill the initial hopes of environmental plaintiffs. Occasionally, the environmental plaintiffs prevailed when an agency prepared an impact statement that gave only cursory consideration to environmental issues. A few cases even expressed a willingness to review the substantive merits of projects, including the benefit-cost analysis. Agencies, however, rarely abandoned projects following preparation of an impact statement, particularly when construction had begun before the NEPA requirements became effective. Moreover, the cases gradually retreated from the suggestions that substantive review might be available. Instead, the federal courts returned to the pre-NEPA position that the benefit-cost analysis was a legislative or administrative decision that the courts would not overturn.

The litigation over the construction of the Gilham Dam in Arkansas provides a useful overview of the decisional trend in NEPA cases. The dam was part of an integrated project that Congress had first authorized in 1958. By September 1, 1970, the total project was approximately two-thirds complete. The spillway and outlet works had been substantially finished, but the Army Corps of Engineers had not actually begun construction on the Gilham Dam structure. Opponents of the dam argued that an impact statement was required because the dam would impound the Cossatot River, one of the last free-flowing streams in the Ouachita Mountains of southeastern Oklahoma and southwestern Arkansas.

Because the Gilham Dam was part of a project begun long before NEPA requirements became effective, the Corps of Engineers initially argued that no impact statement was required. After the district court rejected that position, the corps sought summary judgment on the ground that the impact statement it had submitted after the lawsuit was filed satisfied its NEPA obligations for the Gilham Dam. The district court rejected this argument as well. It granted a preliminary injunction against completion of the dam, agreeing with the plaintiffs "that the impact statement simply does not set forth a detailed study and examination of the important environmental factors involved." The corps appealed those decisions but withdrew the appeal before the Eighth Circuit rendered a decision.

After losing the initial round of litigation, the corps prepared a second environmental impact statement. While this statement was being prepared, the district engineer in charge of preparing it spoke at a meeting of the local chamber of commerce. He assured the audience "that the Gilham Dam would definitely be built" after the corps completed the impact statement.

Following completion of the impact statement, the Corps of Engineers made good on the district engineer's promise to the chamber of commerce. The agency decided that the dam should be completed and filed a motion asking the district court to dissolve the injunction. The district court granted the motion, and the Eighth Circuit affirmed. According to the court of appeals, the impact statement contained "a full and accurate disclosure of the information required by §102(2)(C)" of NEPA. Moreover, the court of appeals held, NEPA only required that federal officials prepare an objective evaluation of the project, not that they be "subjectively impartial." An agency, the court declared, was most likely to display an "institutional bias" in cases where "the project has been partially completed," and "several courts [had] held that an agency involved with an ongoing federal project may approach [NEPA compliance] differently than what might be required with respect to new projects." In the case of the Gilham Dam, "the project was almost two-thirds complete when the procedural requirements of NEPA went into effect," and the agency had already expended nearly "ten million dollars" in federal funds. Under these circumstances, the court regarded as "impractical" the suggestion that the corps should "reassess the basic course of action."

The court of appeals also rejected the contention that it should overrule the decision of the Corps of Engineers on the merits. Echoing

Judge Wright's language in *Calvert Cliffs'*, the Eighth Circuit agreed that limited review of the substantive decision was available, but it held that the scope of review was narrow. A court could overturn the substantive decision of an agency only "if the agency failed to consider all relevant factors in reaching its decision, or if the decision itself represented a clear error in judgment." In the case of the Gilham Dam, the Eighth Circuit concluded it could not set aside the decision of the Corps of Engineers under this standard even "if all factual disputes were resolved in favor of the plaintiffs." To reach this conclusion, the court acknowledged, it had "taken into account . . . that the overall project was authorized by Congress eleven years prior to the passage of NEPA, and was sixty-three percent completed at the date the action was instituted."

Had NEPA been the only obstacle for the Tellico Dam, the case would never have reached the Supreme Court. Furthermore, the dam would probably have been completed and closed several years earlier. Fortunately for the dam opponents, Congress substantially revised federal legal protections for endangered species in December 1973. The new statute imposed substantive limits on federal activities that jeopardized an endangered species or destroyed or modified its critical habitat.

The Endangered Species Act of 1973 made the secretary of the interior responsible for identifying endangered and threatened species of freshwater fish, wildlife, and plants and for administering most of the provisions of the act. The secretary, in turn, delegated most of this authority to the assistant secretary in charge of the Fish and Wildlife Service. That official actually made the decisions implementing the act, so the remainder of the book uses the terms "secretary" and "Fish and Wildlife Service" interchangeably.

Section 2 of the Endangered Species Act articulates the aims of the statute and sets forth the congressional policy. It identifies the three purposes of the act as providing a means for preserving "the ecosystems upon which endangered and threatened species may be conserved," establishing "a program for the conservation of . . . endangered and threatened species," and taking steps to achieve the purposes of various international agreements relating to endangered species. Finally, the section instructs "all federal agencies" to "seek to conserve endangered

species and threatened species" and to use "their authorities in further-
ance of the purposes of [the] Act."

The key provision of the 1973 act is Section 4. It requires the secretary to determine when a species is endangered or threatened. In
making the determination, the secretary is to act "on the basis of the
best scientific and commercial data available." After making the required determinations, the secretary is to compile them into two
lists — one of endangered species and one of threatened species.
When someone petitions for a review of the status of a species, the
secretary has to conduct the review if he or she publishes a finding
that the petitioner has "presented substantial evidence which . . . war-
rants a review."

The title of Section 7 is "Interagency Cooperation." In the 1973
act, it was a short, one-paragraph section that implemented the policy articulated in Section 2 by placing obligations both on the secretary and on other federal agencies. The 1973 version of Section 7
directed the secretary to use other programs administered by the
Department of the Interior "to further the purposes of the Endangered Species Act." In addition, it imposed a positive obligation and
two negative restrictions on "all other Federal departments and agencies." The positive obligation was broad and vague. "In consultation
with the Secretary and with the assistance of the Secretary," federal
agencies were to use "their authorities" to further the purposes of the
act "by carrying out programs for the conservation of endangered . . .
and threatened species listed pursuant to Section 4." The negative
restrictions were equally broad, but they were more precise. Section
7 instructed federal agencies to take "such action necessary to insure
that actions authorized, funded, or carried out by them" would not
"jeopardize the continued existence of [an] endangered . . . or threatened species." It also directed the agencies to ensure that none of their
actions would "result in the destruction or modification of habitat of
such species which the Secretary has determined to be critical."

Section 9 of the act makes certain activities "unlawful for any person,"
and Section 3 defines the term "person" to include "any officer, employee, agent, department, or instrumentality of the Federal Government." One of the proscriptions of Section 9 provides that no person is
to "take" any "fish or wildlife" species that has been listed as endangered

or threatened. Section 3 defines the term "take" to mean "to harass, harm, pursue, hunt, shoot, wound, kill, trap, capture, or collect or to attempt to engage in such conduct."

Section 10 of the Endangered Species Act establishes exceptions to the prohibitions of the act. After the 1973 amendments, the section contained three narrow exceptions to Section 9. One applied only to Alaska natives. The second, which created a "hardship exemption," applied when a person entered a contract with respect to an endangered species before publication of the notice that the Fish and Wildlife Service was considering whether the species should be listed as endangered. The third allowed the Fish and Wildlife Service to issue permits to engage in actions normally prohibited by Section 9 "for scientific purposes or to enhance the propagation or survival of the affected species."

Unlike NEPA, the Endangered Species Act contains specific enforcement provisions. Section 11 allows the secretary to impose civil penalties for violations of the act and permits criminal prosecutions for willful violations of Section 9. More important for the Tellico Dam litigation, Section 11 also includes a citizen suit provision. Subsection 11(g) provides that "any person" may file suit to enjoin "any person, including the United States . . . , who is alleged to be in violation of any provision of this Act." The same subsection also gives federal district courts jurisdiction over such cases.

The Fish and Wildlife Service was fairly cautious in implementing the 1973 act. It listed no new species in 1974 and only eight in 1975. Moreover, the Service did not attempt to force other agencies to comply with the act even when it believed their actions violated Section 7. Indeed, the Service was slow to promulgate binding guidance for the consultation process required by Section 7. It did not issue any official guidance until April 22, 1976, and it sent those informal "guidelines" to federal agencies without publishing them as regulations. The Service said the guidelines were intended as "a starting point for the development and promulgation of regulations." Nine months later, the Service published proposed regulations to implement Section 7, and it issued the final rules on January 4, 1978.

Despite the reluctance the Fish and Wildlife Service showed in enforcing Section 7, the Service did occasionally take administrative action to strengthen the claims of plaintiffs who sought to use the citizen-suit provision of Section 11 to enforce the Endangered Species Act. Section 7 prohibited federal agencies from modifying habitat of an endangered species when the Fish and Wildlife Service had determined the habitat to be "critical," but the 1973 act did not define the term "critical habitat." In 1975, the Fish and Wildlife Service adopted an administrative definition of the term. Moreover, on at least two occasions, the Service designated a portion of an area affected by a development project as critical habitat of an endangered species. In both cases, the Service made its final determination shortly before the beginning of the trial of the citizen suit that sought to enjoin completion of the project.

Although the Service was slow to issue regulations on interagency consultation, the rules it proposed and issued did address an issue of considerable significance for the Tellico project. They indicated that the duties imposed by Section 7 applied to projects begun prior to the enactment of the 1973 statute. In identical language, both the proposed rules and the final rules included this sentence on the applicability of Section 7 to previously initiated actions: "Section 7 applies to all activities or programs where Federal involvement or control remains which in itself could jeopardize the continued existence of a listed species or modify or destroy its critical habitat."

The controversy over the Tellico project produced the first Supreme Court decision under the 1973 amendments to the Endangered Species Act, but two courts of appeal decided Endangered Species Act cases before the Sixth Circuit rendered its opinion in the Tellico Case. The two cases produced differing results. One enjoined further construction of a highway until the Fish and Wildlife Service determined that no violation of Section 7 would occur. The other denied injunctive relief because the plaintiffs had failed to prove that the proposed federal action would jeopardize the endangered species.

The first reported decision came from the Fifth Circuit. It involved a suit to protect the Mississippi sandhill crane, which the secretary had listed as an endangered species six months prior to the adoption of the 1973 amendments to the Endangered Species Act. National and state wildlife federations sought an injunction under the citizen-suit provision of Section 11 to stop construction of an interstate highway that threatened crane habitat which the secretary had determined to be critical on the eve of the trial in federal district court. In the sandhill crane case, the district court ruled that the plaintiffs had failed to establish a violation of Section 7, but the court of appeals reversed. The appellate court held that the Department of Transportation had "failed to take the necessary steps 'to insure' that the highway will not jeopardize the crane or modify its habitat." In light of this conclusion, the Fifth Circuit granted an injunction even though the highway was nearly complete. Noting "the mandatory duty" Section 7 imposed on federal agencies, the court of appeals enjoined further construction until the secretary of the interior determined that the project would not jeopardize the crane or threaten its critical habitat.

The Fifth Circuit decision prompted a settlement that resolved the dispute over the sandhill crane. Following the Supreme Court's denial of a petition for a writ of certiorari, the Department of Transportation modified the highway project. The secretary of the interior then determined that the project no longer jeopardized the crane or threatened its critical habitat, and the district court dissolved the injunction.

The sandhill crane case was an important victory for the environmental plaintiffs because it forced the Department of Transportation to modify its proposed plan for an interstate highway to avoid harm to an endangered species. Nonetheless, the Fifth Circuit opinion was somewhat ambiguous regarding what the Endangered Species Act required. On the one hand, the court emphasized the "mandatory duty" imposed by Section 7, and it required a no-jeopardy determination by the secretary before the injunction could be lifted. On the other hand, the court of appeals declared that Section 7 did "not grant the Department of the Interior a veto over the actions of other federal agencies, provided the required consultation has occurred." It said that the agency proposing the action, not the Department of the Interior, had "the final decision of whether or not to proceed with the action" and that a court could overturn that decision only if it was arbitrary or capricious.

The environmental plaintiffs did not fare as well in the second reported decision. Opponents of Meramec Park Lake Dam in Missouri sought to enjoin the project on the ground that completion of the dam would jeopardize the existence of the Indiana bat. The bat, like the sandhill crane, had originally been listed as endangered prior to the enactment of the 1973 act. Although the Fish and Wildlife Service had not made a determination on critical habitat for the bat, it had requested a moratorium on construction of the dam. Moreover, the plaintiffs introduced testimony of an expert who indicated that the project would jeopardize the bat by destroying its critical habitat. Following an evidentiary hearing, however, the district court denied the plaintiffs' request for an injunction against completion of the dam. It found that the evidence offered by the plaintiffs had failed to prove that any of the "present activities" of the defendants "in constructing the Meramec Park Reservoir [were] adversely affecting Indiana bats in the project area."

The Eight Circuit affirmed the judgment of the district court. On appeal, the plaintiffs argued that the Corps of Engineers had violated the consultation requirement of Section 7 by ignoring warnings from the Fish and Wildlife Service as to the adverse effect of the project on the bats and "a request by the [Service] to declare a moratorium on construction." The court of appeals rejected this claim because it "misread the requirements of the Act." Section 7 required only "consultation," not "acquiescence." When "a difference of opinion [arose] as to a given project, the responsibility for decision after consultation [was] not vested in the Secretary but in the agency involved." That responsibility included the obligation "to take 'such action necessary to insure that actions authorized, funded, or carried out do not jeopardize the continued existence of such endangered species * * * .'" The district court had, however, determined that the plaintiffs failed to prove that the activities of the Corps of Engineers were adversely affecting Indiana bats in the project area, and the appellate court found "no clear error" in that determination.

In light of the decisions summarized in the preceding paragraphs, NEPA and the Endangered Species Act gave opponents of the Tellico Dam new legal arguments to challenge the TVA decision to complete the project. The lawsuits that the new statutes engendered led directly to the Supreme Court decision protecting the snail darter.

CHAPTER 3

The NEPA Litigation

The TVA finished construction of the concrete portion of the Tellico Dam structure before President Nixon signed NEPA into law on January 1, 1970. The dam was far from operational, however. The TVA had not yet completed the much larger earthen dam, which blocked the small, second channel of the river and extended the bank of the reservoir toward Fort Loudon Reservoir. In addition, the TVA still needed to obtain title to approximately one-third of the land that it was acquiring for the project. The Authority was also just beginning work on road projects associated with the building of the dam.

The enactment of NEPA stimulated litigation to stop the Tellico Dam project. The plaintiffs in the lawsuit were the Environmental Defense Fund, the Association for the Preservation of the Little Tennessee River, and Thomas Burel Moser, a landowner whose property was being condemned for the project. They initially argued that the TVA could not complete the project until the Authority prepared the environmental impact statement that NEPA required for every proposal for major federal action significantly affecting the quality of the human environment. Once the impact statement was prepared, the plaintiffs argued that it failed to satisfy the requirements of NEPA and that the TVA decision to proceed with the project was arbitrary and capricious.

The NEPA litigation produced a temporary victory for the dam opponents. The dam opponents obtained an injunction that stopped most work on the dam from January 1972 to October 1973. However, the courts eventually allowed the project to proceed after the TVA prepared a final impact statement.

The TVA responded to the initial NEPA claims in two ways. The Authority's primary argument claimed no impact statement was required for the Tellico project because construction on the dam had begun before NEPA was enacted and because Congress had appropriated funds to continue the project after NEPA became effective. Alternatively, the TVA claimed that it had satisfied the impact statement requirement by filing a "draft" statement with the Council on Environmental Quality (CEQ). As noted in chapter 2, the CEQ had issued Interim Guidelines on April 30, 1970, to help federal agencies comply with the new NEPA requirements. The guidelines undercut the TVA position that no environmental impact statement was required for the Tellico project because they indicated that the duty to prepare an impact statement applied to a project "initiated prior to the enactment of [NEPA]" if the action that came after 1970 would significantly affect the quality of the human environment.

When the CEQ issued its final guidelines in 1971, the agency reaffirmed the position that the impact statement requirement could apply to projects initiated prior to the enactment of NEPA. Less than two months after the CEQ issued its final guidelines, the TVA prepared a "draft" impact statement. It filed the twenty-seven-page statement with the CEQ on June 18, 1971.

Like many early impact statements, the draft statement filed by the TVA was more of an apology for the Tellico project than a serious effort to analyze the project's environmental impacts. The statement extolled the benefits of the project and minimized its adverse consequences. From the statement, one might well have concluded that the Tellico Dam was an uncontroversial project that had engendered virtually no opposition.

The background information for the draft impact statement emphasized the economic importance of the Tellico project, describing it as "one of the most significant developments in the Appalachian east in its potential for combating some of the chronic difficulties of the region." It claimed that the project would create an ideal location for attracting plants because the area was "served not only by the waterway but by highway and rail" and had "large acreages of reasonably available land suitable for the construction of large factories." These advantages and "the experience along the Tennessee River over more than 25 years" led the TVA to a bold prediction of economic development. By the year 2000, the statement estimated, "new industries locating in the Tellico area will create some 9,000 industrial jobs." Coupled with "an additional 16,000 jobs in recreation and service industries," the project would produce "some 25,000 [jobs] in all."

The impact statement was equally expansive in estimating the direct benefits of the project. It predicted that the annual recreational benefits would be "$1,440,000 plus fish and wildlife benefits of $220,000" and "shoreline development benefits of $710,000." The estimates for annual values for other benefits were $505,000 for flood control, $400,000 for power production, $400,000 for navigation, $70,000 for water supply, and $15,000 for redevelopment.

When both direct and secondary benefits were included, the statement declared, "the benefit-cost ratio exceeds 3:1." If the benefit-cost ratio was based on direct benefits alone, it was 1.7:1 according to the statement. The statement did not, however, call attention to the extent the positive ratios depended on the new benefits that the TVA had used for the first time in the Tellico analysis. The largest annual benefits projected by the TVA analysis were $1,440,000 for recreation and $710,000 for shoreline development. For the combined annual benefits for flood control, power production, and navigation — the three benefits on which the TVA had traditionally relied to justify its projects — the statement projected only $1,305,000. That amount was less than 35 percent of the total direct benefits, and using these benefits alone would have produced a negative benefit-cost ratio.

The draft statement acknowledged that the "nonmonetary costs and benefits [of the project] are difficult to assess and quantify." Nonetheless, it confidently asserted the TVA belief "that the environment of the area will be significantly improved by the project and that the improvement will far outweigh the environmental cost of the project."

The twelve-page section of the statement that discussed environmental impacts of the project described most of the impacts as positive. The subsection on land use impacts briefly acknowledged that the farmland being acquired was "high quality," but it focused on the positive aspects of the new industrial and recreational benefits. The statement pledged that the TVA would "not allow industrialization inconsistent with the overall environmental objectives" on the 5,700 acres proposed for industrial development. It also emphasized that the TVA planned to devote most of the land upstream from river mile 20 to recreational uses and noted that the state had "announced plans to create a 1,000-acre state park in the area around historic Fort Loudoun." The land-use subsection of the statement described the TVA "plans for the Timberlake community for 50,000 people." It indicated that "the new community will contain a full range of opportunities required for a balanced community, developed with particular concern for the water, terrain and scenic views." A three-paragraph section on historical values described the Tellico area as one "of some historical interest." Seven "former villages" of the Cherokees had received "limited archaeological attention in the past," and the TVA had made arrangements for "archaeological investigations of those sites that would be inundated." The statement also promised that the TVA would construct a dike between Fort Loudoun and the Tellico Reservoir to ensure that the fort was "protected from the waters of the reservoir." In addition, the statement expressed a commitment to preserve Bowman House and "several other buildings of some historical or archaeological interest."

After discussing the effects of the project on land use, the draft statement analyzed a variety of other environmental impacts. A single paragraph on air quality promised "that no significant adverse impact on air quality will result from the project or related industrial development." The analysis of water quality was a little longer, but the conclusion was the same. "The water of the Little Tennessee River in the project area [was] excellent in most respects," and the TVA did not anticipate "that the project will adversely affect water quality." Perhaps the most positive environmental impact identified in the draft statement concerned fish and wildlife. Even though "fishing in the project area generally [was] good," the TVA expected it to be "improved and diversified following the completion of the project." As a result, the TVA estimated "that the total fishing trips to the lake will increase to over 5 times the present use in the reservoir area." Moreover, the TVA did not anticipate the project would have "any adverse impact on any rare or endangered species."

The final environmental impacts discussed in the draft statement involved "other uses" and "aesthetics." The statement conceded that placing a dam on the Little Tennessee River would eliminate some canoeing and rafting opportunities, but it described the extent of those uses as "relatively small." As far as aesthetics was concerned, the draft statement asserted that the "Tellico Reservoir should be one of the most beautiful reservoirs in the TVA system." With respect to the impact of construction, the draft statement promised that the TVA would "take all necessary precautions to minimize adverse environmental effects of construction," although it conceded "some sporadic and temporary increased turbidity in the river is inevitable."

The title of the next section of the draft statement was "Adverse Environmental Effects Which Cannot Be Avoided." It was very brief, consuming less than a page. The adverse effect on "the trout fishing potential of parts of the Little Tennessee River" would constitute "a very minor reduction in the total trout waters of the area." The impact of the losses of agricultural and timber land and the opportunity for zinc mining, the reduction of terrestrial wildlife, and the decline in hunting trips were all "insignificant" when viewed "as a portion of the land in the region devoted to similar uses." The section closed by noting that canoeing and rafting trips would "decline," construction would "cause some minor temporary increases in the turbidity of the river," and "approximately 275 families [would] have to be relocated."

The premise of the draft statement's analysis of alternatives to the project was the need for industrial development in the area: "The population of the Tennessee Valley cannot be sustained on available agricultural and related employment." Moreover, the draft statement limited its alternatives analysis to "alternative means of supplying the same benefits" as the Tellico proposal. Thus, the analysis only considered alternate sites for the dam and project design alternatives. Although "one other alternative site on the Hiwasse River" was "physically suitable for multipurpose development," that site did "not offer similar potential for industrial growth and would be much less desirable from an environmental standpoint." Finally, topography and the desirability of creating commercial navigability limited the TVA to three sites, and "the environmental consequences of all three . . . [were] virtually the same."

Each of the last two sections of the draft statement consisted of a single paragraph. According to the TVA, the Tellico project did "not represent a short-term use of the environment which will jeopardize long-term productivity." Instead, it was "an investment in the beneficial use of a resource designed to enhance long-term productivity." Finally, the draft statement said the "Irreversible and Irretrievable

Commitments of Resources Associated with the Project" were those detailed in the earlier portions of the impact statement. The draft statement then closed with the assertion that the project would "expand rather than contract the range of beneficial uses of the environment."

Of course, the Tellico project was never as noncontroversial as the draft impact statement suggested, and dam opponents vigorously contested many of the assertions in the statement. Moreover, in the summer following submission of the draft statement, a new critique of the project surfaced.

In 1971, Professor Keith Phillips of the economics department at the University of Tennessee taught a summer school class that prepared a critique of the TVA's benefit-cost analysis on the Tellico project. The report criticized several aspects of the TVA analysis. First, the Phillips Report argued the TVA should not have used discount rates of 4 percent for power generation and 3.25 percent for other benefits when the interest the TVA was paying to the government was approximately 6 percent. Second, the report alleged the TVA had "grossly exaggerated" benefits except for the power generation benefits. In fact, the report suggested, "some of the estimated benefits could be negative"; it particularly mentioned shoreline development as falling in that category. Third, the report found that the TVA "substantially overestimated project benefits" by assuming that the benefits would all accrue "on the day of closure of the proposed impoundment." In light of these criticisms, the Phillips Report expressed "serious reservations" about the prospect that the Tellico project would "pay its own way."

Shortly after the Phillips Report was completed, the opponents of the Tellico Dam filed a lawsuit seeking to halt further work on the project. As explained in chapter 2, NEPA gave opponents a new legal basis for raising their objections; moreover, the opponents obtained important new resources when a national environmental organization, the Environmental Defense Fund (EDF), agreed to assist with the legal challenge. The Tellico Dam suit was one of a number of actions that the EDF filed to challenge ongoing projects in the South.

On August 11, 1971, EDF lawyers filed the NEPA suit in the U.S. District Court for the District of Columbia. The district judge dismissed the suit in October on the ground that it should have been filed in the Northern District of Alabama, the district where the TVA headquarters was located. Instead of appealing that decision, the dam opponents refiled the suit in Alabama. On December 27, that court transferred the case to the Eastern District of Tennessee, the district in which the dam was located.

As the NEPA case was winding its way to the Eastern District of Tennessee, the dam opponents received new political support. On December 7, 1971, Governor Winnfield Dunn of Tennessee wrote a letter to Aubrey Wagner, the TVA chairman, asking the TVA to abandon the Tellico project. "For some months now," the governor wrote, his staff had been "reviewing the implications of the Tellico Dam project." In light of that inquiry, he had "concluded that the interests of the State would best be served if TVA were to discontinue plans to impound the Little Tennessee River."

Ten days later, Chairman Wagner responded with an emphatic defense of the project. The bulk of his seven-page letter extolled the benefits of the project for economic development. He repeated the prediction "that 9,000 industrial jobs and 16,000 service jobs would be created over 25 years" and promised that plans for the new city of Timberlake would "include development of the best available protection technology." He also dismissed the environmental costs of the project as minor. The project would not affect most of the "trout fishing which occurs in Little Tennessee waters," and a number of "counterparts nearby" offered canoeing that was equal or superior to that on the Little Tennessee. As for archaeology, "the Tellico project itself ha[d] made possible the rescue of artifacts still remaining and prevented those artifacts from being completely destroyed and dissipated by unplanned and unmanaged scavenging." Chairman Wagner closed with a promise to "again consider all relevant factors in connection with the final environmental statement." However, he reported, "it now appears to us that the course of action you have proposed would sacrifice the much broader benefits which can be realized through comprehensive planning as provided by the Tellico project."

The plaintiffs in *Environmental Defense Fund v. TVA (EDF I)* argued that the TVA's draft statement failed to satisfy the NEPA requirements because the statement did not adequately describe the environmental impacts of the proposed action, identify the adverse environmental effects that could not be avoided if the proposal was implemented, or analyze alternatives to the proposed action. They sought an injunction halting further work on the dam.

In January 1972, Judge Robert Taylor of the Eastern District of Tennessee conducted a hearing on the request for injunctive relief. The hearing lasted two days — Friday, January 7, and Monday, January 10.

To support its claims that the draft impact statement failed to satisfy the NEPA requirements, the plaintiffs called six witnesses. Paul Douglas Williams identified slides showing the work the TVA had done since NEPA was enacted. Edward Clebsch, an associate professor of botany at the University of Tennessee, testified regarding the need for an ecosystem analysis in the impact statement. David Etnier, an assistant professor of zoology at Tennessee, indicated that at least four rare and endangered species might exist in the Little Tennessee River. L. Price Wilkins, supervisor of hatcheries and trout management for the Tennessee Game and Fish Commission, described the "Little Tennessee River below the Chilhowee Dam" as "an excellent trout stream," one that is "outstanding in the Southeastern United States and probably in the entire eastern section of the United States." Charles McNutt, a professor of anthropology at Memphis State University, classified the area of the Tellico project as "extremely important" from the standpoint of archaeology. James A. Payne, assistant director of the Tennessee Office of Urban and Federal Affairs, summarized the objections voiced in Governor Dunn's December 7 letter. The plaintiffs also introduced an affidavit from the Tennessee state archaeologist identifying inadequacies in the draft statement.

The TVA offered five witnesses in defense of the statement. George H. Kinnon, TVA manager of engineering, reported that the TVA had begun work on the concrete portion of the Tellico Dam in March 1967 and by 1969 had completed the concrete dam and a portion of the much larger earthen dam. Harvey Sproul, county judge of Loudon County and chair of the Tellico Area Planning Council, testified regarding the reasons he and the council supported the project. Charles Hall, mayor of Tellico Plains and president of the Tellico Tri-County Development Association, claimed the project was "the greatest thing to come to Monroe County in its history" and indicated he felt "this way because the jobs that are mentioned our people desperately need." Ashford Todd Jr., director of the Division of Property and Supplies at the TVA, summarized the land acquisition process; he stated that the TVA had acquired two-thirds of the tracts and 60 percent of the acreage by the time of the trial. Reed Elliott, director of the Division of Water Control Planning at the TVA, explained the Authority's role in arranging the archaeological contracts for the Cherokee villages within the project area. In addition, the TVA also introduced affidavits from the county judges of Monroe and Blount counties and one from Alfred Guthe, a professor of anthropology at the University of Tennessee. Guthe's affidavit stated that the archaeological projects, which he headed, would recover "a fair and representative collection of historical and archaeological material for future study and evaluation."

On the day following the completion of the hearing, Judge Taylor issued a preliminary injunction stopping most work on the dam. He also issued an opinion that explained the basis for his decision.

The findings of fact in Judge Taylor's opinion began by summarizing the environmental value of the river that would be inundated by the Tellico Dam. This "lower thirty-three mile, free-flowing stretch of the Little Tennessee River" was "the largest and best trout fishing water east of the Mississippi River." The river's south bank was the site of "Fort Loudon, built in 1756, as England's southwestern outpost in the French and Indian War," and the river bottomlands contained several Cherokee village sites whose "considerable archeological significance" was "largely untapped." These sites included "Chota, the ancient capital of the Cherokees, Tuskeegee, the birthplace of Sequoyah, and Tenassee, [the site] from which Tennessee derives its name." The river was "the likely habitat of one or more of seven rare or endangered fish species," and it flowed through "a picturesque, pastoral setting untouched by urban and industrial blight and pollution." The impoundment of the river would destroy "all of these benefits of the present Little Tennessee River Valley," as well as "some of the most valuable and productive farm land in East Tennessee."

After summarizing the area that would be affected by the dam, Judge Taylor described the Tellico project. The project, he noted, had three main elements: "a concrete and earthfill dam near the mouth of the Little Tennessee River; a navigable canal connecting the proposed Tellico Reservoir with Ft. Loudon Reservoir on the main Tennessee River; and a nine-foot navigable channel extending thirty miles upriver

to a point three miles downriver from the existing Chilhowee Dam."
The TVA planned to acquire 38,000 acres. The reservoir would inundate "16,500 acres of river bottom land," with the remaining 21,500
acres "devoted to industrial, commercial, residential and recreational
developments." The Authority plan anticipated "the creation of a new
community of 50,000 people designed to demonstrate the latest con-
cepts of a high quality urban environment."

Judge Taylor's findings of fact next discussed the status of the project at the time the NEPA suit was filed. Congress had, he found, "appropriated the first funds for construction . . . on October 15, 1966,"
and "the TVA board authorized construction on November 8, 1966."
The Authority had commenced construction of the concrete portion
of the dam on March 7, 1967, and completed it on March 9, 1969.
The TVA had also completed "construction of a four-lane steel span
bridge . . . over the proposed reservoir." In addition, the Authority
had acquired "approximately two thirds of the land tracts for the overall project;" and it had expended "twenty-nine million dollars of the
estimated $69,000,000.00 cost of the project." The preceding Novem-
ber, the TVA had begun "cutting a trench at the proposed location
for the earthfill portion of the dam"; its purpose was to reach the rock
strata some thirty feet below ground level in order to seal the rock to
prevent leakage from the reservoir."

The TVA was also working on its contract "with Monroe County,
Tennessee, to relocate some thirty miles of county roads that will be
flooded by the reservoir." The Authority had completed "some five to
eight miles" and was "presently cutting and burning timber, removing
ground cover and moving earth in constructing the Monroe County
Road." The portion of the road under construction at the time of the
hearing consisted "of denuded land that will erode quickly unless
promptly stabilized," and "the most effective stabilization method at
this time of year [was] completion of the road on the denuded land."

The TVA had, Judge Taylor observed, filed a draft environmental
impact statement on the Tellico Project with the Council on Environmental Quality on June 18, 1971, and expected to complete a final
statement by February 1, 1972. He described the draft statement
as "comprehensive in scope" but found that its "cost benefit analysis
consist[ed] almost entirely of unsupported conclusions." This approach, he declared, denied "a non-expert reader . . . the opportunity

to intelligently evaluate TVA's conclusions" and made it "impossible
. . . to determine the thoroughness of the research upon which TVA
based the conclusions on their relative merit." He particularly cited
two sentences that "suggested" the "lack of careful research and planning." One articulated *"broad conclusions"* that *"can be made at the present
time"*; the other promised "one or more, supplemental environmental
statements, as appropriate, for Tellico land development when detailed
proposals are completed." Because the references "concerned long-
range recreation, residential and industrial development of the area,
they show[ed] a failure to consider the long-range environmental
impact of the project on the area."

According to Judge Taylor, the plaintiffs had offered evidence to
document the significance of the environmental impacts that would
result from the project. They "had introduced expert testimony showing scenic, recreational, archeological, and fish and wildlife losses
threatened by impoundment which are not apparent from a reading
of the draft statement." The defendants, Judge Taylor noted, "disputed the significance of these losses."

Judge Taylor acknowledged the existence of a substantial dispute
regarding the economic benefits that would accrue from the project.
The "TVA concluded that the project's cost-benefit ratio would be
1:3," but other groups had criticized the project. The East Tennessee
Development District was "an organization with a staff of professional
planners concerned with the economic development of a sixteen
county area . . . including the Tellico project area." Its executive committee had issued a statement critical of the project, including ques-
tioning "the location of the reservoir on known earth faults," but the
draft statement did not deal with these objections. Judge Taylor found
the district's comments "of particular significance because its function
is to foster economic growth rather than wilderness preservation."

Judge Taylor also noted that Tennessee Governor Winnfield Dunn
had opposed completion of the dam. His December 7, 1971, letter to
the TVA chairman had "stated his conclusion 'that the interests of the
State would be best served if TVA were to discontinue plans to impound the Little Tennessee River.'" Chairman Wagner's "seven page
reply" extolling the "economic benefits which TVA anticipates from
the project" made it "evident that there is a high level controversy
concerning the merits of the project."

Judge Taylor concluded his factual findings with a determination that "an injunction at this time would cause TVA minimum losses in both time and money." He estimated that halting the project and then starting it back up would cost the TVA approximately $50,000. The cost was so modest because the "wet winter season" would slow work on the project in any event.

After detailing his factual findings, Judge Taylor turned to the legal issue: whether the TVA had to prepare an environmental impact statement for the Tellico project, since the project had been approved and funded and construction had begun prior to the enactment of NEPA. Judge Taylor decided that the requirement to prepare an impact statement could apply to an ongoing project, offering four reasons for rejecting the TVA position that no impact statement was required. First, NEPA required the TVA to prepare a statement on every proposal for "legislation," and "each appropriation request after 1970" was such a proposal. Second, Section 102(2)(C) of NEPA required compliance with the impact statement requirement "to the fullest extent possible," and Judge Taylor quoted a U.S. Supreme Court decision saying compliance was mandatory unless the NEPA mandate caused a "clear conflict" with another "statutory authority." Third, the Council on Environmental Quality had adopted guidelines declaring the impact statement requirement applicable to "projects or programs initiated prior to the enactment of [NEPA]." In Judge Taylor's view, "such administrative regulation cannot be ignored except for the strongest reasons, particularly where the interpretation is a construction of the statute by the [administrators] designated by the statute to put it into effect." Fourth, "the omission of the traditional grandfather clause in NEPA as well as the Act's stress on the inclusive applicability of the policy promulgated by the Act indicate[d] a strong legislative intent to apply [the impact statement requirement] to federal actions initiated prior to January 1, 1970." For all these reasons, Judge Taylor concluded that impact statements "are required for ongoing federal actions . . . , such as the Tellico project."

"A few courts," Judge Taylor acknowledged, had "held that [NEPA] is not retroactive." However, he asserted, none of those opinions analyzed the act "to determine whether the theory has any merit beyond noting the absence of language requiring retroactive application." On the other hand, he cited with approval "a number of cases" that had "enjoined construction on projects" because the federal agencies had not complied with the NEPA mandate to prepare an impact statement. In particular, he noted that construction of the Gilham Dam in Arkansas had been enjoined even though the dam was "one element of a large project authorized in 1958." Relying on these cases, Judge Taylor concluded that the TVA had to prepare an impact statement for the Tellico project even though the project was initiated before NEPA was enacted. He therefore issued an injunction forbidding all work on the dam except for land already cleared for road construction and for the work of mapmaking and reporting employees whose work was not threatening the environment.

The TVA responded to the NEPA injunction in three ways. The Authority continued to work on the final impact statement it was preparing on the Tellico project, it appealed Judge Taylor's judgment to the Sixth Circuit, and it returned to Congress to request additional appropriations for the dam project for fiscal year 1973.

The TVA submitted its final environmental impact statement to the Council on Environmental Quality on February 10, 1972, a month after Judge Taylor issued his injunction and only ten days later than the February 1 deadline it had announced in the NEPA hearing. The form of the final statement differed significantly from the twenty-seven-page draft that it replaced. It consisted of three volumes. Volume 1 included the final impact statement and the draft statement, as well as the comments on the draft submitted by other agencies and the public and the TVA responses to those comments. Volume 2 reproduced the data and studies that the TVA had used in preparing the final statement. Volume 3 contained the Phillips Report and a twenty-four-page rebuttal that the TVA had prepared. Despite the expanded format, the substance of the final statement mirrored the draft: The Tellico project would have a positive impact on the human environment, with only modest loss of natural resources.

The TVA adhered to its prediction that the Tellico project would produce an economic bonanza. "The project," the final statement asserted, "will create an ideal living, working, and recreation environment and pave the way for the economic development of an area of east Tennessee characterized by low incomes and underutilization of human and natural resources." The statement continued to forecast "new industrial employment in the project area for about 9,000 persons plus 16,000 new recreation, commercial, service, and other jobs." To avoid "undesirable development," the TVA was continuing its plans for the new community of Timberlake. According to the statement, the project would produce a "valuable recreational asset," and the TVA anticipated the lake would draw "1,750,000 recreational visits" annually within seven years after impoundment.

The final statement did include one significant change with respect to the economic aspects of the project. Volume 3 contained a detailed rebuttal to the Phillips Report, which had criticized the benefit-cost analysis prepared by the TVA. Basically, the TVA defended its economic predictions and claimed that the analysis had been prepared in compliance with the directives of Senate Document 97.

A key theme of the final statement was to emphasize the impact of the previous development on the Little Tennessee River. "The 2,627-square-mile Little Tennessee River Basin," the statement noted, "is one of the most highly developed hydroelectric regions in the Nation with 16 hydroelectric generating developments on the river and its tributaries." With respect to the "project area," the final statement called attention to the ways "that man's occupation of the area, particularly during the last 175 years, has substantially altered it from its natural state." Even the trout fishing that the plaintiffs sought to protect was an artificial creation. It was the product of the construction of the Chilhowee Dam and required annual restocking to continue.

According to the final impact statement, four factors mitigated "the seriousness of the impact of the Tellico project on fishing." First, the TVA did not consider the reduction of an artificial fishery "as environmentally serious as reduction of a natural trout fishery." Second, the completion of the project would still leave "3 to 4 miles of trout waters," and the TVA promised "to take the measures necessary to provide for the continuation of the stocking program." Third, completion of the dam would provide 16,500 acres for fishing as compared with the 2,100 acres of the Little Tennessee River. Fourth, the area around the project contained "many miles of other trout streams."

The final statement had only a brief section titled "Rare and Endangered Species." Professor Etnier, the statement noted, had identified four species "that might be affected by the impoundment of Tellico Dam," but "none of those species is known to exist in the project area." Moreover, the impact of the dam would not be great even if any of the species were present. According to the statement, the southeastern United States has "many hundreds of miles of rivers and streams . . . in which there appears at least as great a probability that these species exist as in the area affected by the Tellico project."

The final statement contained a three-page discussion of water quality, and its conclusion was identical to the one offered in the draft statement. In the project area, the Little Tennessee River had "excellent" water quality "in all respects." The TVA did not expect "that the project will adversely affect water quality to any significant extent."

The section titled "Historical and Archaeological Values" consumed almost three pages in the final statement. It described the area as having "considerable archaeological value," but noted that it had "received virtually no archaeological attention until 1967," when the TVA and other federal and state agencies had initiated excavation actions. Despite the limited archaeological interest prior to the Tellico project, "the present archaeologist of the State of Tennessee and others have suggested that the value of these sites outweighs the value of the Tellico project." The TVA rejected this position as "an extreme point of view, particularly in view of the extensive archaeological work being undertaken before impoundment."

The final statement conceded that "the creation of a lake will change the setting" of Fort Loudoun. However, the statement noted, "the view at present is not that which existed when the fort was erected." In "the intervening two centuries," settlers had cleared bottoms and hillsides and built houses. In addition, the Tellico project would create "a new buffer zone around the fort," and the fort would become part of a 1,000-acre state park.

The section titled "Adverse Environmental Effects That Cannot Be Avoided Should the Proposal Be Implemented" remained brief. The loss of the trout fishery would "amount to a very minor reduction in the total trout waters of the area." The impacts on lands used for agriculture, timber, zinc mining, wildlife, and hunting would be "insignificant" as a percentage "of the land in the region devoted to similar uses." The project would "virtually" eliminate "the availability of the river for canoeing and rafting," adversely affect "certain archaeological values," and possibly impact some wells. Construction would cause "minor, temporary increases in siltation and turbidity" of the river, and approximately 275 families would have to relocate.

As for the "possible losses of rare and endangered species," that risk did not appear to be significant.

The final statement also added a new section not required by NEPA. Entitled "Adverse Environmental Impacts That the Project Will Relieve," it identified the "principal adverse impact that may be relieved by the project" as "the adverse human environmental impact associated with a low-income economy." The project, the statement asserted, will "bring dramatic improvement" to "the human environment." The project would "both greatly improve living opportunities in the area and help relieve pressure caused by migration to other regions."

The section on alternatives continued to limit its focus to "alternative means of supplying comparable benefits." A single paragraph rejected "the possibility of developing the unimpounded parts of the river for public fishing, boating, and scenic uses," the feasibility of developing "the thirty-three miles of river in its present state for scenic use," and "abandonment of the project." The statement explained in conclusory fashion that it rejected all three alternatives because they "would result in the failure to realize the benefits that will be provided by the Tellico project."

The statement closed with a positive assessment of the project's impact on the environment. The Tellico project, it emphatically proclaimed, "will substantially expand the range of beneficial uses of the environment."

The TVA did not immediately seek a dissolution of Judge Taylor's preliminary injunction on the ground that the final impact statement was complete. Instead, it appealed the district court judgment to the Sixth Circuit and requested an expedited hearing.

As the appeal to the Sixth Circuit was pending, TVA officials returned to Congress seeking additional funds for the Tellico project. In April 1972, TVA representatives appeared before Congress in support of the Authority's request for a $15 million appropriation for the Tellico project in fiscal year 1973. Testifying before the Public Works Subcommittee of the Senate Appropriations Committee on April 18, Chairman Wagner noted that Judge Taylor's injunction had halted all "construction work, except for work on two highway relocations," but that "mapping and land acquisition were continuing." According to the TVA chairman, "the delays up to this point have been relatively minor — not sufficient to prevent completion of the project in 1975 as scheduled." As a result, the total funding estimate for the project remained at the $69 million figure projected in January 1973; the projected benefit-cost ratio was 1.6 to 1.

Congress did include funds for the Tellico project in the appropriation act for the 1973 fiscal year. Curiously, however, neither the House Appropriations Committee nor the Senate Appropriations Committee mentioned the NEPA litigation in its report on the appropriation bill.

The House of Representatives initially enacted a bill reducing the TVA request for the Tellico project for the 1973 fiscal year by $7.5 million. The terse explanation of the committee report stated that the reduction was "based on delays being encountered in the construction schedule." According to nonofficial sources, the real reason for the reduction was to fund a $5 million increase to expedite construction of the Duck River project. After the reduction for Tellico, the House bill appropriated a total of $60.8 million to the TVA Fund.

The Senate was more generous, passing an appropriation bill that included $64.5 million for the TVA. The larger amount in the Senate bill reflected the recommendation of the Appropriations Committee to retain the $5 million increase for the Duck River project while restoring $3.75 million (one-half of the House reduction) to the Tellico project. The report of the Senate committee gave no specific justification for the increased amount. Ultimately, a conference committee recommended the larger amount proposed by the Senate. On August 25, 1972, both houses passed the bill proposed by the conference committee.

The Sixth Circuit heard oral argument in April 1972 and issued its opinion affirming the district court judgment in *EDF I* on December 13, 1972. Its decision enjoined further construction until the TVA prepared an environmental impact statement that complied with the requirements of NEPA. The appellate court concluded that the lower court was correct in holding that neither congressional approval of the Tellico Dam project prior to enactment of NEPA nor congressional appropriations for the project after NEPA became effective exempted the TVA from the duty to prepare an environmental impact statement. Moreover, the court of appeals agreed that an impact statement was required for two reasons. First, the "continuing construction of the project [was] still a 'proposal for action'" because substantial work was still required to complete the Tellico Dam project. Second, the TVA's annual requests for appropriations after January 1, 1970, were proposals for legislation that obligated the authority to prepare an environmental impact statement on the Tellico Dam project.

Judge McCree's opinion for the Sixth Circuit began by summarizing the facts of the case and confirming that two of the plaintiffs — the individual landowner and Trout Unlimited — had standing to bring the suit. It then turned to the central issue of the case: whether NEPA required the TVA to prepare an impact statement for the Tellico project.

The TVA argued that it had made "no 'proposals' . . . with respect to the Tellico project" after Congress began appropriating funds for the project in 1966. Following congressional approval of the project, "all aspects of construction [had proceeded] as a single unified project rather than in separate stages," and the Authority had completed one-third of the project by January 1, 1970, the date NEPA became effective. "The nature, scope, and design" of the project had, the TVA claimed, "not changed since 1967," and construction had begun "prior to the effective date of the NEPA." In light of these considerations, the Authority argued, applying "the NEPA — especially [the impact statement requirement] — to Tellico would amount to a prohibited retroactive application of the Act."

Judge McCree rejected the TVA contention for three reasons. In his view, the Authority's position "ignore[d] the language and policy of the NEPA, violate[d] regulations promulgated both by the Council on Environmental Quality and by the TVA itself," and was inconsistent with "the clear weight and trend of the case law that has developed under the Act."

Expressly following Judge Skelly Wright's opinion in *Calvert Cliffs*, Judge McCree broadly construed the new obligations imposed by NEPA. The "congressional mandate" of Section 101 was, he declared, "clear." It required "federal officials . . . to appraise continuously all of their activities not only in terms of strict economic or technical considerations but also with reference to broad environmental concerns." To "assure federal agency consideration of the policies and goals enunciated in section 101," Congress included the procedural obligations of Section 102. The legislative history, Judge McCree noted, emphasized the importance of the "action-forcing require-ments" of Section 102 and confirmed that the requirements applied to "the *ongoing activities* of the regular federal agencies."

Section 102(2), Judge McCree emphasized, obligated federal agen-cies to comply with its procedural requirements "to the fullest extent possible." This language, he declared, did not qualify "the obligation to comply with the requirement in section 102." To the contrary, he followed a decision of the Fourth Circuit which had construed the phrase "as an injunction to all federal agencies to exert utmost efforts to apply NEPA to their own operations." This "clearly expressed con-gressional purpose that federal agencies accord environmental values a high priority in their decision-making process" led Judge McCree to conclude that the impact statement requirement of Section 102(2)(C) applied to the Tellico project.

Section 101(b) made it "apparent that the Congress envisaged ongoing agency attempts to minimize environmental harm caused by implementation of agency programs." Achieving this congressional vision would require "not only constant reevaluations of projects already begun to determine whether alterations can be made in exist-ing features or whether there are alternatives to proceeding with the projects as initially planned but also the consideration of the envi-ronmental impact of all *proposed* agency action." The TVA's "position regarding the applicability of the NEPA generally to projects begun before January 1, 1970, ignore[d] the mandate to engage in continu-ous review of federal programs." Likewise, the Authority's "proffered interpretation of the term 'proposal' substantially weaken[ed] the Act's effectiveness by making it virtually impossible to update and improve effectively projects begun before the effective date of the Act but not revised since [that date]."

Interpreting NEPA to apply to ongoing projects, Judge McCree next argued, was not only consistent with the text and structure of the statute; it also followed the administrative construction of the act. The Council on Environmental Quality Guidelines demonstrated "that the Council regarded the date of approval or initiation of a project to be unimportant for purposes of fostering the informed decision-making required by the NEPA." They also confirmed that the coun-cil rejected "the narrow construction of section 102(2)(C) urged by appellants." Even more significantly, the TVA interpretation was inconsistent with the Authority's own NEPA regulations, and the appellate court termed it "axiomatic that TVA is bound by the terms of its own regulations." The TVA's regulatory definition of "actions" included "continuing activities" and provided that they "can be either 'proposed' or 'ongoing.'" In addition, the regulations "recognized that the NEPA has 'declared congressional policy that agencies should administer their statutory authorities so as to restore, preserve and enhance the quality of the environment.'" Thus, the Authority's own regulations required "an expansive interpretation of the requirements of section 102(2)(C), and [made] no distinction with respect to the obligation to apply the Act to proposed or ongoing activities for projects initiated before January 1, 1970." Because the Tellico project was "clearly an 'ongoing activity' and . . . the flooding of the Little Tennessee valley [was] still a 'proposed action,'" the regulations required the TVA to prepare an impact statement for the project.

Next, Judge McCree turned to the judicial decisions construing NEPA. Requiring the TVA to prepare an impact statement for the Tellico project was, he concluded, consistent "with the trend of the case law in this area." A number of cases had refused to apply the NEPA requirements "retroactively to invalidate or reopen decisions made or other federal action completed prior to January 1, 1970." However, "these decisions [did] not require a conclusion that the NEPA is inapplicable to any federal project initiated before January 1, 1970, or that a project that has advanced to the stage of completion that the Tellico has reached necessarily falls outside the specific terms of section 102(2)(C)." Moreover, at least two courts had enjoined "further construction on projects well advanced by January 1, 1970." In the Gilham Dam case, the district court for the Eastern District of Arkansas had required the Corps of Engineers to prepare an impact statement for a project "that had been authorized in 1958 and was, by the time of the lawsuit, 63% complete." When the injunction was granted, "all that remained was the construction of the embankment across the river and the clearing of the lake area." Similarly, the District Court for the District of Columbia had "granted a preliminary injunction against further construction of the Cross-Florida Barge Canal." Congress had authorized that project in 1942; "construction had begun in 1964"; and "by the time of the lawsuit, about one-third of the project had been completed."

The TVA attempted to distinguish the Gilham Dam case on the ground that the letting of the construction contract in that case "constituted a separate and distinct stage of the project for which an impact statement should be required." Judge McCree rejected this distinction for three reasons. First, "the court in the Arkansas case did not rest its decision on this fact." Second, "the 'separate stage' analysis would not only attach an unwarranted importance to the accounting or construction methods utilized by particular agencies . . . , but would also . . . be difficult to apply." Third, "even if a segmented analysis should be employed, we would conclude that the only significant 'stage' of construction is that which directly causes the significant environmental effects anticipated by the project planners." For all these reasons, the Sixth Circuit affirmed Judge Taylor's ruling that the Tellico project required an impact statement because it involved a proposal for major federal action significantly affecting the quality of the human environment.

The Sixth Circuit also indicated that it reached the "same result" when it focused on the TVA's continuing requests for appropriations. "Unquestionably," construing annual requests for appropriations "as proposals for legislation within the meaning of the NEPA would facilitate Congress' expressed purpose of constant revision and reevaluation of ongoing projects." Moreover, that construction was consistent with the NEPA Council on Environmental Quality Guidelines and the NEPA regulations of the TVA. Judge McCree acknowledged that the rules of the House of Representatives and the Senate distinguished "legislation" from "appropriations," but he refused to use the distinction to interpret NEPA. In the first place, applying the distinction would ignore the TVA's own regulations, which "require[d] the preparation of an impact statement for reports relating to appropriations as well as for reports relating to other 'legislation.'" "More significantly," the TVA interpretation contradicted both the "commonly accepted meaning of the word 'legislation'" and "the clearly expressed congressional purpose of the NEPA."

Construing NEPA to apply to requests for appropriations would not, Judge McCree insisted, "place an enormous administrative burden on federal agencies." After preparing and circulating an initial statement, an agency could often make annual revisions or additions "with little effort or expense." Only if unforeseen environmental effects had developed would "extensive revision and supplementation be required."

Nor was Judge McCree persuaded that no impact statement was required because "Congress [had] authorized appropriations for Tellico in 1970 and 1971 even though environmental impact statements had not been filed." Following "other federal courts," the Sixth Circuit concluded "that congressional appropriations for a project subject to NEPA are not to be taken as expressing any view with respect to compliance with NEPA."

The TVA did not seek review of the Sixth Circuit's decision in the Supreme Court. Instead, the Authority returned to the district court. On January 29, 1973, the TVA asked Judge Taylor to dissolve the injunction and to dismiss the plaintiffs' claims on the merits because the final impact statement had been prepared on the Tellico project. After several months of discovery, the hearing on the defense motion began before Judge Taylor on September 17, 1973.

Prior to the 1973 hearing, TVA officials again returned to Washington to testify in support of the Authority's request for additional appropriations for the 1974 fiscal year. On May 1, 1973, TVA chairman Aubrey Wagner appeared before the Public Works Subcommittee of the House Appropriations Committee with Lynn Seeber, the TVA general manager. Chairman Wagner's statement celebrated the fortieth anniversary of the creation of the TVA and the many accomplishments of the Authority in those years. Representative Joe Evins, the subcommittee chair, was most interested in the sharp rise in TVA electricity rates over the previous five years. Nonetheless, the hearings did include a few references to the Tellico project.

A "temporary injunction," the TVA chairman advised the subcommittee, had halted all work on the project "except for land acquisition and some engineering design." Despite the delay, he estimated that the Authority would spend $7.5 million on the project in the 1974 fiscal year and that completion of the project would take "about 2 years" once the injunction was lifted. The spending estimate presumed, Chairman Wagner emphasized, "a successful completion of the suit and lifting of the injunction" after the September hearing before Judge Taylor. The chairman acknowledged that the Authority "couldn't spend the money" it was requesting unless the injunction was lifted, but he expressed confidence that the injunction would be lifted and that the final impact statement was adequate to satisfy the requirements of NEPA. Representative Evins seconded Wagner's confidence with the comment: "You have a good lawyer and are going to win that lawsuit."

In the congressional hearings of 1973, the testimony of both Wagner and Seeber emphasized the potential flood control benefits of the Tellico project. In March 1973, Wagner noted, "one of the greatest rainstorms of record struck the Tennessee Valley." "Had the Tellico project been in operation" at that time, the flood damages in Chattanooga would have been reduced by $15 million. Similarly, Seeber testified that "the Tellico project, had it been in operation, would have been worth $15 million to Chattanooga" by cutting "2 feet off the top of an expensive flood." Neither the chairman nor the general manager reminded the committee that the project would not have ameliorated the 1973 flood, because the TVA had projected a 1975 completion date for the Tellico project even before the NEPA litigation. Nor did either of them remind the committee that such an unusual rain was unlikely to occur again in the near future.

The TVA proposed to fund the $7.5 million it requested for the Tellico project in the 1974 fiscal year with carryover funds. Because of Judge Taylor's injunction, the TVA had spent only $2.95 million of the $11.25 million that Congress had appropriated for the previous fiscal year.

The official budget estimate for the Tellico project remained at $69 million, and Wagner also reaffirmed the estimate that proceeds from the sale of shoreline lands for industrial and residential development would total approximately $10 million. The chairman did, however, acknowledge that "the total project cost estimate [was] likely to increase" because of the delay in construction. However, he had "no estimate of the impact at this time."

Both the House Appropriations Committee and the Senate Appropriations Committee recommended approval of the TVA request for a $7.5 million appropriation for the Tellico project. Neither committee report discussed the project or the litigation challenging the project, although both called attention to the need for the TVA to control its rising electricity rates. As usual, the appropriation act included only the total appropriated to the TVA Fund without specifying the particular projects for which the money was appropriated.

The September trial in the Eastern District of Tennessee lasted four days. A little more than a month later — on October 25, 1973 — Judge Taylor issued his second decision in *Environmental Defense Fund v. TVA (EDF II)*. It dissolved the temporary injunction and dismissed the lawsuit.

The plaintiffs used the testimony of expert witnesses to challenge the final impact statement from a variety of perspectives. They focused particularly on archaeological impacts and economic analysis, but they also attacked the statement with respect to impacts on water quality and fishing, as well as the projections regarding recreational uses, the computation of agricultural income, and the analysis of alternatives. The TVA countered with testimony defending the project from senior TVA officials and outside experts.

At the September 1973 hearing, the plaintiffs initially called nine witnesses. Mark Prichard, Tennessee state archaeologist, testified that the statement did not contain a detailed discussion of the cultural or historic significance of the project area. Dr. Joseph Carroll, a former TVA employee who was now a professor at Pennsylvania State University, said that he had identified inadequacies in the economic analysis when it was initially prepared. Dr. Paul Roberts, an assistant professor of economics at the University of Florida, opined that the impact statement did "not contain a critical economic analysis of the Tellico Project." Dr. Edward Clebsch, an associate professor of botany at the University of Tennessee, described the statement's list of species that are known to occur in the project area as "grossly inadequate, incomplete." Dr. Edward Thackston, associate professor of environmental engineering at Vanderbilt University, claimed that the statement's evaluation of water quality impacts was deficient in a number of respects. James Payne from the Tennessee Office of Urban and Federal Affairs testified that the statement had not "given adequate consideration" to the possibility of a recreational development plan for the Little Tennessee River. L. Price Wilkins, the state supervisor of hatcheries and trout management, complained that the statement failed to account for the loss of current fish and wildlife benefits that would be caused by impoundment. Walter Criley, director of the Division of Planning and Development of the Tennessee Department of Conservation, questioned the methodology used in determining projected visits to the reservoir. Robert Sigler of the Agricultural Extension

Service at the University of Tennessee testified that the statement's information about agricultural incomes was no longer accurate and gave his opinion that the statement failed to discuss the quality of the agricultural lands in adequate detail.

The TVA defended the impact statement with eight witnesses. Reed A. Elliot, director of the TVA Division of Water Control Planning, described the Little Tennessee River as "the most highly regulated [stream] in the Tennessee Valley" and explained how the benefit-cost analysis for the project was prepared in accordance with Senate Document 97. Dr. M. I. Foster, director of the TVA Division of Navigation Development and Regional Studies, specifically defended the methodology used to compute transportation and navigation benefits and the secondary benefits of the Tellico project. He said the final statement gave "a good, succinct picture of the benefits and costs" of the project. Dr. William E. Cole, a professor of sociology at the University of Tennessee, agreed with the statement's conclusion that the Tellico project would bring a dramatic improvement in the human environment and said the statement adequately described the industrialization impacts that would result from the project. Milo A. Churchill, a water quality specialist at the TVA, indicated that the TVA had arranged for outside experts from Johns Hopkins University and Michigan State University to review the section of the impact statement discussing water quality impacts. Dr. Peter Ashton Krenkel, a professor of environmental engineering at Vanderbilt University, testified that the impact statement adequately discussed the "significant impacts" of the Tellico Project with respect to water quality. Dr. Frank R. Holland, assistant to the director of the TVA Division of Fisheries and Wildlife Development, offered his opinion that the discussion of the ecology and ecosystem in the statement had "gone to the limits of our knowledge" and covered "every aspect possible." Dr. Alfred K. Guthe, an archaeology professor at the University of Tennessee and director of the excavation work in the project area, testified that the impact statement provided "an accurate, objective, and sufficiently detailed discussion of the archaeological and historical aspects of the reservoir project." Lynn Seeber, TVA general manager, provided an overview of the process by which the final impact statement was developed and explained how he had used the statement to reevaluate the project before deciding that the TVA should proceed.

The hearing closed with a single rebuttal witness from the plaintiffs. Greer C. Tidwell, chief of the Tennessee-Kentucky Liaison Office for the EPA, explained that a letter from the regional administrator did not indicate the EPA was completely satisfied with the final statement that the TVA had prepared.

The district court decision in *EDF II* paralleled NEPA decisions in challenges to other governmental development projects. Once the Authority prepared a second impact statement, the court ruled it was sufficient to satisfy the requirements of Section 102(2)(C) without extensive review of the Authority's analysis. In addition, the court refused to second-guess the decision of the Authority on the question of whether the project should proceed.

The plaintiffs claimed that the TVA's final impact statement was deficient in a variety of respects. They argued the statement gave insufficient attention to "the historical and archaeological loss" that would occur, as well as to "the impact resulting from family relocation," the "ecological impact of the project," "the water quality changes" the project would produce, the development of the shoreline, "the economic aspects of the project," and the alternatives to the project. They also alleged the TVA had not complied with NEPA's mandate to develop procedures to ensure that unquantifiable environmental amenities be given appropriate consideration.

Like most other federal courts, Judge Taylor ruled that the adequacy of the final impact statement was subject to judicial review in two important respects. First, the impact statement had to "discuss in detail the significant environmental impacts resulting from the proposed project." Second, the statement had to provide a "searching" discussion of the "alternatives available to [the] proposed action." In "determining the scope of reasonable alternatives to the [Tellico] project," however, one had to consider that the project "was authorized and approximately one-half completed prior to the enactment of NEPA."

Judge Taylor analyzed and reacted to each of the objections that the plaintiffs offered to the final impact statement for the Tellico project. He gave the most detailed attention to the claims involving three matters: the statement's discussion of the environmental impacts associated with historical and archaeological loss and shoreline development, the economic analysis, and the evaluation of alternatives.

On the question of the discussion of environmental impacts, Judge Taylor deferred to the TVA. He acknowledged the difference of opinion between the plaintiffs' experts and those of the defendant regarding historical and archaeological loss, but he did not try to resolve that dispute. The disagreement among experts was not, he concluded, sufficient to demonstrate "a lack of disclosure on the part of TVA or a lack of objective analysis of the loss." Even though plaintiffs attacked the treatment of shoreline development in the final statement as "virtually identical" to the draft statement Judge Taylor had previously ruled was inadequate in the draft statement, Judge Taylor found to the contrary: "The treatment afforded this topic has been expanded from that in the draft statement and represents, as far as practicable at the time the discussion was filed, a detailed discussion."

The plaintiffs sharply contested the TVA's economic analysis, but Judge Taylor ruled that it was also adequate. He concluded that "the treatment afforded the economic aspects of the project in the impact statement more than [satisfies] the disclosure requirements of Section 102(2)(C) of NEPA."

Judge Taylor also upheld the statement's evaluation of alternatives. Emphasizing that "the extent of completion is a factor limiting the breadth of alternatives," he rejected the suggestion that the impact statement ignored several "reasonable alternatives" and failed to discuss "the impacts of the alternatives that were discussed." The statement did, he ruled, discuss a "number of alternatives," and the "absence of discussion of nonstructural alternatives" was "not fatal to the analysis since testimony by witnesses for the defendants demonstrated that these alternatives could not provide complete protection." In addition, the "discussion of the impacts of the alternatives although not definitive [was] sufficient to satisfy NEPA." Thus, "the statement as a whole" gave "sufficient information concerning all reasonable alternatives for evaluation of their relative merits."

In addition, Judge Taylor addressed, albeit somewhat more briefly, other challenges to the statement. Although the discussion of family relocation was "limited to the financial compensation available through present federal legislation," the "plaintiffs provided little proof on how the quality of the discussion could have been improved." With respect to the broad question of the ecological impacts of the project, Judge Taylor conceded that "more detailed studies could have been performed." Nonetheless, he ruled "that the material presented [in the impact statement] was sufficient to alert an expert to the potential impacts." The plaintiffs' challenge to the discussion of water quality complained that the statement "was deficient in predicting future water quality," but Judge Taylor declined to "find the failure to predict the areas outlined [by the plaintiff's expert] fatal to the analysis of the topic." Furthermore, he rejected the contention "that defendants failed to circulate the [impact statement] to all interested parties and failed to respond in adequate detail to comments of other agencies."

Judge Taylor also denied the claim that the TVA had failed to satisfy the mandate of NEPA Section 102(2)(B), which directed every agency to "develop methods and procedures" to "insure that presently unquantified environmental amenities be given appropriate consideration in decisionmaking." The plaintiffs argued that the testimony at trial and TVA's regulations showed this requirement had not been "satisfied" even though three and one-half years had elapsed since NEPA was enacted. Judge Taylor took a different view of the statutory provision, however. In his view, the mandate did not obligate an agency "to compute in dollar figures every environmental loss." It "merely" required that *methods and procedures* be developed for *appropriate consideration* of presently unquantified amenities, not the development of mathematical equivalencies.

Next, Judge Taylor addressed the plaintiffs' right to challenge the substantive decision "to continue with the project as designated." Although he recognized such a right, he defined it quite narrowly. Following the decision of the Eighth Circuit in the Gilham Dam case, he concluded NEPA did not change the traditional rule that made the calculation of the benefit-cost ratio immune from judicial review. The limited substantive review available under NEPA did not encompass "a complete review of all economic factors involved in a project." Issues "such as the projected electric power benefits, flood control benefits, etc. and whether their computation conforms to the requirements of Senate Document 97 are legislative matters and not reviewable." Instead, the reviewing court was to scrutinize "any environmental benefits claimed by an agency" to determine "whether the costs and benefits struck were arbitrary according to the standards set forth in sections 101 and 102 of NEPA." Applying that lenient standard to the evidence produced at the September 1973 hearing, Judge Taylor concluded "that defendants' decision to proceed was not arbitrary." He emphasized that, in making this determination, he considered both "the narrow scope of review under NEPA," as well as the facts "that the project was authorized several years prior to the passage of NEPA, and [that] almost $35,000,000 ha[d] been expended on the project."

In his concluding paragraph, Judge Taylor acknowledged that "the Tellico project has engendered a great deal of controversy." That controversy did not, however, authorize the court "to substitute its judgment for that of TVA as to the wisdom of proceeding with a project in which almost one-half of the funds have been appropriated." As he had explained previously in considerable detail, the authority of the reviewing court was "considerably more limited."

On October 25, 1973, Judge Taylor signed the judgment dissolving the preliminary injunction and dismissing the plaintiffs' claim. Because the TVA was now free to resume work on the dam, the plaintiffs quickly asked the Sixth Circuit to stay the judgment of the district court. The appellate court denied that request, and the Supreme Court also denied a petition for an injunction pending appeal. The Sixth Circuit did, however, schedule the case for a prompt hearing on December 7, and the court of appeals issued its decision on the merits on February 22, 1974.

The court of appeals affirmed the decision of the lower court. On this appeal, the appellate court did not examine NEPA issues in detail. After summarizing the history of the litigation and quoting Judge Taylor's description of the project, the Sixth Circuit panel issued a brief per curiam opinion that announced the appellate court found "no error on the part of the district court in dissolving the preliminary injunction and in dismissing the action." It therefore affirmed the judgment of the lower court "for the reasons fully set forth in [the] well-reasoned opinion" of the district court. In a footnote the court of appeals did reiterate its agreement with Judge Taylor regarding the impact statement that the TVA had prepared. The footnote declared that the impact statement was "as thorough and complete on all pertinent features as could be reasonably expected." As for the plaintiffs' objections to the final statement, they appeared to the Sixth Circuit to be "overly technical and hypercritical."

Perhaps because the Supreme Court had already rejected a request for a stay of the district court's order pending appeal, opponents of the Tellico Dam did not seek further review of the Sixth Circuit decision. The Sixth Circuit decision in *EDF II* did not end the legal opposition to the dam, however. Instead of appealing to the Sixth Circuit decision, dam opponents returned to the district court with new claims based on the Endangered Species Act, and that lawsuit is the one that eventually reached the Supreme Court.

CHAPTER 4

The Discovery of the Snail Darter

Dr. David Etnier was the expert ichthyologist for the opponents of
the Tellico Dam in the NEPA litigation. An associate professor of
zoology at the University of Tennessee, Etnier was an expert on the
fishes of eastern Tennessee. In the first NEPA hearing, he testified
that several rare or endangered species of fish lived or might live in
the portion of the Little Tennessee River to be impounded by the
dam. The plaintiffs also listed Etnier as a potential expert for the second NEPA hearing, and the defendants took his deposition during
the discovery phase of the litigation.

In the fall of 1972, Etnier went duck hunting on the Little Tennessee
River. The day was so foggy that he and his hunting companion did not
even find the river until 10:00 A.M. Then the fog lifted, and they put
their canoe into a beautiful shoal area that Etnier had never visited previously. Although the hunters did not see any ducks that day, Etnier
thought the section was one to which he should return to determine
what kind of fish lived there. As the time for the second NEPA hearing
approached, Etnier was uncertain whether he would be called as a witness. To prepare for his possible testimony, he returned with one of his
graduate students on August 12, 1973, to examine the area he had discovered on the hunting trip. They came with snorkels and face masks
to see if they could find any of the rare or endangered species that
Dr. Etnier thought might live in the Little Tennessee River.

Etnier did not find any of the fish for which he was searching, but
he did discover a new species. As he recalled in a January 2005 interview, the first fish he saw looked like a skullfin but it was a bit too slen-
der. When he pulled it out of the water, he immediately realized he was
looking at a darter that no one had ever seen previously. He remembered being elated because he thought he might have found something
that had a chance to save the river. A few days later, he returned with

more efficient collecting equipment. The samples he took back to his laboratory after that trip confirmed his initial impression.

Etnier called the fish he found a snail darter because snails in the fast-moving shoals were its principal food, and he eventually assigned it the scientific name *Percina (Imostoma) tanasi*. A type of perch, the snail darter reaches a maximum length of three and one-half inches, and its color varies from brown to olive. The snail darter most closely resembles the stargazing darter, which is found only in the Ozark region of Arkansas and Missouri. The snail darter's distinguishing characteristics include twelve anal fin rays and round pectoral and pelvic fins. The life span of a snail darter is four years or less.

Despite the discovery of the snail darter, the plaintiffs did not call Etnier as a witness for the second NEPA hearing, and the attorneys never told him why. The likely reasons are Judge Taylor's instruction to the parties to limit the number of expert witnesses and the seemingly stronger evidence regarding the inadequacies of the environmental impact statement with respect to economic and archaeological issues. The second NEPA hearing began slightly more than a month after Etnier discovered his new species, at a time when he had not yet submitted his findings for peer review and publication.

Although the discovery of the snail darter did not affect the NEPA litigation, it did prompt a new legal challenge to the Tellico project. This one stopped the TVA from completing the dam until Congress eventually enacted a special exemption for it in the Energy and Water Development Appropriation Act of 1980.

During the second half of 1973, two other events occurred that gave new significance to Etnier's discovery. First, Zygmunt Plater joined the law faculty at the University of Tennessee as an assistant professor. A property law professor, Plater also taught environmental law, an emerging field in American law schools during the 1970s. Second, Congress enacted the Endangered Species Act of 1973. As explained in chapter 2, the statute prohibited the federal government from jeopardizing a species or modifying its critical habitat once the Fish and Wildlife Service had listed the species as endangered and determined its critical habitat. It also provided that no person could "take" any listed species.

Hiram "Hank" Hill, a law student at the University of Tennessee, had learned about the discovery of the snail darter from friends who were graduate students in the university's zoology department. In the fall semester of 1974, Hill enrolled in Professor Plater's environmental law class. He had to write a ten-page paper for the course and asked Plater whether the snail darter and the Endangered Species Act would be a suitable subject for the paper. Plater approved the topic, and — by the end of the semester — both the student and the professor were convinced that the Endangered Species Act precluded the damming of the Little Tennessee River. Eventually, they became plaintiffs in a new lawsuit challenging the dam, and Plater argued the case before the U.S. Supreme Court.

To trigger the protections of the Endangered Species Act, the Fish and Wildlife Service had to list the snail darter as an endangered species and to designate the Little Tennessee River as its critical habitat. The initial problem was to secure recognition of the snail darter as a species, a problem Etnier had begun working on as soon as he made his discovery. He and his graduate students collected about sixty specimens, and Etnier began assembling the data to present his discovery to the scientific community. By the end of the semester in which Hank Hill prepared his paper, the Biological Society of Washington, D.C., had accepted Etnier's description of the snail darter for publication in its peer-review journal.

On January 20, 1975, Joseph P. Congleton, a Knoxville attorney, joined Plater and Hill in filing a petition under Section 4 of the Endangered Species Act. The petition asked the secretary of the interior to list the snail darter as an endangered species. It also requested that the secretary act under the emergency provisions of Section 4 of the act because the planned completion of the Tellico Dam would destroy the entire species.

Six weeks later, the acting director of the Fish and Wildlife Service responded with the preliminary notice that he was considering adding the snail darter to the list of endangered species. The notice, which appeared in the *Federal Register* on March 12, declared that the petitioners had "presented substantial evidence to warrant a review of the situation" and indicated that "action is being initiated immediately on this matter."

On the same day that the acting director signed the preliminary notice, he also sent a letter to the general manager of the TVA. The letter advised the general manager that the Fish and Wildlife Service was reviewing the evidence to determine whether the snail darter should be listed as threatened or endangered in light of the planned completion of the Tellico Dam. The letter also stated the position of the Interior Department that Section 7 of the Endangered Species Act "would operate as a mandatory prohibition of any Federal or federally authorized action which would result in jeopardy to the darter's continued existence" if the snail darter were listed as a threatened or endangered species.

The TVA general manager responded to the Fish and Wildlife Service in a letter dated March 12, 1975. The response declared the TVA's disagreement with the construction of the Endangered Species Act which the letter from the acting director "seemed to imply." In addition, the general manager described efforts the "TVA had taken, and is taking, with respect to conservation of the fish if at all possible short of stopping the project." In particular, he called attention to TVA funding of a study by the University of Tennessee on "the life history of the darter, including reproduction, feeding habits, etc., so that a record could be left of its existence after the closing of the Tellico Dam and so that the possibility of transplanting it to other areas could be studied."

In April and May 1975, TVA officials appeared before Congress to make the Authority's annual request for appropriations. The TVA now projected a total cost of $100 million for the Tellico project, and the Authority requested an appropriation of $23,742,000 for the 1976 fiscal year.

Aubrey Wagner, the TVA chairman, offered his most complete justification of the Tellico project in testimony before the Public Works Subcommittee of the House Appropriations Committee. His statement to the committee defended the TVA's appropriation request and announced a new schedule for the project: filling of the reservoir would begin in January 1977, and the project would be completed by December. Total costs for the project, he advised the committee, had escalated to $100 million, a $31 million increase over the estimate provided in the previous year. To explain the increase, he noted that the project had been "the subject of extensive litigation," which had resulted in "considerable delay and increased costs." Despite these increased costs, Wagner emphasized the importance of the project. Completion of the dam would bring three important "benefits to the people of the region." First, the project would "add an average of 200 million kilowatt hours a year to meet energy needs without the construction of a powerhouse." Second, completion of the dam would "extend navigation some 30 miles up the Little Tennessee River, opening the door in an undeveloped area to quality growth of industry, commerce, recreation, and the resulting new jobs and homes." Third, the project would add "120,000 acre-feet of flood storage . . . to TVA's flood control system."

In response to questions from Representative Evans, the chairman of the subcommittee, Wagner provided additional information regarding the Tellico project. Funding limits and litigation had, he noted, delayed the project for two years; as a result, the project had reached the following stage at the time of his testimony: "Land acquisition is about 90 percent complete; design about 85 percent complete; and construction about 55 percent complete." He also explained that the $31 million increase in costs was attributable to four factors:

- "land and construction price escalation";
- "extended supervision and overheads, and other costs associated with an interrupted construction program and a 2-year prolongation of the construction schedule";
- "project scope changes"; and
- "other estimate increases, including higher highway relocation estimates . . . and provision for severe foundation problems encountered in construction of the earth dam."

Wagner did not offer any breakdown of what proportion of the increase was attributable to each of the factors.

Chairman Wagner's only oral testimony on the snail darter controversy came when he appeared before the Public Works Subcommittee of the Senate Appropriations Committee. Noting that the Authority had experienced some environmental "problems on the Tellico project," he explained that the "project was stopped with a lawsuit[,] a challenge to the adequacy of our environmental impact statement." Although the TVA had prevailed in litigation, "certain groups are unwilling to still admit that project is going ahead, and there is a movement that has been started where someone has found a 3-inch minnow that they call a snail darter." The groups opposing the project were now "making efforts to have this included in the endangered species list by the secretary of the interior, and some actions have been taken there to again try to interfere with this project." In lieu of a more detailed oral explanation of the snail darter controversy, the TVA chairman received permission to insert a written statement into the hearing records of both subcommittees. The initial paragraph of the written statement was noncommittal about the significance of the snail darter discovery. According to the statement, the new environmental questions involved "an *'undescribed' fish species*, a small member of the perch family, which was *reportedly collected* in August 1973 . . . in the Little Tennessee River by Drs. David A Etnier and Robert Stiles." Dr. Etnier, the statement noted, had "dubbed" the fish "a 'snail darter' pending its scientific status and description, and he claimed it [was] a distinct species."

The remainder of the written statement summarized the status of the snail darter controversy and explained why the TVA thought that the discovery of the darter should not stop it from completing the project. After summarizing the NEPA litigation, the statement noted that the "possible presence of 'undescribed' species of darters in the portion of the Little Tennessee River to be impounded and the possible adverse impact of the project" had already been considered and litigated. Both the "testimony before the court and also TVA's impact statement for the project" had "specifically recognized" those issues.

The TVA chairman indicated to the appropriations subcommittees that the Authority believed "that opponents of the project may again be planning to litigate," despite the preparation of the final impact statement and the decision of the Sixth Circuit upholding the statement. He said the opponents apparently expected to base the new litigation on the claim that completion of the dam "would destroy the habitat of the darter in question, which they say would violate the Endangered Species Act of 1973 if the fish is eventually listed as endangered." Although Wagner's written statement acknowledged that the Endangered Species Act "certainly requires us to do what we can to preserve endangered species," it emphatically rejected the claim that discovery of an endangered species should stop an ongoing project. The Endangered Species Act does not, the written statement noted, "repeal prior Congressional approval and funding of the Tellico project, because the habitat or range of an endangered species will necessarily be destroyed, altered, or curtailed by the completion of the project." According to the TVA statement, construing the act in that manner would give the secretary of the interior "absolute veto power over any congressionally authorized and funded project if any opponent of the project could obtain additions to the endangered species list of any species of fish, wildlife, or plant which could not be conserved except by stopping the project."

The written statement also advised the committee of the exchange of letters between the Fish and Wildlife Service and the TVA general manager regarding the possibility that the snail darter might be listed as endangered. The statement reiterated the TVA position that listing should not prevent the TVA from completing the Tellico dam.

The next action concerning the snail darter came from the Fish and Wildlife Service. On June 17, its director issued a proposed rule listing the snail darter as endangered. The sole basis for the proposal was the impact of the planned completion of the Tellico Dam: "The proposed impoundment of water behind the proposed Tellico Dam would result in total destruction of the snail darter's habitat." The proposed rule invited public comments and set a deadline for comments of August 18, 1975.

Three days after the Fish and Wildlife Service proposed listing the snail darter as endangered, the House Appropriations Committee submitted its report on the public works appropriation bill. The report recommended that the TVA's funding request for the Tellico Dam should be approved. The report did not mention the Endangered Species Act or the proposed listing of the snail darter. It did, however, note that "an environmental impact statement has been completed" and provided that the "Committee directs that the project . . . should be completed as promptly as possible for energy supply and flood protection in the public interest."

As the Fish and Wildlife Service was awaiting comments on its proposed rule listing the snail darter as endangered, Professor Plater filed a new lawsuit. He sought an injunction halting further construction on the dam until the Fish and Wildlife Service made its final decision as to whether the snail darter should be listed. Further construction while the listing decision was pending would, Plater argued, violate the spirit of the Endangered Species Act, as well as the affirmative duty that Section 7 imposed on the TVA to carry out "programs for the conservation of endangered species" that had been listed by the Fish and Wildlife Service.

The Fish and Wildlife Service received sixteen comments on its proposed rule listing the snail darter as an endangered species, with twelve comments supporting the listing, and four opposing it. The comments that supported listing the snail darter as endangered came from two groups — biologists and concerned citizens. Several ichthyologists and other professors supported the recognition of the snail darter as an endangered species. The citizen comments came primarily from longtime opponents of the Tellico project. Three individuals objected to the proposal of the Fish and Wildlife Service to list the snail darter as endangered, but the most substantial challenge to the proposed listing came from the TVA. In its comments, the TVA summarized four grounds for objecting to the proposal:

- Listing the snail darter "would have no valid basis since the taxonomic status of the fish has not been determined, . . . no known publication of its description" exists, and the fish "has never been classified as a new and distinct species."

- "No present threat exists to the darter which would justify shortcutting the customary scientific procedures" given the "scientific opinion" supporting the position "that the fish undoubtedly exists elsewhere in the Tennessee River system."

- "Listing the snail darter would not enhance the likelihood that this fish would survive and therefore would not further the purposes of the Endangered Species Act."

- Because "the Endangered Species Act does not require, nor does it even permit," the proposed listing, the Fish and Wildlife Service should not "inject itself into the longstanding controversy surrounding the wisdom of the Tellico project."

On October 9, 1975, the secretary of the interior issued the final rule listing the snail darter as endangered. Effective November 10, the rule amended the *Code of Federal Regulations* to add the snail darter to the list of endangered species. The basis for the listing was identical to the one expressed in the proposed rule: the destruction of the snail darter's habitat that would result from the "proposed impoundment of water behind the proposed Tellico Dam." The *Federal Register* notice containing the final rule did, however, respond to comments the Fish and Wildlife Service had received.

Two brief paragraphs contained the responses to fifteen of the sixteen comments. According to the summary by the Fish and Wildlife Service, "Twelve persons completely supported the proposed rulemaking." The supporters consisted of two groups: "several ichthyologists and biology professors who felt [the snail darter] was a valid species and did need protection" and "several concerned citizens decrying the possible destruction of the species which is threatened by the Tellico Dam." On the other hand, "three letters oppos[ed] the listing" without providing any information "relevant to the biological evaluation."

The Fish and Wildlife Service responded at much greater length to the "letter and attached appendices" from the TVA. Following a lengthy quotation that detailed the Authority's "specific objections," the discussion in the *Federal Register* offered a detailed response to each of them.

The Fish and Wildlife Service response began by rejecting the claim that "the lack of a published formal description of the snail darter with the designation of a name-bearing holotype" precluded listing. According to the Fish and Wildlife Service, listing was appropriate because "the weight of scientific opinion recognizes the snail darter as a distinct species." To support that conclusion, the *Federal Register* discussion cited three sources of evidence: "the original data submitted in the petition to list the snail darter," the lack of contrary evidence in the comments objecting to the proposed rule, and a manuscript, which "had been reviewed and accepted by a panel of ichthyologists at the Smithsonian Institute" and which "further substantiat[ed] the validity of the snail darter as a distinct species."

The response in the *Federal Register* next addressed the TVA's claim that the snail darter "undoubtedly exists elsewhere in the Tennessee River system." The Fish and Wildlife Service refused to embrace that position because the TVA "offer[ed] only opinion rather than specific scientific evidence" to support it. Moreover, the Fish and Wildlife Service emphasized, the available evidence contradicted the claim: "More than 1,000 collections in recent years and additional earlier collections from central and east Tennessee have not revealed the presence of the snail darter outside the Little Tennessee River."

The Fish and Wildlife Service gave two reasons for its determination that the TVA's program for transplanting the snail darter to the Hiwassee River did not preclude listing the snail darter as endangered. First, the TVA had presented "little evidence that [the Authority had] carefully studied the Hiwassee to determine whether . . . biological or other factors" might "negate a successful transplant." Second, the TVA program failed to conserve "the ecosystem upon which the only known established population of snail darter depends."

The *Federal Register* response also found that the environmental impact statement that the TVA prepared for the NEPA litigation was insufficient to preclude listing. The statement, the Fish and Wildlife Service noted, "was finalized prior to passage of the Endangered Species Act of 1973." Moreover, the preparation of the environmental impact statement and "all litigation of the Tellico project occurred prior to the discovery of the snail darter." As a result, neither the impact statement nor the litigation "indicate[d] that the Tennessee Valley Authority ha[d] given adequate consideration to the snail darter with respect to the Tellico project."

Finally, the Fish and Wildlife Service rejected the assertion that congressional appropriations for the Tellico Project precluded listing. Instead, the Service relied on the findings and policies of Section 2 of the Endangered Species Act and the obligations imposed on all federal agencies by Section 7 as the controlling legal authority.

The TVA refused to alter its plans for the completion of the Tellico Dam in light of the listing decision of the Fish and Wildlife Service and the proposed designation of critical habitat. Instead, the Authority focused its efforts on completing the dam as soon as possible and implementing the plan to relocate the snail darter in the Hiwassee River.

Although the Fish and Wildlife Service concluded that completion of the Tellico Dam would violate the Endangered Species Act, it took no formal action to enforce its interpretation of the act. Section 11 of the Endangered Species Act gave dam opponents another alternative, however. As explained in chapter 2, Section 11(g) contained a citizen suit provision that allowed individuals to file a civil action "to enjoin any person, including the United States . . . , who is alleged to be in violation of any provision of this Act."

The citizen suit provision imposed a preliminary requirement. At least sixty days prior to initiating an action under Section 11(g), the plaintiffs had to "give written notice" to the secretary of the Department of the Interior and to "any alleged violator." To satisfy this notice requirement, Zygmunt Plater, Hank Hill, and Donald S. Cohen — an associate dean at the University of Tennessee Law School — wrote to the TVA and to the Department of the Interior on October 20, 1975. The initial paragraphs of the two letters were identical. The first called attention to the decision to list the snail darter as endangered and noted that the TVA work on the project continued to threaten the species. The second quoted Section 7 of the Endangered Species Act. The final paragraph in each letter described the TVA actions as "a violation of Section 7" and requested appropriate action from the addressee. The letter to the TVA "respectfully request[ed]" the Authority to discontinue the actions that threatened the snail darter. The letter to the Department of the Interior asked "that the Department of the Interior take all action necessary to enforce the Act."

On December 5, 1975 — a little less than two months after the plaintiffs sent their sixty-day-notice letters, the Senate passed the 1976 Public Works for Water and Energy Research Appropriation Act. Notwithstanding the Fish and Wildlife Service decision to list the snail darter, the appropriation for the TVA included the amount requested for the Tellico project. However, neither the committee report nor the floor debate included any specific reference to the snail darter or to the Tellico project. The Senate bill differed from the House bill on matters other than the Tellico project, and so a conference was necessary. Because the differences did not involve the Tellico project, neither the conference report nor the floor debate on the conference bill discussed the dam or the snail darter. The conference bill passed both houses of Congress on December 12, and President Ford signed the appropriation act on December 26.

Just after Congress completed final action on the appropriation act, the Fish and Wildlife Service initiated a new rule-making procedure to provide further protection for the snail darter. On December 16, 1975, the Service issued a proposed rule that designated the critical habitat of the snail darter and five other species that had been listed as endangered. The area designated for the snail darter was "river mile

0.5 to river mile 17 of the Little Tennessee River," all of which would be flooded by the closing of the Tellico Dam.

The dam opponents did not wait for the Fish and Wildlife Service to finalize the critical-habitat rule before filing their legal action. On February 28, 1976, they filed suit against the TVA in the Federal District Court for the Eastern District of Tennessee. The plaintiffs in the new suit were Hill, Plater, and Cohen — the three individuals who had signed the notice letters to the TVA and the Department of the Interior — plus the Association of Southeastern Biologists and the Audubon Council of Tennessee. The attorney of record for the plaintiffs was W. P. Boone Dougherty, a highly respected trial attorney in Knoxville, who had agreed to take the case on the promise that the plaintiffs would raise the money to pay his fee. The complaint alleged that completion of the dam would violate the Endangered Species Act and that Section 7 required the district court to enjoin the violation.

The plaintiffs in the Endangered Species Act suit sought an expedited hearing "as soon as practicable" and asked the court to issue temporary and permanent injunctions against further work on the Tellico project "following such hearing." Once again, Judge Robert Taylor was the presiding judge. On February 25, he heard oral arguments from the attorneys on the request for a temporary injunction, and he issued an opinion from the bench the next day. Although Judge Taylor rejected the TVA argument "that the Endangered Species Act [did] not apply to the Tellico Project," he denied the request for a preliminary injunction. He gave two reasons for reaching this result. First, he could not say "at this time that plaintiffs have demonstrated a probability of success on the merits." Second, he could not find "that the injury which the plaintiffs will suffer unless a preliminary injunction is granted outweighs the harm that would result to the TVA." In support of this second finding, he cited a statement by counsel that the original NEPA injunction had "cost the TVA approximately $15 million, an amount which was shocking to the Court." He did, however, schedule a trial on the merits for April.

As the parties were preparing for trial, the Fish and Wildlife Service strengthened the case of the opponents by completing the designation of the critical habitat for the snail darter. On April 1, 1976, the Fish and Wildlife Service issued a final rule designating mile 0.5 to mile 17 of the Little Tennessee River as critical habitat for the snail darter. The final rule covered only the snail darter. The Authority said it would complete the critical-habitat designations for the other species covered by the proposed rule at a later date.

Nineteen individuals and organizations had filed comments on the proposed designation of critical habitat for the snail darter. Seventeen supported the proposal. One individual and the TVA opposed the designation of critical habitat. The TVA gave two reasons for its opposition. First, the "river mile designation appears to be in error" because snail darters have been discovered between river mile 0.1 and river mile 0.4 as well as between river mile 0.5 and river mile 17. Second, the identification of "the critical needs of the snail darter" is not yet complete, and so designation should await the completion of a study that the TVA was conducting with Jones & Stokes Associates, Inc., a biological consulting firm.

The preamble to the final rule responded briefly to all the comments except those submitted by the TVA. It acknowledged that "seventeen of the 19 comments received completely supported the proposal" and did not analyze them except to note that they came from "professional biological societies, national and state conservation associations, a national sportsman organization," the "State of Tennessee, through the Tennessee Wildlife Resources Agency," and "several citizens from the area." Although the Fish and Wildlife Service received "one letter opposing the proposal from an individual living in the area," the response published in the *Federal Register* did not address it because the individual presented "no factual information . . . to warrant any change of the proposed critical habitat."

The Fish and Wildlife Service addressed the comments from the TVA in more detail. It dismissed the sightings of snail darters in river miles 0.1 to 0.4 as irrelevant to whether river miles 0.5 to 17 should be designated as critical habitat. Although the new sightings by the TVA might indicate the existence of "additional critical habitat," it did not have "any bearing on the present proposal." Nor was the Fish and Wildlife Service persuaded that it should defer action until the completion of the TVA study. In its view, "the year-round occurrence of adult snail darters" in "the area proposed as critical habitat" was adequate "evidence that the area is critical habitat." Although the Fish and Wildlife Service acknowledged that "the identification of most of the links between the snail darter and its abiotic and biotic environment have not been specifically determined," the absence of that information did not "prevent the designation of critical habitat."

Three weeks after designating the critical habitat for the snail darter, the Fish and Wildlife Service circulated a document entitled "Guidelines to Assist the Federal Agencies in Complying with Section 7 of the Endangered Species Act of 1973." Prepared "as a starting point for the development and promulgation of regulations," the document indicated that the Service intended the guidelines as "a broad flexible framework within which federal agencies may prepare internal procedures to fulfill their responsibilities under section 7." The guidelines did, however, address the applicability of Section 7 to existing projects. In deciding whether Section 7 applied to actions that were being implemented but had not been completed, a federal agency was to determine whether "substantial work remain[ed] to be done which would, independent of the effect of earlier work performed, in and of itself jeopardize the continued existence of a listed species or modify . . . critical habitat of a listed species." If the remaining work on a project could have such an effect, the guidelines provided that "the requirements of section 7 should be satisfied."

Once the Fish and Wildlife Service issued the critical-habitat designation for the snail darter and guidelines for the implementation of Section 7, the struggle over the snail darter shifted back to the litigation pending in the Eastern District of Tennessee. In that litigation, the plaintiffs argued that completion of the Tellico Dam would violate both Section 7 and Section 9 of the Endangered Species Act. They placed most emphasis on the Section 7 claim. Completion of the Tellico Dam would, they contended, violate Section 7 by jeopardizing the continued existence of the snail darter and by destroying its critical habitat. The plaintiffs gave much less emphasis to the argument that completing the dam was a violation of Section 9 because it would "take" members of the endangered species by harming or harassing them.

In light of the violations of the Endangered Species Act, the plaintiffs insisted that an injunction was the appropriate remedy. Their primary argument claimed that an injunction was mandatory because the court was obligated to implement the policy that the Endangered Species Act established. Alternatively, they contended that an injunction was appropriate even if the decision of whether to issue the injunction was committed to the court's discretion. They cited four factors to show that granting the injunction would serve the public interest: the importance of preserving ecological habitats and species, the congressional recognition of this ecological interest in the Endangered Species Act, the value of preserving the existing river, and the limited loss that would be caused by an injunction.

In response, the TVA argued that no violation of the Endangered Species Act had occurred and that a permanent injunction against completion of the dam was inappropriate even if completion of the Tellico Dam would amount to a "technical violation" of the act. The Authority gave two reasons for its position that completion of the dam would not violate the Endangered Species Act. First, the TVA claimed that the legislative history for the 1976 appropriation act showed a congressional intent that the dam should be completed. Second, the TVA contended, the Endangered Species Act vested the ultimate decision as to whether to proceed with a project in the agency responsible for the project, not the Fish and Wildlife Service. Given the extensive efforts of the TVA to locate, study, and transplant the snail darter, its decision to complete the Tellico Dam was not arbitrary, capricious, or otherwise not in accordance with law. Moreover, even if completion of the dam would violate the act, the TVA argued that the decision regarding whether to grant or to deny an injunction was committed to the sound discretion of the trial court. Given the advanced stage of the project, the good faith efforts of the TVA to conserve the snail darter, and the congressional appropriations after discovery of the snail darter, the TVA argued that Judge Taylor should exercise his discretion to deny the injunction.

The trial on the merits of the Endangered Species Act claim began before Judge Taylor on April 29, 1976. Dr. Etnier was the principal witness for the plaintiffs. He testified regarding his discovery of the snail darter and the TVA grant for his graduate student, Wayne Starnes, to study the fish. He estimated that 5,000 to 15,000 snail darters lived in the Little Tennessee and said he had "no doubt" that the "snail darter will become extinct in the Little Tennessee River following impoundment of the Tellico Reservoir." He described the transplant to the Hiwassee River as having "a chance but a slight chance" of success. Zygmunt Plater appeared briefly as a witness as well as counsel; he identified a letter that the Department of the Interior had hand delivered to him the previous day. Wayne Starnes, a graduate student in zoology at the University of Tennessee, testified regarding his study of the life cycle of the snail darter; he said that closure of the dam would mean that "the majority or all of the reproducing population of the snail darter will be exterminated." John Ramsey, an employee of the research unit of the Fish and Wildlife Service at Auburn University, agreed that "the closure of the Tellico Reservoir and impoundment will jeopardize the continued existence of the snail darter and destroy or modify its critical habitat in the Little Tennessee River." Dr. James D. Williams Sr., the ichthyologist for the Office of Endangered Species of the Fish and Wildlife Service, said that the evidence on the transplant program to the Hiwassee was "inconclusive" at this point and that the TVA had failed to restrict clearing around Coytee Springs as it had promised. The plaintiffs presented the testimony of two witnesses by reading from their depositions. Dr. Royal D. Suttkus, a professor of biology at Tulane University, questioned the current qualifications of the defense expert; Dr. Suttkus also agreed that creation of the Tellico Reservoir would destroy the habitat of the snail darter in the Little Tennessee River. Dr. Herbert Boschung Jr., a professor of biology at the University of Alabama, refuted the defense suggestions that the snail darter "was not a good species" and that the range of the snail darter was "probably more widespread" than just the Little Tennessee River.

The TVA offered testimony from six witnesses. George H. Kimmons, the TVA manager of engineering design and construction, indicated that the project was approximately 78.6 percent complete as of March 31, 1976, and that it was scheduled for closure in January 1977. Dr. Thomas H. Ripley, director of the Forestries, Fisheries and Wildlife Development Division at the TVA, testified regarding the TVA transplant program. Richard B. Fitz, a fisheries biologist for the TVA and supervisor of the TVA snail darter conservation team, described the discovery of snail darters below the mouth of the Little Tennessee River and in Watts Bar Reservoir. He opined that "the evidence we have gathered thus far indicates the transplant [to the Hiwassee River] will be successful." Charles F. Saylor, the TVA employee who was responsible for the program for transplanting the snail darter, testified regarding the transplant program; he said that the sexual progress and condition of the fish on the Hiwassee were "parallel" to those in the Little Tennessee and that "today it appears that there is successful transplant" on the Hiwassee River. David Turner, a TVA employee on the snail darter conservation team, said that he had observed snail darters in approximately fifteen feet of water in the Chickamauga Reservoir. Dr. Edward Raney, a professor of zoology emeritus at Cornell University, was the principal outside expert for the TVA. He described the TVA transplant effort as "an excellent program" that is "being done in depth" and said "the evidence to date indicates that [the transplant] is successful." He also suggested that "the upper Tellico River, at a depth of approximately 5 to 10 feet, will serve as a satisfactory habitat for the snail darter after the dam has been closed." The TVA also introduced the deposition of Gray Hickman, a TVA employee whose testimony was stipulated to be substantially the same as that offered by Charles Saylor.

The trial concluded with a single rebuttal witness from the plaintiffs. Dr. Alan Randall, an associate professor of agricultural economics at the University of Kentucky, testified regarding the economic cost of halting the Tellico Project. If the project were abandoned, he estimated that "non-recoverable obligations would be of the order of $30 million, say plus or minus $5 million," of the $78 million the TVA had spent.

On May 25, 1976, Judge Taylor issued his decision. He found the plaintiffs had established that completion of the dam would violate Section 7 of the Endangered Species Act. Nonetheless, he refused to enjoin completion of the dam.

Judge Taylor conceded that TVA witnesses had testified they had sighted a few snail darters outside the area that had been designated as critical habitat. These sightings did not, however, "alter the fact that [the area designated] constitutes a significant portion of the snail darter's range and is a critical habitat for the species." "Undisputed" evidence established "that the best estimates of the snail darter population are 10,000 to 15,000 and that this population is presently in the critical habitat area." If the dam were completed, "all of the portion of the Little Tennessee River which is presently designated as critical habitat will be inundated by the waters of the Tellico Reservoir." Moreover, "the water depth at Coytee Springs, the place of the snail darter's discovery, will increase from its present depth of two or three feet to a depth of thirty or forty feet." According to Judge

Taylor, the snail darter might "continue to exist for several years after the proposed impoundment." However, he labeled "highly doubtful" the prospect that the snail darter would reproduce once the habitat were changed from a free-flowing stream to a reservoir. Thus, Judge Taylor concluded, "the preponderance of the evidence" demonstrated that closure of the dam would "result in the adverse modification if not the complete destruction of the snail darter's critical habitat."

Judge Taylor also concluded it was "highly probable" that completion of the dam would "jeopardize the continued existence of the snail darter" as a species. Neither the TVA's efforts to transplant the snail darter to the Hiwassee River nor the sightings of a few darters outside the reservoir area negated the threat to the species. Although the TVA had transplanted more than 700 snail darters, the relocation project would succeed only if the snail darter were able to reproduce in the new environment and the Authority had offered "no conclusive proof on that issue." The TVA, Judge Taylor noted, had "searched unsuccessfully" for snail darters in the upper reaches of the Little Tennessee River as well as "in 60 or 70 other watercourses in Alabama and Tennessee." The failure to discover populations meant that filling the Tellico Reservoir would eliminate "almost all of the known population of snail darters."

Despite finding that completion of the Tellico Dam would violate Section 7, Judge Taylor refused to grant an injunction. In his view, the evidence showed that the TVA had "made a good faith effort to conserve the snail darter while carrying out its plan to complete the [Tellico] project." In particular, he cited the Authority's support of research projects concerning the snail darter. The TVA, he noted, had funded a proposal by Dr. Etnier's graduate student for "a biological study of the snail darter, including its life history and habitat." In addition, the authority had initiated its own program to "study the snail darter, attempt transplantation[,] and search for new populations."

The plaintiffs also claimed that the TVA had "not properly consult[ed] with the Department of the Interior within the meaning of that term as used in § 7 of the [Endangered Species] Act." In particular, they argued, the Authority had "never seriously considered alternatives to completing the dam and impounding the river." Assuming that the refusal to consider alternatives was "true," Judge Taylor found that the TVA decision to "take such a course of action" was "reasonable" for three reasons. First, "when the snail darter was listed on the endangered list in November 1975," the TVA "was fairly close to completion of the project." Second, "the nature of the project" gave the TVA "no alternative to impoundment of the reservoir, short of scrapping the entire project." Third, the TVA had "continued work on the project under the supervision and direction of Congress." To reinforce this last point, Judge Taylor quoted at length from the congressional hearings and committee reports from 1975 and 1976.

The advanced stage of the project also led Judge Taylor to conclude that the violations of the Endangered Species Act did not mandate an injunction against completion of the Tellico Dam. Congress had, he said, authorized the Tellico Dam "on October 15, 1966 as a multipurpose water resource and development project." By "March 31, 1976, the main dam, spillway and auxiliary dams were 85% complete, and the entire project was about 80% complete." The TVA had continued on the project "since work was first begun in 1965, except for the delays caused by the litigation" initiated by opponents of the dam. The federal government had invested more than $78 million in public funds on the dam, and enjoining the project would result in a loss of approximately $53 million. Opponents of the dam argued that the loss could be mitigated by modifying the project to leave the river undisturbed, but Judge Taylor noted in a footnote that the TVA lacked authority to use the funds appropriated by Congress for any purpose other than completion of the dam.

The Endangered Species Act problem did not arise, Judge Taylor emphasized, until long after the TVA had begun work on the Tellico Dam. Congress had initially authorized the project more than seven years before the Endangered Species Act became effective in December 1973 and nine years before the snail darter was listed as endangered. "Under these circumstances," Judge Taylor found it unreasonable "to conclude that Congress intended the [Endangered Species] Act to halt the Tellico Project at its advanced stage of completion." Such an interpretation of the Endangered Species Act would, he argued, conflict with the principle that "the Act should be construed in a reasonable manner to effectuate the legislative purpose."

Citing several decisions rendered under the National Environmental Policy Act, Judge Taylor declared that "at some point in time a federal project becomes so near completion and incapable of modification that a court of equity should not apply a statute enacted long after inception of the project to produce an unreasonable result." In particular, a court "should proceed with a great deal of circumspection" when Congress has made "an irreversible and irretrievable commitment of resources . . . to a project over a span of almost a decade." Judge Taylor completed his opinion by rejecting several specific arguments advanced by the plaintiffs. He refused to defer to the guidelines recently issued by the Fish and Wildlife Service, and he explained why it was appropriate to give weight to appropriation acts in construing a substantive statute. He also distinguished several recent decisions interpreting the Endangered Species Act and rejected the claim that a judge had limited discretion in deciding whether to issue an injunction under the act.

The Fish and Wildlife Service had, Judge Taylor acknowledged, "very recently promulgated guidelines to assist federal agencies in carrying out their responsibilities under [Section] 7." The guidelines provided that "the requirements of section 7" applied whenever "substantial work remains to be done" and the remaining work would jeopardize a species or destroy its critical habitat. Although a court was "ordinarily" required to give "considerable weight" to the interpretation of a statute "by an agency charged with administering it," Judge Taylor decided that that rule was inapplicable to the guidelines. When the Fish and Wildlife Service promulgated the guidelines, the agency "noted that they were intended as a 'starting point' for the promulgation of regulations" that would be issued later. This statement led Judge Taylor to conclude that the guidelines might not be the agency's "final statement of the manner in which [Section] 7 is to be applied to ongoing projects." Alternatively, he suggested that the guidelines "might be directed toward ongoing projects which, with reasonable alterations, could be completed without violating" Section 7 or that the guidelines might not have "contemplated" the "situation presented in this case." In any event, he declined to give the guidelines "much weight in [their] present tentative form."

Judge Taylor next defended his reliance on congressional appropriations for the Tellico project as an aid to construction of the Endangered Species Act. He acknowledged "the rule that congressional approval of appropriations does not, standing alone, repeal provisions of law in effect at the time the appropriations are approved." Moreover, he conceded Congress had not yet acted on the only appropriation request that the TVA had submitted since the critical habitat of the snail darter was determined in April 1976. Nonetheless, he noted, Congress had approved "additional funding of the Tellico Project" after "being informed" that the TVA "did not construe the Endangered Species Act as preventing the project's completion." In addition, a House committee directed the TVA "to complete the project 'in the public interest.'" These actions convinced him "that Congress was thoroughly familiar with the project when additional appropriations were made since it had been dealing with the project over a number of years."

Opponents of the dam also relied on decisions issued by the Fifth, Eighth, and Ninth Circuits in the months before the district court decision in the snail darter case. They contended these decisions established "that the Act should be applied with full force and effect to the Tellico Project." Judge Taylor rejected this contention because he found the cases factually distinguishable. A Ninth Circuit case dealt "only tangentially" with the Endangered Species Act. The Fifth Circuit decision (described in chapter 2) involved a species that had been named as endangered under an earlier version of the Endangered Species Act and a project in the initial stages of construction. In addition, the plaintiffs sought "relatively minor alterations" to the highway segment being challenged. The Eighth Circuit decision (also described in chapter 2) involved a species that had been designated as endangered prior to the Endangered Species Act of 1973, and it concerned a project on which "actual construction" did not begin until July 1974.

The plaintiffs also argued that a district court had only limited discretion in deciding whether to grant an injunction. They claimed that the court was "limited to fashioning a remedy to insure compliance with the Act, not to excuse a violation thereof." Judge Taylor rejected that contention as applied to the Tellico project. Under the "particular facts and circumstances," he ruled, "the Act does not operate in such a manner as to halt the completion of this particular project." The situation would be, he declared, "far different . . . if the project were capable of reasonable modification that would insure compliance with the Act or if the project had not been underway for nearly a decade." Carrying the plaintiffs' argument "to its logical extreme" would, he noted, "require a court to halt impoundment of water behind a fully completed dam if an endangered species were discovered in the river on the day before such impoundment was scheduled to take place." He rejected this interpretation because he could not "conceive that Congress intended such a result."

Rejection of the arguments described in the preceding paragraphs led naturally to Judge Taylor's ultimate conclusion: the request for a permanent injunction should be denied. The TVA actions "in continuing further implementation of the Tellico Project" were not arbitrary, capricious, "or otherwise not in accordance with the law." To the contrary, the TVA had "made a good faith effort to conserve the snail darter" and had "consulted with other agencies about the problem rather than taking the immutable position that it was not required to comply with the Act."

The plaintiffs appealed Judge Taylor's refusal to enjoin completion of the dam to the Sixth Circuit. The immediate problem was to stop the TVA from completing the dam while the appeal was pending, and so the plaintiffs filed a motion asking the appellate court to enjoin further work on the dam until the appeal was decided on the merits. On July 26, 1976, the court of appeals issued an injunction pending appeal and scheduled oral arguments for the October session. The TVA immediately asked the court of appeals to reconsider the decision to grant the injunction. In response to the TVA motion, the Sixth Circuit stayed its injunction until the parties were given a chance to present oral arguments in the chambers of Judge Oakes. Following the oral argument, Judge Weick authored an August 2 opinion that ordered a modified injunction. Relying on the findings of fact by the district court, he concluded "that the only conduct which would result in destruction of the [snail darter] is closure of the dam." Accordingly, the modified injunction allowed the TVA to continue its construction activities. It did, however, "enjoin pending appeal, any closure of the dam."

As the appeal to the Sixth Circuit was pending, Congress acted on the TVA's appropriation request for the 1977 fiscal year. The appropriation committees of both houses of Congress recommended that $9.7 million be appropriated for the project, but only the Senate report discussed the snail darter litigation. That report briefly summarized the TVA presentation in its subcommittee hearings. It then noted that "the subcommittee brought this matter as well as the recent U.S. District Court's decision to complete the project, to the full committee." Based on this information, the Senate report emphatically endorsed "the full $9.7 million budget request for the Tellico project." It declared that "the Committee does not view the Endangered Species Act as prohibiting the completion of the Tellico project at its advanced stage and directs that this project be completed as promptly as possible in the public interest."

The Sixth Circuit heard oral argument on the appeal of Judge Taylor's decision on October 14, 1976, and rendered its decision on January 31, 1977. The appellate court reversed the district court's judgment and remanded the case with instructions to issue "a permanent injunction halting all activities incident to the Tellico Project which may destroy or modify the critical habitat of the snail darter." This injunction was to "remain in effect until Congress, by appropriate legislation, exempts Tellico from compliance with the Act or the snail darter has been deleted from the list of endangered species or its critical habitat materially redefined."

Judge Anthony Celebrezze authored the opinion of the court of appeals. All three judges agreed with the decision, but Judge Wade McCree added a brief concurring opinion.

The analytic structure of Judge Celebrezze's opinion had three parts. First, the court found that completion of the Tellico Dam would violate the Endangered Species Act. Second, the court determined that no adequate ground existed for exempting the Tellico project from the statutory requirements. Third, the court concluded that an injunction was "the proper remedy to effectuate the purposes of the Act."

Like the district court, the appellate court ruled that completion of the dam would violate Section 7 of the Act. The TVA conceded that converting the free-flowing river to a reservoir would alter "a significant portion of the designated 'critical habitat' of the snail darter." In addition, the record supported the claim "that the intrinsic environmental difference between river and reservoir bottom will inexorably destroy large numbers of snail darter eggs as well as inhibit the species' spawning instinct." In light of this concession and evidence, the Sixth Circuit upheld the district court's finding that inundation of the area designated as critical habitat would significantly reduce, if not completely eliminate, "the known population of the snail darter."

The Sixth Circuit held that the district court's finding was sufficient to establish that the TVA's Tellico operations violated Section 7. In reaching this conclusion, Judge Celebrezze relied on the critical-habitat regulation that the secretary of the interior had adopted in 1975. The regulation provided that an action affecting a critical habitat violated Section 7 if its impact on the species would "place the species in further jeopardy or restrict the potential and reasonable expansion of [the] species." Courts were not, Judge Celebrezze noted, "compelled to follow agency constructions of a regulatory measure." Nonetheless, the court normally showed "great deference" to the interpretation of the agency charged with responsibility for administering the statute, and the Interior Department was that agency for the Endangered Species Act. Section 7 gave the interior secretary a "pivotal role" in securing "voluntary compliance" with the act from federal agencies, and the secretary's interpretation of Section 7 was "both reasonable and consistent with [the court's] reading of the Act's legislative history." Moreover, giving effect to the secretary's definition of "critical habitat" would have "positive benefit" for administration of the statute. The judicial endorsement would "expedite the adjudication of future cases as well as assist the Secretary in achieving a uniform federal conservation posture with minimal reliance upon the courts."

The TVA offered two arguments for exempting the Tellico project from the requirements of Section 7, but Judge Celebrezze rejected both. He rejected an exemption "for the terminal phases of ongoing projects," because such an exemption would be "inimical" to achieving the objectives of the act. Nor was he willing to "condone non-compliance on the theory . . . that congressional approval of Tellico appropriations, upon full disclosure of the plight of the snail darter, constitutes legislative acquiescence in or express ratification of TVA's *laissez faire* interpretation of the Act." Such congressional attempts to control the interpretation of an existing statute by subsequent legislation amounted to "advisory opinions by Congress."

The TVA admitted that "a predictable causal relationship" existed between "the impoundment of the Little Tennessee [River] and the ultimate depletion of the snail darter population." Although this admission was sufficient to bring Section 7 "into play," the TVA argued "that closure of the Tellico Dam, as the last stage of a ten year project, falls outside the purview of the Act if it is rationally construed." The Sixth Circuit, however, refused to embrace "so restrictive an interpretation" of Section 7 "in the absence of positive reinforcement from the Act's legislative history." Instead, the court of appeals chose "to give the term 'actions' its plain meaning in the belief that [this] interpretation will best effectuate the will of Congress."

"The complexity of the ecological sciences suggests," Judge Celebrezze asserted, "that the detrimental impact of a project upon an endangered species may not always be clearly perceived before construction is well underway." Moreover, when "a project is on-going and substantial resources have already been expended, the conflict between national incentives to conserve living things and the pragmatic momentum to complete the project on schedule is most incisive." Thus, a judicial decision to treat "the extent of project completion" as "relevant in determining the coverage of the Act . . . would effectively defeat responsible review in those cases in which the alternatives are most sharply drawn and the required analysis most complex."

Judge Celebrezze concluded that "current project status cannot be translated into a workable standard of judicial review," and he supported that conclusion with two reasons. First, he noted that "whether a dam is 50% or 90% complete is irrelevant in calculating the social and scientific costs attributable to the disappearance of a unique form of life." Second, he found courts "ill-equipped to calculate how many dollars must be invested before the value of a dam exceeds that of the endangered responsibility." The judicial responsibility, he declared, was "merely to preserve the status quo where endangered species are threatened, thereby guaranteeing the legislative or executive branches sufficient opportunity to grapple with the alternatives." The district court had resisted this interpretation because of the consequences of following the argument to its "logical extreme." Logically, the interpretation adopted by the court of appeals would require "a court to halt impoundment of water behind a fully completed dam if an endangered species were discovered on the day before such impoundment was scheduled to take place." Judge Taylor had "dismissed this proposition out of hand as unreasonable and inconsistent with the intent of Congress." By contrast, the Sixth Circuit embraced it: "Conscientious enforcement of the Act requires that it be taken to its logical extreme."

Judge Celebrezze also claimed that the appellate court's decision was consistent with previous judicial decisions. He cited with approval the Fifth Circuit's decision, which interpreted the Endangered Species Act to protect the sandhill crane, as well as the Sixth Circuit's own decision requiring the TVA to prepare an environmental impact statement for the Tellico Dam. On the other hand, he "reject[ed] as inapposite" the other NEPA cases cited by TVA. They were "readily distinguished by one fact which they all share: any judicial error in a NEPA case is subject to later review and remedial reversal before permanent damage is done to the environment." That opportunity for later review and reversal would not "exist for an erroneously granted exemption from the Endangered Species Act." If the TVA were allowed "to complete and close the dam as scheduled, the most eloquent argument would be of little consequence to an extinct species."

The argument that congressional approval of Tellico appropriations, "upon full disclosure of the plight of the snail darter," amounted to legislative approval of the interpretation of Section 7 advanced by the TVA was equally unpersuasive to Judge Celebrezze. Congressional declarations "concerning the 'proper' application of an *existing* statute cannot influence our review because they lack the force of law." Crediting them "would be tantamount to permitting the legislature to invade a province reserved to the courts by Article III of the [C]onstitution."

The Sixth Circuit rejected the TVA position regarding the effect of congressional appropriations as inconsistent with "separation of powers doctrine." That doctrine required each branch to perform its assigned responsibility. In the words of the Sixth Circuit, "Congress must be free to appropriate funds for public works projects with the expectation that resulting executive action will pass judicial muster." At the same time, "courts must defend their prerogative to apply the law as they find it 'to require the Executive to abide by the limitations prescribed by the Legislature.'"

According to Judge Celebrezze, the TVA interpretation was especially inappropriate because it ignored the distinction between substantive laws and appropriations, a distinction recognized in the congressional rules. Congress itself had "recognized the dangers of bypassing plenary consideration of proposed modification to existing laws by adding amendments to appropriations bills." To avoid this danger, House Rule XXI provided that any provision in an appropriation bill that changed existing law was subject to challenge on a point of order.

The Sixth Circuit also rejected the claim that an earlier decision sustaining land condemnations by the TVA supported its argument.

The TVA claimed that the earlier case established that "congressional spending decisions" could provide "indicia of approval of the application of existing laws by the executive branch." The court of appeals, however, took a narrower view of the earlier decision. In its view, the previous case "viewed the continued financing of TVA's on-going land acquisition activities as implied ratification by Congress of a system of rules and regulations promulgated by TVA to give effect to enabling legislation which the Authority was charged with administering." The Endangered Species Act question was very different. The TVA was "neither charged with administering the Act nor [was] its conduct compatible with the measure's conservationist aims."

Because the Endangered Species Act contained no exemption for the Tellico Dam project, the court of appeals ruled that the district court had "abused its discretion in refusing to permanently enjoin all further actions by TVA which may detrimentally alter the critical habitat of the snail darter." According to the Sixth Circuit, "halting further construction pending intervention by Congress or additional rule making by the Secretary of the Interior" was not an "inequitable remedy" for "a clear violation of federal law."

The TVA claimed "to have done everything possible to save the snail darter, short of abandoning work on the dam." Although the TVA regarded abandonment of the dam as "innately unreasonable," the appellate court disagreed. "The welfare of an endangered species might," the Sixth Circuit concluded, "weigh more heavily upon the public conscience, as expressed by the final will of Congress, than the writeoff of those millions of dollars already expended for Tellico in excess of its present [salvageable] value."

Judge Celebrezze also rejected the TVA claim that its effort to transplant snail darters to the Hiwassee River discharged its obligation under Section 7. He insisted the relocation efforts would not have altered the court's "decision to enjoin further Tellico Dam construction" even if the TVA had offered "conclusive evidence" confirming that the transplanted population was "thriving and reproducing." According to the Sixth Circuit, the secretary of the interior, not the judiciary, had "the responsibility for maintaining the endangered species list and designating the critical habitats of listed species." The act required the secretary to issue rules when listing species and designating critical habitat. By contrast, nothing in the act authorized the courts "to override the Secretary by arbitrarily 'reading' species out of the endangered list or by redefining the boundaries of existing critical habitats on a case-by-case basis." To obtain relief, the TVA would have "to petition the Secretary . . . to blunt the impact of the Act by curative rule-making." Until the secretary removed the snail darter from the endangered list or redefined its critical habitat, the courts had "no recourse but to enjoin creation of the reservoir."

Despite the Sixth Circuit's reversal of the district court, Judge Celebrezze's opinion indicated that the appellate court was "sympathetic to [Judge Taylor's] analysis of the equitable factors present here which would normally militate against granting injunctive relief." The TVA, the opinion noted, "had not acted in bad faith." Indeed, the Authority's "efforts to preserve the snail darter appear to [have been] reasonable." However, the court of appeals regarded the "separation of powers doctrine" as "too fundamental a thread in our constitutional fabric for us to be tempted to preempt congressional action in the name of equity or expediency." As a result, the Sixth Circuit concluded that "the district court abused its discretion when it refused to enjoin a clear violation of federal law."

Judge McCree's concurring opinion consisted of a single paragraph. The starting point for his analysis was the district court's finding "that completion of the Tellico Dam would 'jeopardize the existence of the snail darter.'" That finding, he said, required the conclusion "that completion of the project would violate the Endangered Species Act." According to McCree, neither the beginning of the project before the enactment of the Endangered Species Act nor the continued appropriations after "a congressional committee was aware of the fact that the snail darter would be threatened by completion of the dam" was sufficient to exempt the Tellico project from the act. Thus, he agreed "that the case should be remanded with instructions to issue an injunction forbidding project activity that would threaten the existence of the snail darter."

The Sixth Circuit's decision once again halted the TVA's work on the Tellico Dam. It did not, however, alter the Authority's determination to complete the project. The appellate court ruling simply directed the struggle into new directions — back to the Fish and Wildlife Service and Congress and on to the Supreme Court.

CHAPTER 5

Battle before the Supreme Court

The TVA launched a three-pronged response to the Sixth Circuit injunction forbidding the completion and operation of the Tellico Dam. First, the TVA asked the Fish and Wildlife Service to delist the snail darter and to remove the designation of the Little Tennessee River as its critical habitat. Second, representatives of the Authority testified before congressional subcommittees seeking continued appropriations for the Tellico project. Third, TVA attorneys sought review of the decision of the Sixth Circuit in the U.S. Supreme Court.

Just over a month after the Sixth Circuit rendered its decision enjoining completion of the dam, the TVA initiated an administrative petition designed to end the Endangered Species Act restrictions. On February 28, 1977, the TVA petitioned the Fish and Wildlife Service to remove the snail darter from the list of endangered species and to eliminate the designation of the Little Tennessee River as the snail darter's critical habitat. The TVA also applied for a permit to transplant additional snail darters.

The Fish and Wildlife Service denied the request to transplant the darters on July 6, 1977, and the August 1977 General Accounting Office (GAO) report on the TVA economic analysis of the Tellico project contained an August 2 letter from the Service indicating that the delisting petition had been denied. On November 14, the TVA general manager wrote to the Fish and Wildlife Service inquiring about the status of the delisting petition. The Service responded in a December 5 letter formally denying the petition. The Fish and Wildlife Service letter apologized for not having provided a direct response to the delisting petition, but said it thought denial "was inherent" in its rejection of the application to transplant additional snail darters.

In the spring of 1977, the TVA general manager and members of the board of directors appeared before subcommittees of the appropriation committees of both houses of Congress. They explained the status of the project, including the recent decision of the court of appeals.

In his testimony before the Public Works Subcommittee of the House Appropriations Committee, TVA chairman Wagner cited the Tellico project as "a prime example of balanced perspective gone awry." The project was "more than 90 percent complete" and "more than $100 million of the project's estimated $116 million cost" had already been spent. When completed, the project would produce "substantial" benefits, including "126,000 acre-feet of flood control storage," the annual "production of 200 million kilowatt hours of electric energy," and the "creation of a navigation channel" that would provide opportunities for industrial development. Despite the advanced stage of the project and the public benefits that would be achieved by completing the dam, the Sixth Circuit had enjoined impoundment of the Tellico Reservoir. The court of appeals had issued its injunction because impoundment "would destroy the habitat of the 'snail darter,' a 3-inch minnow which was designated an endangered species by the U.S. Department of the Interior."

The Sixth Circuit had not issued its injunction, Wagner emphasized, when the Tellico project remained "on the drawing boards or in the preliminary phases of construction." Instead, the court stopped the project when the gates were ready "to be closed and the reservoir filled." Moreover, the statute on which the injunction was based "did not become law until the project was more than half completed," and the fish that led to the injunction was "not listed as endangered until the project was three-quarters completed."

Wagner next noted that the TVA had "conducted a comprehensive conservation program" for the snail darter. That program included "transplanting more than 770 snail darters to two rivers in an effort to assure their continued existence." The transplanted fish were "doing well and [had] reproduced," but even a successful transplant would not allow "completion of the project so long as the fish's critical habitat remains the Little Tennessee River."

The TVA, its chairman concluded, needed Congress's help to "resolve the special dilemma we face today with the Endangered Species Act in our efforts to complete the Tellico project." The Authority faced conflicting directions. "In the appropriation process, Congress ha[d] said, 'Go ahead. Build and develop benefits for men.'" At the same time, the Sixth Circuit had interpreted the Endangered Species Act to say "Stop building. Save the snail darter." The TVA needed to know what Congress wanted it to do.

In his presentation to the subcommittee, the TVA chairman requested an additional $11.5 million to complete the Tellico project. This request raised the total cost of the project to $116 million. A footnote to the cost estimate prepared in the TVA explained that five factors contributed to the cost escalation: "some foundation problems" on the main earthen dam, additional costs for reservoir clearing, additions to the project scope for highway modification and protection of the Tellico Blockhouse, more extensive archaeological investigations and actions related to the snail darter, and overhead services "being required over a more prolonged period." Notwithstanding the rising cost, the TVA still projected a positive benefit-cost ratio of 1.7 to 1.

In his 1977 testimony, the TVA chairman did significantly reduce the indirect benefits claimed for the project. His testimony did not include an independent estimate of the economic development that would occur. He did, however, say that the completion of the navigation channel would result in "4,000 basic industrial jobs and 2,000 trades and service jobs being created along the reservoir over a 25-year development period." That total of 6,600 was only about 25 percent of the 25,000 jobs that the TVA estimated would be created when it prepared the environmental impact statement.

By their comments and questions, the members of the House subcommittee showed their support for the completion of the Tellico project. At the conclusion of Wagner's presentation, Representative Bevill declared that the subcommittee wanted the TVA "to build these projects." He also agreed with the claim that the system was "out of balance as far as the Tellico Dam is concerned." Several members of the subcommittee also appeared sympathetic to the optimistic assessment of the Authority's transplant project offered by a TVA biologist. Finally, in comparing the $116 million construction cost with the small number of snail darters in the Little Tennessee River, Representative Myers calculated the cost of protecting the snail darter as "$50,000 to $100,000 for each snail darter."

The testimony apparently persuaded the subcommittees and the appropriation committees to which they reported. Both committees recommended appropriations sufficient to fund the full amount requested for the Tellico project, and they issued reports that recommended completion of the dam notwithstanding the threat to the snail darter.

The Appropriations Committee of the House of Representatives issued its report on June 2, 1977. Suggesting that the Sixth Circuit had erred in construing the Endangered Species Act, it declared "the Committee's view that the Endangered Species Act was not intended to halt projects such as these in their advanced stage of completion." In light of that view, the committee "strongly" recommended "that these projects not be stopped because of misuse of the Act." To solve the problem of the snail darter, the committee suggested that the TVA cooperate with the Department of the Interior "to relocate the endangered species to another suitable habitat so as to permit the project to proceed as rapidly as possible." To assist those relocation efforts, the House committee recommended an additional appropriation beyond the amount recommended by the TVA. The special appropriation gave the TVA an additional $2 million to facilitate relocation of the snail darter and other endangered species that threatened to delay or to stop TVA projects.

The Senate Appropriations Committee agreed with the recommendations of the House committee. Its June 25 report recommended approval of the amount requested by the TVA, as well as the supplemental appropriation proposed by the House committee for transplanting endangered species. The Senate report also declared its disagreement with the position adopted by the Sixth Circuit: "This committee has not viewed the Endangered Species Act as preventing the completion and use of these projects which were well under way at the time the affected species were listed as endangered." In any event, the committee favored completion of the projects even if the act did apply to projects that were under way when the species was listed. Reiterating that this effect was "contrary to the Committee's understanding of the intent of Congress in enacting the Endangered Species Act," the Senate report declared that "funds should be appropriated to allow these projects to be completed and their benefits realized in the public interest, the Endangered Species Act notwithstanding."

Dam supporters also sought an express statutory exemption for the Tellico project. Congress deferred action on those proposals until the committee responsible for the Endangered Species Act had an opportunity to hold hearings on the issue.

While it was seeking additional congressional appropriations for the Tellico project, the TVA also sought to have the Supreme Court reverse the decision of the Sixth Circuit. On May 31, 1977, the Authority filed a petition for a writ of certiorari with the Supreme Court. The opponents of the dam responded on July 1 with a brief opposing Supreme Court review. The National Resources Defense Council and the Eastern Band of the Cherokee Indians also filed briefs urging the Supreme Court to deny certiorari.

Most federal lawsuits end with the decision of the court of appeals even when one of the parties desires further review. The Supreme Court considers the merits of only a tiny fraction of the cases that are presented to the federal courts. The first hurdle for the party seeking review is to convince the Court that the appeal is one that should be addressed on the merits. In almost all cases, the party begins this process by filing a petition for a writ of certiorari. By a long-standing, unwritten tradition, the Court grants the writ of certiorari and considers the case on the merits if four or more justices think the case is worthy of review.

The Supreme Court has broad discretion in deciding which cases to hear. The Supreme Court rules do, however, identify some general considerations on which the Court relies in deciding which cases to address on the merits. The rules indicate that the Court focuses on those cases where lower courts have rendered conflicting decisions, where a lower court has apparently departed from Supreme Court precedent, or where the issues on which the case turns present important, unresolved questions of federal law. In addition, studies of the Supreme Court have shown that the Court grants review more frequently when the solicitor general seeks review on behalf of the United States than when private parties request review.

Judged by the criteria set forth in the Supreme Court rules, the Tellico Dam litigation seemed a possible candidate for review by the Supreme Court. Arguably, the case presented important, unresolved issues of federal law regarding the applicability of the Endangered Species Act of 1973 to projects begun before the act was passed, the significance of subsequent appropriations for a project after an endangered species was discovered, and the scope of a federal judge's power to deny an injunction in cases involving statutory violations.

The key feature in obtaining Supreme Court review was to convince the Office of the Solicitor General to approve the TVA application for a writ of certiorari. When the Sixth Circuit issued its opinion on January 31, 1977, the position of solicitor general was temporarily vacant following the election of Jimmy Carter as president. In March, Wade McCree — the concurring judge on the Sixth Circuit panel in *TVA v. Hill* and the author of the appellate opinion in the first NEPA case — assumed the position. His previous participation in the case as a judge obviously disqualified him, and so Daniel Friedman signed the petition for the writ of certiorari on behalf of the United States. Obtaining the support of the Office of the Solicitor General made it far more likely that the Supreme Court would grant review; indeed, whether an independent agency like the TVA can seek Supreme Court review without the support of the solicitor general is unclear.

Once a writ of certiorari has been granted, the process of considering the case on the merits normally consumes several months. The party seeking reversal of the lower court's decision first submits a brief explaining how it believes that court erred. The party that prevailed in the court of appeals files a brief indicating why it believes the lower court should be affirmed, and the party seeking reversal prepares another brief responding to the arguments in the brief by the party that prevailed. In addition, persons who are not parties but who are interested in the outcome of the lawsuit may file briefs as amici curiae, or "friends of the court." After the briefs are submitted, the parties have the opportunity to support their positions in oral arguments before the Court. Following oral argument, the Supreme Court discusses the case in a closed session, reaches a tentative decision, and assigns one justice to prepare the opinion in the case. Once a majority of the justices have approved the opinion and any concurring or dissenting opinions have been prepared, the Court announces the decision and publishes its opinion or opinions.

On rare occasions, the Court follows a more streamlined procedure that dispenses with oral argument and issues the opinion on the merits at the same time that it grants the petition for a writ of certiorari. The Supreme Court Rules say that the disposition of a petition for writ of certiorari can "be a summary disposition on the merits," but it provides no guidance as to when the Court will use this procedure. The Court obviously uses this summary disposition procedure only when a majority of the justices think that the lower court made a clear error in its decision. Citing an anonymous interview with a

Supreme Court justice, one recent study of the Court's process says the Court has a custom that requires six justices to agree on a summary disposition on the merits.

Ordinarily, the parties, their attorneys, and the public receive no information regarding the Court's deliberations with respect to whether the petition for certiorari should be granted and whether summary disposition is appropriate. The Court deliberates in private, and the only documents available to the parties or to the public are the order granting or denying the writ of certiorari and — in cases involving summary disposition — the opinion resolving the case on the merits. However, the 1993 opening of the papers of Justice Thurgood Marshall lifted the shroud of secrecy for *TVA v. Hill*, and the more recent opportunities to review the papers of Justice Blackmun and Justice Brennan have further amplified a most interesting story.

The papers of the Supreme Court justices reveal that the Court almost used the summary disposition procedure to reverse the decision of the Sixth Circuit in *TVA v. Hill*. When the justices first considered the petition for a writ of certiorari in September 1977, four members of the Court — Justices Stewart, Brennan, Marshall, and Stevens — voted to deny the petition. The other five justices — Chief Justice Burger and Justices White, Blackmun, Powell, and Rehnquist — favored granting the writ; moreover, four of the five justices who voted to grant the petition of certiorari favored a summary reversal without oral argument. Only Justice Blackmun favored scheduling the case for oral argument, and even he wanted to lift the injunction to allow construction of the dam to continue as the Supreme Court was considering the case.

During the month of October 1977, both Justice Rehnquist and Justice Powell tried to obtain majority support for opinions that would summarily reverse the Sixth Circuit and uphold the refusal of the district court to grant an injunction. In addition, a letter from Chief Justice Burger suggested a third rationale that would achieve the same result. None of them was able, however, to obtain the support of a majority of the justices for his position. Ultimately, the Court granted the petition for a writ of certiorari and scheduled the case for oral argument.

Justice Rehnquist first circulated a draft opinion summarily reversing the Sixth Circuit on October 5. The per curiam opinion he circulated emphasized that an injunction was an equitable remedy. A 1944 decision construing the Emergency Price Control Act of 1942 had ruled, he argued, that a grant of jurisdiction to enjoin statutory violations was insufficient to establish "that Congress intended an injunction to issue as a matter of right." Thus, the judicial enforcement provisions of Section 11 of the Endangered Species Act did not "require automatic issuance of an injunction . . . once a violation is found." Instead, the district court "possessed discretion to refuse injunctive relief" even though it had found a violation of the act; and Judge Taylor had not abused his discretion by refusing to enjoin the completion of the Tellico Dam. In exercising his discretion, Judge Taylor recognized that the Endangered Species Act "made the preservation of the habitat an important public concern." But he also found that a permanent injunction would mean the irretrievable loss of funds appropriated by Congress" and that, "after the snail darter was discovered," the TVA had continued to work on the project "at the direction of Congress." Moreover, the district court had also found that the TVA had acted "in good faith" by repeatedly bringing the snail darter to the attention of the appropriation committees of the Senate and the House, by "funding projects" to save the snail darter, and by "consulting frequently" with federal and state fish and wildlife officials. Finally, the opinion that Justice Rehnquist circulated rejected the argument that denying an injunction "somehow threatened the separation of powers" between the branches of the federal government. To the contrary, the district court had performed its traditional function of "balancing the equities" in deciding whether to enjoin a project for which Congress had appropriated funds "annually for more than a decade" because the completion of the project "would violate another Act of Congress passed seven years after the original authorization and appropriation" for the project.

Justice Rehnquist's draft opinion in support of summary reversal of the Sixth Circuit prompted Justice Stewart to draft a dissent that he circulated on October 12. His three-page opinion argued that injunctive relief was appropriate because it was "the only means available to forestall the precise irreparable harm the [Endangered Species] Act was designed to prevent — the destruction of the critical habitat of an endangered species." He distinguished the 1944 case on which Justice Rehnquist relied because in that case the Court had found that an injunction was not necessary to effectuate the purpose of the statute that the lawsuit sought to enforce. In the case of the snail darter, an injunction offered "the only means available to forestall the precise irreparable harm the Act was designed to prevent — the destruction of the critical habitat of an endangered species." Justice Stewart conceded that "some may wonder at a system of values that puts the survival of a three-inch fish ahead of the completion of a multi-million dollar public works project." In his view, however, any reordering of those priorities was a job for Congress, not the courts. The day after Justice Stewart circulated his opinion, Justices Brennan and Marshall indicated that they would join the dissent.

One day later, Justice Rehnquist added two footnotes to his draft opinion responding to the dissent. One challenged the dissent's reading of the 1944 case on which Justice Rehnquist had relied in the original draft. According to Justice Rehnquist, the 1944 decision affirmed a broad principle "affording federal courts a 'full opportunity' to exercise 'the sound discretion which guides the determinations of courts of equity.'" The second new footnote criticized the dissent for not addressing the statutory conflict that the district court had faced. The dissenters, Justice Rehnquist asserted, "failed to confront the fact that Congress had also recognized the public importance of the Tellico Project and mandated that the Project be completed 'as promptly as possible.'"

Justice Stevens had also voted to deny the petition for a writ of certiorari. A week after Justice Rehnquist revised his opinion, Justice Stevens circulated a brief, but acerbic, dissent. The petition for certiorari, he asserted in a footnote, presented only two issues for the Court's consideration: whether the Tellico Dam could be completed because Congress had continued to approve the project by appropriating funds necessary for its completion," and whether the Endangered Species Act applied "to a project substantially completed at the time of its enactment." Even on these grounds, the government had sought only plenary review, not summary reversal. Now the majority proposed to reverse summarily "on an entirely different ground." "Perhaps," Justice Stevens admitted, "it is somewhat odd for Congress to place such a high valuation on the preservation of the snail darter." However, he found it "even more odd for this Court to place a higher value on the investment in the Tellico Dam and Reservoir Project than on the proper allocation of decisional responsibility in the structure of our Government." The majority's action of approving "proposed executive action that [would] admittedly violate a federal statute" was "not only unprecedented." It was "lawless."

At this point, two other justices who favored summary reversal indicated that they favored alternate grounds to reach that result. Justice Powell circulated a draft that concluded the Endangered Species Act did not apply to projects already under construction when the statute was enacted. Chief Justice Burger argued for yet a third approach in a memorandum to Justice Powell. He suggested that the repeated congressional appropriations could be viewed as an amendment of the Endangered Species Act insofar as it applied to the Tellico Dam.

Justice Powell initially circulated his proposal to the five justices who had voted to grant certiorari. Apparently, Justice Powell failed to persuade the other members of the majority, because he circulated his alternative to the entire Court as a concurring opinion on October 21. In it, Justice Powell announced his "agreement with the result of the Per Curiam opinion" circulated by Justice Rehnquist. He indicated, however, that he reached the result by a "different line of analysis." In his view, the Endangered Species Act did "not apply to projects that are substantially completed."

As Justice Powell read the Endangered Species Act, Section 7 did "not require abandonment of projects duly authorized and under construction where a threat to an endangered species cannot be avoided by measures short of abandonment." Thus, the TVA did not have to abandon the construction of the Tellico Dam because it was "substantially complete."

Justice Powell gave two brief rationales for his position. First, the "language of § 7" was "at least ambiguous," and he found "strong support" for resolving the ambiguity "in favor of nonretroactivity" in "the 1976 appropriation and express congressional affirmation that § 7 does not apply retroactively to this nearly completed project." Second, the legislative history, particularly the views expressed by Senator Tunney and the Interior Department, "support[ed] this interpretation of § 7."

In an undated, handwritten note to Justice Blackmun, Chief Justice Burger wrote that "[Justice] Byron [White] has just about persuaded me that the Appropriation Act . . . operates as an amendment to the 'Snail Darter Act.' " He also wrote that Justice White had indicated that — despite his dissent — Justice Stewart "would not make a 4th to insist on oral argument." Thus, the chief justice said, he was inclined "to stay with a summary and [to] try to get [Justice Stevens] to 'cool it' on his rhetoric."

On October 25, the chief justice shared his view regarding the appropriation acts by sending all the justices copies of a typewritten note to Justice Powell. He proposed relying "entirely on the Appropriation Act of Congress enacted subsequent to the 'Snail Darter Act' as amending the latter." He also suggested a footnote to document "the fact that Congress showed *full awareness* of the conflict between the 'Snail Darter Act' and the action it was taking." Finally, he concluded with a sentence declaring that "the 'rabbit' capacity of the perch species to launch a new species 'in even numbered years' shows how absurd it would be to ignore the *positive* Act of Congress in Appropriation Acts, subsequent to the 'Snail Darter Act.' "

On October 26, the day after the chief justice circulated his note to Justice Powell, Justice Blackmun announced his willingness to join a summary reversal. His memorandum to the conference said he still preferred to grant certiorari while staying the injunction of the court of appeals. "The several opinions in circulation, however, clearly indicate[d] that no one else [was] of this mind." In this circumstance, he decided to join the concurring opinion of Justice Powell.

Justice Brennan then circulated a lengthy memorandum that urged the Court to avoid summary disposition of the snail darter case. The memorandum challenged the rationales of the draft opinions circulated by Justices Rehnquist and Powell and reiterated that Justice Brennan still favored denying review altogether. In any event, he argued, "the wealth of writing surely proves that a summary disposition is most inappropriate." Indeed, he indicated that he would "be writing something myself" if anyone "commands a court" for summary disposition.

Shortly thereafter, the Supreme Court accepted Justice Brennan's advice and decided to hear oral argument in *TVA v. Hill*. On November 14, 1977, the Court issued a brief order granting the petition for a writ of certiorari, and the Court later scheduled oral argument for April 18, 1978. Neither the order nor the papers of the justices explain exactly why the Court reached that result. Perhaps the other members of the Court accepted Justice Brennan's suggestion that summary disposition was inappropriate when the Court was so divided. Or perhaps Justice Stewart retreated from his earlier willingness to forgo oral argument, and he and the other three justices who wanted to affirm the Sixth Circuit combined to preclude summary disposition under the unwritten policy that requires the concurrence of six justices.

The grant of certiorari in *TVA v. Hill* prompted a major confrontation in the Carter administration. White House advisers initially persuaded President Carter that he should direct the Department of Justice to file a brief supporting the position of the Department of the Interior. In a subsequent meeting, Attorney General Griffin Bell argued that the department could not ethically switch positions after endorsing the TVA position in the application for a writ of certiorari, and he convinced the president to reverse his decision. The attorney general did, however, agree that the position of the Interior Department could also be presented to the Court. Daniel Friedman, the acting solicitor general, and three TVA lawyers signed the brief filed on behalf of the TVA. They made two basic claims: that Section 7 did not prohibit completion of the Tellico Dam and that the appropriation acts demonstrated a congressional intent that the project should be completed.

The TVA brief offered four reasons to support the argument that Section 7 did not apply to the dam: (1) Section 7 covered only actions for which reasonable alternatives were available, (2) this construction of the section was fully consistent with earlier cases construing NEPA, (3) the legislative history of the Endangered Species Act indicated that agencies could continue with a project when the public interest warranted it, and (4) the appropriation acts passed after the Endangered Species Act showed that Congress did not intend for Section 7 to stop the Tellico project.

The second argument in the TVA brief focused directly on the appropriation acts passed in 1975, 1976, and 1977. Prohibiting completion of the Tellico Dam, the TVA contended, would directly conflict with the purpose of these acts and the intent of Congress as reflected in the acts and their legislative histories.

As part of the compromise that allowed the Justice Department to continue to support the TVA, the brief filed in the snail darter legislation included an unusual attachment: a second brief prepared by the solicitor of the Department of the Interior. It directly contradicted the arguments in the brief filed on behalf of the TVA. The Department of the Interior brief argued that the TVA had not complied with Section 7 because the Authority had refused to consider viable alternatives and had failed to comply with the section's consultation requirement. It also argued that the appropriation acts did not exempt the Tellico Dam from the Endangered Species Act because none of the statutes contained any express reference to the dam.

Zygmunt Plater, Boone Daugherty, and Donald Cohen were the attorneys of record on the brief filed by the dam opponents. The brief emphasized four points. First, it claimed that Section 7 prohibited impoundment of the Tellico project because the prohibition against species extinction was absolute and because the TVA had failed to satisfy the consultation requirement. Second, the brief gave three reasons to support the contention that Section 7 applied to ongoing projects such as the Tellico Dam: the absence of an exemption provision in the statute, the adoption of this construction in the Interior Department regulation, and the consistency of this approach with the cases applying NEPA to ongoing projects. The opponents' brief also rejected the claim that the appropriation acts had implicitly amended the Endangered Species Act. None of the appropriation acts contained any express mention of the Tellico project, the brief noted, and so the TVA should be required to seek legislative relief from Congress. Finally, the brief argued that the appropriation acts were not inconsistent with the Endangered Species Act because they did not direct the TVA to proceed with the Tellico project notwithstanding the violation of Section 7.

The TVA also filed a reply brief responding to arguments advanced by the opponents. The reply brief dismissed assertions that the costs of the project exceeded its benefits as irrelevant to the issue before the Supreme Court. On the other hand, it disputed the assertion that the TVA had not consulted with the secretary of the interior. According to the reply brief, the TVA had acted in good faith to save the snail darter, but the only alternative the Authority was unwilling to consider was abandoning the project. Finally, the TVA claimed that the Endangered Species Act did not require stopping the final phases of a project that had been substantially completed.

Various groups filed amicus briefs on behalf of both parties. Several local governments and a local chamber of commerce filed a brief supporting the TVA, as did the Pacific Legal Foundation. On the other side, various national environmental organizations, the East Tennessee Valley Landowners Association, and the Eastern Band of the Cherokee Indians filed briefs opposing completion of the dam. For the most part, these briefs mirrored the arguments of the parties or made factual and legal arguments not directly resolved in the lower courts. One exception was the brief of the Pacific Legal Foundation. It filed the only brief directly addressing the issue on which Justice Rehnquist wanted the Court to base its decision: whether the district court had discretion to deny an injunction even if a statutory violation were established.

At the oral argument on April 18, Attorney General Bell argued the case for the TVA, and Professor Plater argued for the opponents of the dam. The solicitor general normally represents the United States in the Supreme Court, but the attorney general traditionally argues at least one case each term. Attorney General Bell did not explain why he chose to argue personally in the snail darter case. One possible explanation is the disqualification of Solicitor General Wade McCree, who had been a member of the panel that had decided the case in the Sixth Circuit, coupled with Bell's personal insistence that the federal government support the position of the TVA rather than the Department of the Interior. An attorney who formerly worked in the Office of the Solicitor in the Department of the Interior said the story in the department indicated that the attorney general had chosen the case because he was confident that the Supreme Court would reverse the Sixth Circuit.

The attorney general began his oral argument with a brief explanation of the unusual procedure of filing two briefs prepared by the government. He said he had agreed to allow the secretary of the interior to submit a brief taking a position contrary to the one urged by the Department of Justice on the understanding that this procedure did not violate "any policy of the Court." "Historically," he noted, this procedure had been followed "on rare occasions" going back to the Eisenhower administration. Although he would, "of course, not argue the Secretary of Interior's position," he described it as "well stated" and expressed confidence that "the Court will take note of it."

After explaining the reason for two briefs from the United States, the attorney general briefly summarized the Tellico project, noting that construction had begun in 1967 and had been temporarily halted in 1972 by the NEPA injunction. He also held up Exhibit 7 from the trial, a bottle containing a three-inch fish that he said was "supposed to be a full grown snail darter." Later he described the "dam itself" as "completed." All that remained was "to shut the gate, close the gate, it's over with."

Proceeding to his legal argument, the attorney general acknowledged that the Endangered Species Act could apply to some projects initiated prior to the enactment of the statute. But he contended that one had to consider the "stage of development" of the project to determine whether a violation had occurred. In the case of the Tellico Dam, he offered three arguments to support his claim that completion of the dam would not violate the act. First, "the language of the statute itself [could] be construed to support the District Court." Section 7 referred to an action "authorized, funded, or carried out" by an agency. These words, he claimed, suggested that "the agency had to have choices." In this case, the TVA had "none," and so the Authority did not have to abandon the project. Second, the attorney general claimed that the position he was urging was consistent with the secretary's regulatory guidance, "which was in effect when the District Court decided this case." That "tentative regulation" disavowed any intent to construe Section 7 to "bring about the waste that can occur if an advanced project is halted." Third, the attorney general relied on the appropriation acts and the accompanying committee reports. "Three times," he claimed, Congress had said "in committee reports" to the TVA: "Go forward and complete the project. We know abut the snail darter."

Justice Stevens was the member of the Court most willing to challenge the attorney general's position with probing questions. When the attorney general called attention to the small size of the snail darter, Justice Stevens forced him to concede that the Endangered Species Act offered the same protections to all species on the endangered list. Later, the attorney general asserted that the record "shows clearly that the snail darter has been transplanted to the Hiwassee River." Again, Justice Stevens forced him to admit that the secretary — not the courts — had the responsibility for defining the critical habitat of the snail darter. Near the end of the government's oral argument, Justice Stevens secured the attorney general's agreement that only the secretary of the interior could remove a species from the list of endangered species.

Justice Brennan and Justice Stewart challenged the interpretation of the appropriation acts offered by the attorney general. Justice Brennan offered a contrary interpretation of the $2 million appropriation for the TVA program to transplant the snail darter. In his view, the appropriation suggested that the TVA could not "go on with the dam" if completion would place the snail darter in jeopardy. In response to a question from Justice Stewart, the attorney general admitted that Congress had considered but not enacted a statute exempting the Tellico Dam from the Endangered Species Act.

For the most part, the questions from the other justices were more supportive of the government. Justice Blackmun inquired whether the program to transplant the snail darter allowed the attorney general to describe the transplant effort as "successful." Chief Justice Burger asked the attorney general to confirm that "three times, this project and the snail darter problem [had] been called to the attention of Congress." Justice Powell wondered how many congressional representatives would vote for a bill clarifying "that Section 7 shall apply to every completed project." The only negative signals from these justices came when the chief justice and Justice Powell indicated their disapproval of the decision to allow two briefs to be filed on behalf of the United States.

Appearing for the dam opponents, Professor Plater argued that the case "essentially turns on traditional questions of separation of powers and administrative law." The Sixth Circuit's position, which was also "the position taken by the Department of the Interior and by the respondent," came down, he asserted, "essentially to two basic points." First, completion of the dam would be a clear violation of Section 7. Second, Congress had not "changed the law" even though that body was still "reviewing public interest resolution for the conflict" over the Tellico project. Because Congress had not acted, Plater argued, the Court should reject the TVA's request "for some sort of informal statutory amendment, overriding the Endangered Species Act, based on appropriations funding."

In response to questions, Plater offered some significant additions to his basic argument. At one point, Justice Marshall suggested that a remand might be appropriate to determine the status of the transplant program. Plater responded by noting that only the secretary of the interior had authority to change the designation of the Little Tennessee River as the critical habitat of the snail darter. Similarly, Plater challenged Chief Justice Burger's assertion that the conflict was between protecting the snail darter and "a $120 million dam." The $120 million figure, he emphasized, was "the total project cost," while the cost of "the dam structure" was only "$5 million." The total cost figure, Plater noted, included "the purchase of 38,000 acres, less than half of which was to be flooded," and "25,000 acres of those [were] prime agricultural lands." The total cost, he insisted, also included "land purchases, roads, and bridges," which would be "immensely beneficial to the people." Finally, Plater noted that the TVA had aggressively pursued its construction efforts after the snail darter was discovered. Since 1973, when the TVA "took the position that [it] would not comply with the Endangered Species Act," the Authority had "trebled the rate of expenditure" and "doubled the amount of money spent."

Several justices peppered Plater with questions throughout his presentation. Early in the argument, Justice Blackmun objected to Plater's reference to the unanimous "opinion" of the Sixth Circuit because Judge McCree had submitted a brief opinion concurring in the result. Then Chief Justice Burger suggested that Plater's interpretation of the Endangered Species Act could require the government to dismantle an existing dam if an endangered species were discovered because "the continuance of the dam would be sufficient federal action to trigger Section 7." Plater declined to "take a position on that argument."

Justice Powell asked a series of questions trying to demonstrate the unreasonableness of refusing to close the dam. "Apart from the biological interest," he asked, "what purpose is served, if any, by these little darters." Although Plater acknowledged that the darters were not suitable for human food or as bait, he refused to concede that the snail darters were valueless. They were important for scientific reasons and for preserving the "philosophical" objection to eliminating a species. Moreover, the presence of the snail darter was an indicator of "clean, clear, cool flowing river water," an ecology much reduced by the sixty-eight dams the TVA had built on the Tennessee River system. Justice

Powell also called attention to the recent report of the Senate Appropriation Committee. In response, Plater noted that "the appropriation bill, on its face, . . . says nothing about Tellico."

Justice Rehnquist questioned Plater about the district court's discretion to deny an injunction even if a statutory violation were proved, the theory the justice had advanced in the opinion he circulated to the Court the previous October. The district court had ruled, he reminded Plater, that "you don't get an injunction automatically for a statutory violation." Plater argued that an injunction was mandatory for a statutory violation unless the violator "agreed to obey the law voluntarily," but the exchange obviously failed to convince Justice Rehnquist.

Following the oral argument, the Supreme Court voted again on the merits of the snail darter case. Two justices reconsidered the positions they had taken when the Court first voted on the petition for writ of certiorari in September, and their votes were sufficient to change the outcome. Chief Justice Burger and Justice White joined the four justices who had favored denying the petition to produce a 6-to-3 majority in favor of affirming the decision of the Sixth Circuit. Justices Powell and Rehnquist submitted revised versions of the opinions they had circulated in October, and Justice Blackmun again joined Justice Powell's opinion.

The Blackmun and Brennan papers offer the clearest summary of the voting switch that led to the Supreme Court's final decision. The conference notes of the justices indicate that the Court was closely divided. Justices Stewart, Brennan, Marshall, and Stevens — the four justices who had originally voted to deny the petition for a writ of certiorari — all adhered to their position that the decision of the Sixth Circuit should be affirmed. Similarly, Justices Powell and Rehnquist, both of whom had circulated per curiam opinions for summary reversal of the Sixth Circuit, also maintained their positions. Justice White, however, declined to take a final position, as did the chief justice. According to Justice Brennan's notes, the comments of the chief justice favored reversal, but he concluded by saying that "maybe" he "could go with [a] unanimous court to affirm."

According to the conference notes, Justice White promised to cast his vote by the following Monday, but he actually voted more quickly. The same day as the conference, he circulated a one-sentence memorandum in which he cast his vote to affirm the judgment of the Sixth

Circuit. A week later, a postscript to a memorandum from the chief justice indicated that he would "send a memo on 'snails' shortly." On May 3, Chief Justice Burger circulated the promised memorandum indicating that he had decided "to come down on the side of separation of powers" by voting to affirm. The May 3 memorandum also announced that the chief justice would write the majority opinion himself "even though [his] bid to 'join 8' to affirm failed to get 8."

The Marshall, Blackmun, and Brennan papers offer no explanation why the chief justice and Justice White changed their minds between October and April. Nonetheless, the timing of their votes suggests that the decision of the chief justice was a tactical one. By tradition, the Supreme Court votes in reverse order of seniority, with the chief justice voting last. In addition, when a member of the majority, the chief justice also decides which justice will write the opinion of the Court; if the chief justice is part of a minority, the senior associate justice in the majority assigns the opinion. Thus, when the conference vote in *TVA v. Hill* reached Chief Justice Burger, he knew that Justice White's vote was the crucial one for determining the outcome in the case. By delaying his vote until after Justice White voted, the chief justice was able to assign the opinion to himself and to draft a narrow opinion that focused on the Endangered Species Act as an exceptional statute. Had the chief justice joined the dissenters, Justice Brennan — the senior associate justice in the majority — would have assigned the majority opinion. He would probably have asked Justice Stewart to convert his October dissent into an opinion for the Court, but he might have chosen Justice Stevens, who had drafted an even more acerbic dissent. In either case, the opinion probably would have differed from the one ultimately prepared by Chief Justice Burger. It almost certainly would have focused more on the general principle mandating injunctive relief when such relief is necessary to correct a statutory violation and less on the specific language of the Endangered Species Act.

Chief Justice Burger began his majority opinion with an introductory paragraph summarizing the issues presented for decision and then turned to an extensive analysis of the background giving rise to the litigation before the Supreme Court. He used more than fifteen pages to describe the river and the dam, the NEPA lawsuits, the discovery of the snail darter, the administrative proceedings under the

Endangered Species Act, the litigation in the lower courts, and the congressional appropriations that continued throughout the judicial proceedings.

After this extensive factual introduction, Chief Justice Burger identified the "premise" on which his decision was based: "Operation of the Tellico Dam will either eradicate the known population of snail darters or destroy their critical habitat." From that premise, he identified two questions that the Court had to decide to resolve the case.

1. "Would TVA be in violation of the [Endangered Species] Act if it completed and operated the Tellico Dam as planned?"
2. "If TVA's actions would offend the Act, is an injunction the appropriate remedy for the violation?"

The remainder of the opinion explained why the Court answered yes to each of these questions.

The chief justice began the analysis of the first question — whether the TVA would violate the act by completing and operating the dam — with the concession that some might find the result that the Court reached "curious." By virtue of the Court's decision, "the survival of a relatively small number of three-inch fish among all the countless millions of species extant would require the permanent halting of a virtually completed dam for which Congress has expended more than $100 million." Moreover, that result would come to pass despite appropriations of "large sums of public money for the project, even after congressional Appropriation Committees were apprised of its apparent impact on the survival of the snail darter." The Court mandated that outcome, the chief justice insisted, because "the explicit provisions of the Endangered Species Act require precisely that result." Explaining the rationale for that conclusion consumed almost all the remainder of the majority opinion.

The chief justice conceded that the Court's construction of the act would "produce results requiring the sacrifice of the anticipated benefits of the project of many million dollars in pubic funds." Nonetheless, "an examination of the language, history, and structure" of the statute required that result. All three indicated "beyond doubt that Congress intended endangered species to be afforded the highest of priorities."

As one would expect in a case involving the interpretation of a statute, Chief Justice Burger started his analysis of the Endangered Species Act with the text of Section 7. "One would be hard pressed," he asserted, "to find a statutory provision whose terms were any plainer that those in § 7." Its affirmative command covers "all federal agencies," applies to any "actions *authorized, funded,* or *carried out* by them," and directs the agencies "to *insure*" that their actions will not have either of two effects. The agencies must avoid actions that will "*'jeopardize'* the continued existence" of an endangered species, as well as those that will "*result* in the destruction or modification of [critical] habitat" of an endangered species.

"This language," the chief justice insisted, "admits of no exception." He refused, therefore, to accept the TVA's argument that the statute should be interpreted "reasonably" by excluding from its coverage any "federal project which was well under way when Congress passed the Endangered Species Act in 1973." According to Chief Justice Burger, accepting that position would require the Court "to ignore the ordinary meaning of plain language." The TVA could not "close the gates of the Tellico Dam without 'carrying out' an action that has been 'authorized' and 'funded' by a federal agency." Nor could the TVA's action satisfy its duty to " 'insure' that the snail darter's habitat is not disrupted." Indeed, the "proposed operation of the dam will have precisely the opposite effect, the *eradication* of an endangered species."

After parsing the text of Section 7, Chief Justice Burger turned to the historical development of the statute. Congress was not, he noted, "legislating on a clean slate" when it enacted the Endangered Species Act of 1973. A 1966 statute had declared "the preservation of endangered species a national policy." That law "directed all federal agencies to protect these species." It also instructed agencies to preserve the habitats of "threatened species on land under their jurisdiction" but only " 'insofar as is practicable and consistent with the[ir] primary purposes.' "

Congress strengthened the 1966 act with amendments in 1969. This legislation was " 'the most comprehensive of its type enacted by any nation' up to that time." Nonetheless, proponents of the 1973 statute persuaded Congress "that a more expansive approach was needed if the newly declared national policy of preserving endangered species was to be realized."

{ *Chapter 5* }

As Congress was crafting the expanded approach in 1973, various witnesses testified that the greatest threat to endangered species "was destruction of natural habitat." That advice led directly to the new language in Section 7 of the 1973 act. "Virtually every bill introduced in Congress during the 1973 session" incorporated "language similar, if not identical to that found in the present § 7" with one important difference. Almost all "contained a qualification similar to the one in the 1966 Act."

Advocates of "strong endangered species legislation" encouraged Congress to eliminate the qualification. The chair of the National Wildlife Committee of the Sierra Club, for example, strenuously opposed the "consistent with the primary purpose" exception to the duty to avoid jeopardizing endangered species or destroying their critical habitat. That qualification, the representative argued, "could be construed to be a declaration of congressional policy that other agency purposes are necessarily more important than protection of endangered species." Under that interpretation, the normal agency mission "could always prevail if conflict were to occur."

In light of "this sequence" in the legislative history, Chief Justice Burger termed the "final version" of Section 7 "very significant." The text of the statute enacted by Congress "carefully omitted all of the reservations" in the prior legislation and in the bills that formed the basis for the 1973 act. The bill initially passed by the Senate only required federal agencies to "carry out such programs *as are practicable* for the protection of [listed] species." By contrast, the bill that the House of Representatives passed deleted "all phrases which might have qualified an agency's responsibilities." On most issues, the conference committee appointed to resolve the differences between the bills "basically adopted the Senate Bill." However, in the case of Section 7, "the conferees rejected the Senate version . . . and adopted the stringent, mandatory language in [the House Bill]."

The conference report made no specific reference to Section 7, but Representative Dingell — one of the managers of the legislation in the House of Representatives — referred to the section in a floor speech. He suggested that the new language would have an impact on two specific, ongoing controversies. It would require the secretary of defense "to take the proper steps" to protect the whooping crane, which was "being threatened by Air Force bombing activities." In addition, "the appropriate Secretary" would have *"to take action"* to see that grizzly bears "are not driven to extinction."

This "legislative background" formed the basis for the majority's rejection of the TVA's call for a "reasonable" construction of the statute. The TVA claimed "that the Act was not intended to stop operation of a project which, like Tellico Dam, was near completion when an endangered species was discovered in its path." The majority conceded that "no discussion in the legislative history" addressed "precisely this problem." Nonetheless, "the totality of congressional action [made] it abundantly clear" to the majority that applying Section 7 to the Tellico Dam was "wholly in accord with both the words of the statute and the intent of Congress." The "stated policies of the Act" as well as "literally every section of the statute" reflected the "plain intent of Congress . . . to halt and reverse the trend toward species extinction, whatever the cost." Furthermore, "the legislative history undergirding § 7 reveal[ed] an explicit congressional decision to require agencies to afford first priority to the declared national policy of saving endangered species." The chief justice gave particular emphasis to "the pointed omission of the type of qualifying language previously included in endangered species legislation." That omission showed "a conscious decision by Congress to give endangered species priority over the 'primary missions' of federal agencies."

The chief justice declined "to speculate, much less [to] act, on whether Congress would have altered its stance had the specific events [surrounding the Tellico Dam] been anticipated." He did, however, note that "the deliberations of Congress relating to the 1973 Act" contained "no hint" of any evidence "that would compel a different result" than the one the Supreme Court reached. To the contrary, the legislative history contained "repeated expressions of congressional concern over what it saw as the potentially enormous danger presented by the eradication of *any* endangered species." In addition, the comments of Representative Dingell and the House committee report were particularly important. They made it "clear" that "Congress foresaw that § 7 would, on occasion, require agencies to alter ongoing projects in order to fulfill the goals of the Act."

The majority acknowledged that "one might dispute the application of these examples to the Tellico Dam." One could say "that in this case the burden on the public through the loss of millions of unrecoverable dollars would greatly outweigh the loss of the snail darter." However, that decision was not one for the judiciary. "Neither the Endangered Species Act nor [Article] III of the Constitution provides federal courts with authority to make such fine utilitarian calculations." To the contrary, the act "show[ed] clearly that Congress viewed the value of endangered species as 'incalculable.' " This valuation would "quite obviously" make any balancing "difficult" if it were part of the Supreme Court's "power to engage in such weighing process," a suggestion that the chief justice "emphatically" rejected.

As a final argument to support the majority's construction of the Endangered Species Act, the chief justice called attention to "a number of limited 'hardship exemptions' " contained in Section 10 of the act. These exemptions showed that "Congress was also aware of certain instances in which exceptions to the statute's broad sweep would be necessary." None of the exemptions, however, "would even remotely apply to the Tellico Project." Therefore, "the maxim *expressio unis est exclusio alterius*" (listing one excludes others) applied, and the Court had to presume that the hardship cases of Section 10 were "the only ones Congress intended to exempt."

The preceding paragraph completed the chief justice's analysis of the Endangered Species Act as it was enacted in 1973. He next turned to the claim he had championed the previous October, "that the continuing appropriations for the Tellico Dam constitute[d] implied repeal of the 1973 Act, at least insofar as it applies to the Tellico Project." In support of that argument, the TVA cited statements in "various House and Senate Appropriations Committee Reports" issued during the course of the litigation over the dam. The majority "assumed" the statements indicated "that these Committees believed that the Act simply was not applicable in this situation." Nonetheless, the statements failed to convince the majority "that the Act has been in any respect amended or repealed."

"Nothing in the appropriation measures," the chief justice emphasized, stated "that the Tellico Project was to be completed irrespective of the requirements of the Endangered Species Act." In fact, the acts themselves did not itemize the appropriations for the Tellico Dam act or even "identify the projects for which the sums had been appropriated." Moreover, the amounts appropriated for the Tellico project "represented relatively minor components of the lump-sum amounts for the *entire* TVA budget." Under these circumstances, finding a repeal would "do violence to" a "cardinal rule" of statutory construction, the principle that repeals by implication are disfavored.

"The doctrine disfavoring repeals by implication," the chief justice emphasized, applies "with even *greater* force when the claimed repeal rests solely on an Appropriation Act." An appropriation act has "the limited and specific purpose of providing funds for authorized projects." Allowing appropriation acts to repeal substantive laws by implication would "lead to the absurd result of requiring members to review exhaustively the background of every authorization before voting on an appropriation." Moreover, allowing implied repeals of substantive laws by appropriation acts would "flout the very rules that Congress carefully adopted to avoid this need." The rules of both houses of Congress declared that substantive amendments by appropriation acts were not "in order." Thus, to accept the TVA argument would require the Supreme Court to conclude that Congress intended an implicit repeal of Section 7 "by means of a procedure expressly prohibited under the rules of Congress."

The chief justice also refused to embrace a narrower formulation of the implied repeal argument. The TVA contended that "an exception to the rule against implied repealers" was appropriate where "Appropriations Committees have expressly stated their 'understanding' that the earlier legislation would not prohibit the proposed expenditure." The majority rejected that proposition because "expressions of committees dealing with requests for appropriations cannot be equated with statutes enacted by Congress, particularly not in the circumstances presented by this case." Under congressional rules, "the Appropriations Committees had no jurisdiction over the subject of endangered species." Furthermore, neither of the committees had conducted "the type of extensive hearings which preceded passage of the earlier Endangered Species Act, especially the 1973 Act," and nothing in the record indicated "that Congress as a whole was aware of TVA's position."

As a final reason for rejecting the implied repeal argument, the chief justice emphasized that implied repeal was appropriate only where the new statute is "irreconcilable" with the prior law, and that one could construe the appropriation acts in a way that did not conflict with the

Endangered Species Act. Representatives of the TVA had appeared before appropriations committees several times after the snail darter was listed as endangered. In all those appearances, the TVA representatives "confidently reported . . . that efforts to transplant the snail darter appeared to be successful." This testimony, the chief justice argued, gave those committees "some basis for the impression that there was no direct conflict between the Tellico Project and the Endangered Species Act." In this context, the committees' expressions of the "view" "that the Act did not prevent completion of the Tellico Project" represented only the personal views of individual legislators. Such views, "however explicit," were never sufficient to change the legislative intent of Congress expressed in the prior legislation.

After exhaustively analyzing the applicability of the Endangered Species Act, the chief justice needed less than three pages to resolve the second issue of whether an injunction was the appropriate remedy. The Court's responsibility, he concluded, was not to "balance the equities" between the project and the snail darter, but to enforce the balance that Congress had established. Because completion of the Tellico Dam would violate the Endangered Species Act, an injunction had to issue.

"Of course," Chief Justice Burger conceded, "a federal judge . . . is not mechanically obligated to grant an injunction for every violation of law." To support this proposition, he cited a general treatise on remedies and the 1944 Supreme Court decision discussed in the opinion Justice Rehnquist had circulated in October. The treatise declared that "the balancing of equities is appropriate in almost any case." The 1944 decision refused to grant an injunction against a private company when the injunction would have no impact on future compliance and it would be unjust to the person who was the subject of the injunction.

Those "principles," the chief justice insisted, "take a court only so far." The separation of powers established in the federal Constitution required the courts to enforce statutes enacted by Congress. Although the Constitution granted the courts the power to interpret federal law, it also granted the power to enact those laws to Congress. "The exclusive province of Congress" includes not only the power "to formulate legislative policies and mandate programs and projects, but also [the power] to establish their relative priority for the Nation." Moreover, "once Congress has decided the order of priorities in a given area," the courts must "enforce them when enforcement is sought."

The majority specifically rejected the claim that its function included a responsibility "to view the Endangered Species Act 'reasonably'" and to "shape a remedy that accords with some modicum of common sense and the public weal." According to the chief justice, the Supreme Court lacked both "expert knowledge on the subject of endangered species" and "a mandate from the people to strike a balance of equities on the side of the Tellico Dam." In the Endangered Species Act, "Congress [had] spoken in the plainest of words," making "it abundantly clear that the balance has been struck in favor of affording endangered species the highest of priorities." This clarity required individual justices to set aside their personal appraisals "of the wisdom or unwisdom of a particular course consciously selected by Congress."

To bolster his position, the chief justice inserted an extensive quotation from Robert Boalt's play *A Man for All Seasons*. In the passage, Sir Thomas More is speaking to Roper about the importance of fidelity to the law. More confesses an inability to "navigate" the "currents and eddies of right and wrong." However, "in the thicket of the law," he claims to be "a forester." He urges Roper to avoid cutting "a great road through the law [even] to get after the Devil." If such a road is cut, More asks, "when the last law was drawn and the Devil turned round on you — where would you hide, Roper, the laws all being flat?" Yes, More concludes, he would "give the Devil benefit of law, for my own safety's sake."

Fidelity to the constitutional structure, the chief justice concluded, required an injunction. "In our constitutional system the commitment to the separation of powers is too fundamental for us to pre-empt congressional action by judicially decreeing what accords with 'common sense and the public weal.'" Under the Constitution, responsibility for making those determinations belongs to "the political branches."

Three justices dissented from the Supreme Court's decision. Justice Powell, joined by Justice Blackmun, disagreed with the majority on the first issue analyzed by the opinion of the chief justice; he argued that the limitations of Section 7 of the Endangered Species Act did not apply to the Tellico Dam. Justice Rehnquist dissented with respect to the second issue. He contended that the district judge had not exceeded his discretion when he refused to grant an injunction. The dissenting opinions essentially repeated the arguments that Justice Powell and Justice Rehnquist had stated in the opinions they circulated when the Supreme Court was considering a summary disposition in October.

According to Justice Powell, the decision of the majority "casts a long shadow." It affected "the operation of even the most important projects, serving vital needs of society and national defense." When "continued operation would threaten extinction of an endangered species or its habitat," Section 7 of the Endangered Species Act — as construed by the majority — required a federal court to issue a permanent injunction halting the project.

The majority justified its position because it implemented "the 'plain intent of Congress' as well as . . . the language of the statute." Justice Powell, however, rejected both prongs of the majority's rationale. In his view, Section 7 could not "reasonably be interpreted as applying to a project that is completed or substantially completed when its threat to an endangered species is discovered." Nor did he "believe that Congress could have intended this Act to produce the 'absurd result' of this case." If "the language of the Act and the legislative history" had made it clear that "Congress intended this result," Justice Powell conceded that the Court "would be compelled to enforce it." But the Court's duty was different in cases "where the statutory language and legislative history, as in this case, need not be construed to reach such a result." In these cases, the Court's duty was "to adopt a permissible construction that accords with some modicum of common sense and the public weal."

Although Justice Powell praised the majority opinion for "stat[ing] the facts fully and present[ing] the testimony and action of the Appropriations Committees relevant to this case," he still felt it necessary to "repeat some of what has been said" to set forth "the complete record." That record, he argued, "compell[ed] rejection of the Court's conclusion that Congress intended the Endangered Species Act to apply to completed or substantially completed projects such as the [Tellico] dam and reservoir."

Justice Powell's supplemental factual summary extended for more than six pages and emphasized three factors. First, Congress had authorized the Tellico Dam seven years before the snail darter was discovered and had appropriated funds for the project in each of the intervening years. Second, "the Tellico Project was 75% completed" when the secretary of the interior listed the snail darter as an endangered species and designated the reservoir area as its critical habitat. Third, Congress "continued to appropriate funds for the completion of the Tellico Project" after being informed about the project's "effect on the snail darter and the alleged violation of the Endangered Species Act."

The majority opinion, Justice Powell declared, gave Section 7 "a retroactive effect" and disregarded twelve years "of consistently expressed congressional intent to complete the Tellico Project." The result represented "an extreme example of literalist construction, not required by the language of the Act and adopted without regard to its manifest purpose." In addition, achieving that result required the majority to ignore "established canons of construction."

Like the majority, Justice Powell began his analysis with "the language of § 7 itself." He disagreed, however, with the proper construction of the phrase "actions authorized, funded, or carried out by [federal agencies]." The "Court's reasoning," he asserted, would "cover every existing federal installation, including great hydroelectric projects and reservoirs, every river and harbor project, and every national defense installation — however essential to the Nation's economic health and safety." Furthermore, the actions prohibited by Section 7 "would include the continued operation of such projects or any change to preserve their continued usefulness." In the dissenter's view, the result produced by the majority's opinion made "it unreasonable to believe that Congress intended that reading," particularly since Section 7 "may be construed in a way which avoids an 'absurd result' without doing violence to its language."

Recognizing that "the critical word in § 7 is 'actions,'" Justice Powell contended "its meaning is far from 'plain.'" The word "is part of the phrase: 'actions authorized, funded, or carried out.'" In context, "the 'actions' referred to are not all actions that an agency can ever take, but rather actions that the agency is *deciding whether* to authorize, to fund, or to carry out." Thus, "these words may be reasonably read as applying only to prospective actions, i.e., actions with respect to which the agency has reasonable decision-making alternatives still available."

If Section 7 were construed in this manner, Justice Powell argued, it would not apply to the Tellico Dam. When "respondents brought this lawsuit, the Tellico Project was 80% complete at a cost of more than $78 million." Applying this "prospective reading of § 7, the action had already been 'carried out' in terms of any remaining reasonable decision-making power."

The "presumption against construing statutes to give them a retroactive effect" provided an additional reason for adopting this "reasonable construction of the language" of Section 7. The Supreme Court had long recognized this presumption as "very strong," and Justice Powell found it "particularly" persuasive "where a statute enacts a new regime of regulation." As an example, he noted that the presumption had "been recognized in cases arising under the National Environmental Policy Act."

After rejecting the majority's textual arguments, Justice Powell also adopted a different reading of the legislative history. That history, he acknowledged, "establish[ed] that Congress intended to require governmental agencies to take endangered species into the planning and execution of their programs." But, he insisted, the legislative history contained "not even a hint . . . that Congress intended to compel the undoing or abandonment of any project or program later found to threaten a newly discovered species."

In a lengthy footnote, Justice Powell argued that, when "reasonably viewed," even "the quotations from the legislative history relied upon by the Court" supported his construction of Section 7. They "demonstrat[ed] that Congress was thinking about agency action in prospective situations, rather than actions requiring abandonment of completed projects."

Justice Powell also regarded the silence of the legislative history with respect to the impact of Section 7 on existing projects as powerful evidence that the act did not apply. The silence in the legislative history suggested that "the relevant Committees that considered the Act" and "the Members of Congress who voted on it" were not "aware that the Act could be used to terminate major federal projects authorized years earlier and nearly completed or to require the abandonment of essential and long-completed installations." Otherwise, "we can be certain that there would have been hearings, testimony, and debate concerning consequences so wasteful, so inimical to purposes previously deemed important and so likely to arouse public outrage." The lack of such consideration indicated "quite clearly that no one participating in the legislative process considered these consequences as within the intendment of the Act."

"This view of legislative intent," Justice Powell insisted, was "abundantly confirmed by the subsequent congressional actions and expressions." Nor was the force of these actions diminished by prior decisions giving "post-enactment statements by individual members of Congress" or "subsequent Appropriation Acts" little weight in determining the meaning of a statute. Those precedents were "inapposite" with respect to the applicability of the Endangered Species Act to completed or nearly completed projects. Supporters of the Tellico Dam presented "testimony on this precise issue . . . before congressional committees." Moreover, "for three years," those committees prepared reports that "addressed the problem." In the reports, the committees "affirmed their understanding of the original intent." These reports were available to "Congress, when it continued to approve the recommended appropriation," and the majority had no basis for its assumption that Congress "was unaware of the contents of the supporting Committee Reports." Thus, this legislative activity provided "strong corroborative evidence that the interpretation of § 7 as not applying to completed or substantially completed projects reflects the initial legislative intent."

In a brief concluding section of his dissent, Justice Powell offered a prediction. "Congress will," he declared, "amend the Endangered Species Act to prevent the grave consequences made possible by today's decision." In his view, "few if any members of that body" would favor wasting "at least $53 million" or denying "the people of the Tennessee Valley area the benefits of the reservoir that Congress intended to confer." He foresaw "little sentiment to leave this dam standing before an empty reservoir, serving no purpose other than a conversation piece for incredulous tourists."

Justice Powell did, however, see an impact of the Court's decision "more far reaching than the adverse effect on the people of this economically depressed area." The majority's interpretation of the Endangered Species Act established "a continuing threat to the operation of every federal project, no matter how important to the Nation." Expeditious action to amend the statute, "as may be anticipated," would probably keep the Court's decision from having "any lasting adverse consequences." Nonetheless, Justice Powell objected to the Court "forc[ing] Congress into otherwise unnecessary action by interpreting a statute to produce a result no one intended."

Justice Rehnquist's much shorter dissent focused on the remedial issue. Its substance was the same as the opinion he had circulated the previous October when he urged the Court to reverse the Sixth Circuit judgment summarily without hearing oral argument. In his view, the prohibitory language of Section 7 did not limit the district court's normal discretion to decide whether an injunction should issue, and the trial judge had not abused his discretion in refusing to issue an injunction in the Tellico Dam litigation.

Justice Rehnquist began his analysis by indicating that — in light of Justice Powell's opinion — he was "far less convinced than is the Court that the Endangered Species Act . . . was intended to prohibit the completion of the dam." However, "the very difficulty and doubtfulness of the correct answer to this legal question" convinced him "that the Act did *not* prohibit the District Court from refusing, in the exercise of its traditional equitable powers, to enjoin [the TVA] from completing the dam." For Justice Rehnquist, the crucial provision of the Endangered Species Act was not Section 7 but Section 11, the provision that allowed citizens to sue to enforce the act. As he read Section 11, the citizen suit provision had two essential provisions. First, it allowed "any person" to file "a civil suit on his own behalf . . . to enjoin any person, including the United States and any other governmental instrumentality or agency . . . , who is alleged to be in violation of any provision" of the act. Second, it granted "jurisdiction" to federal district courts "to enforce any such provision."

According to Justice Rehnquist, the language of Section 11 was insufficient to require the district court to issue an injunction for every violation of the Endangered Species Act. In his view, the Supreme Court's 1944 decision in an action to enforce the Emergency Price Control Act of 1942 compelled the conclusion that no injunction was required. The 1944 decision involved a statute that contained language lending "far greater support to a conclusion that Congress intended an injunction to issue as a matter of right than does the language" of the Endangered Species Act. Nonetheless, the Court refused to mandate an injunction "without regard to established equitable considerations."

Moreover, the 1944 opinion specifically declared that "a grant of jurisdiction to issue compliance orders hardly suggests an absolute duty to do so under any and all circumstances." To construe Section 11 of the Endangered Species Act to "require automatic issuance of an injunction by the district courts once a violation is found" thus required "sharply retreating from the principle of statutory construction announced in [the 1944 decision]." Justice Rehnquist said he preferred to adhere to the "teaching" of the earlier case.

Having determined that an injunction was not automatic, Justice Rehnquist concluded his dissent by addressing the question of whether the district court had abused its discretion when it refused to enjoin the completion of the Tellico Dam. The district court, he noted, "denied . . . injunctive relief because of the significant public and social harms that would flow from such relief and because of the demonstrated good faith of petitioners." As the majority itself recognized, "such factors traditionally have played a central role" when an equity court decides "whether to deny an injunction." Moreover, the "conflicting evidence of congressional purpose" provided the district court "even stronger ground" to refuse the injunction in the Tellico Dam case. The district court "recognized that Congress, when it enacted the Endangered Species Act, made preservation of the habitat of the snail darter an important public concern." Nonetheless, the lower court concluded that "other equally significant factors" more than outweighed "the public interest in preserving the habitat of an endangered species." Those factors were also sufficient for Justice Rehnquist to conclude "that the District Court's refusal to issue an injunction was not an abuse of its discretion."

The Supreme Court opinion ended the snail darter litigation. Despite the dissents, the Court affirmed the Sixth Circuit's order that an injunction should issue forbidding TVA from taking any actions that would jeopardize the snail darter or destroy its critical habitat. The Authority had exhausted its judicial avenues for relief, but it remained unwilling to abandon or to modify the Tellico project. Instead, the TVA returned to the political arena and asked Congress to exempt the project from the requirements of the Endangered Species Act.

CHAPTER 6

Completion of the Dam

Ultimately, Justice Powell's prediction was accurate: Congress did authorize the completion of the Tellico Dam. The path to that result was, however, far less straightforward than the justice suggested it would be. S. David Freeman, the new chairman of the TVA Board of Directors, indicated a willingness to compromise with opponents of the reservoir project. However, the congressional supporters of the project continued to insist that the dam and reservoir be completed as planned, and they eventually prevailed.

The congressional response involved a prolonged struggle. Support for the dam was always greater in the House of Representatives than in the Senate, and the House consistently favored an exemption for the dam. The Senate tried to craft an exemption procedure that would maintain the basic structure of the Endangered Species Act while establishing an administrative mechanism for exemptions. When the Senate procedure failed to produce an exemption for the Tellico project, the Senate eventually accepted an appropriation act provision exempting Tellico from the requirements of the Endangered Species Act. The outcome, however, remained in doubt until the very end of the legislative process.

Although the details of the congressional fight are complex, its main events are fairly straightforward. Less than six months after the Supreme Court decision in *TVA v. Hill*, Congress amended the Endangered Species Act to create a committee with the authority to grant exemptions from the absolute prohibition of Section 7. As directed by the 1978 amendments, the committee considered whether to grant an exemption for the Tellico Dam, but it decided that no exemption was warranted. The congressional supporters of the dam then exercised their political muscle to override the judicial and administrative decisions. The Energy and Water Development Appropriation Act for fiscal year 1980 directed that the dam be completed "notwithstanding [the Endangered Species Act] or any other law," and President Carter failed to make good on his promise to veto the legislation. A final constitutional challenge filed by the Eastern Band of the Cherokee Indians failed, and the dam became operational on November 29, 1979.

As noted in chapter 5, the legislative struggle to exempt the Tellico project from the Endangered Species Act began before the Supreme Court issued its decision upholding the injunction against completing the Tellico Dam. The Endangered Species Act of 1973 had only authorized appropriations to support its provisions through the 1976 fiscal year. In June 1976, Congress authorized additional appropriations for the 1977 fiscal year and also for the 1978 fiscal year, which ended on September 30, 1978. Thus, Congress was beginning to consider another reauthorization of appropriations as the snail darter case was pending before the Supreme Court.

Early in 1977, several members of Congress requested that the GAO review the Tellico project. In January, Representative John Duncan of Tennessee suggested "that a GAO cost-benefit study of the Tellico Project would be most appropriate." On March 2, the chairman of the Merchant Marine and Fisheries Committee of the House of Representatives, the ranking member of the committee, and the chair of the subcommittee on wildlife conservation formally asked the GAO to prepare a review of the TVA analysis of the Tellico project. Two weeks later, Senator James Sasser of Tennessee also wrote a letter supporting "a study of the facts by the GAO." As the GAO was preparing its report, Representative Duncan sent a second letter indicating that a survey of local residents by his office revealed overwhelming support for the dam.

The GAO submitted its report in October 1977, but the report did little to resolve the controversy over whether the dam should be completed. The agency did "not take a position for or against the Tellico project." It did, however, suggest "that more information is needed to allow the Congress to act on the questions before it."

The GAO report criticized the benefit-cost analysis prepared by the TVA: "Some of the assumptions and logic of the Authority's projection would not accurately predict actual benefits. In some instances the methodology did not conform to Federal guidelines and in other instances the statistical projections were not valid." In response to the

TVA claim that further analysis of alternatives would be "a waste of public funds already invested in the project," the GAO noted that "many important issues . . . have surfaced since the project was conceived." These new issues included the threat to the survival of the snail darter, the destruction of "a rich archaeological valley," the rendering "useless" of 16,500 acres of prime agricultural land, the conversion of "the last large flowing river in the region into a reservoir," and the discovery that a "scenic riverway rather than a reservoir would more effectively alleviate overcrowding at Great Smoky Mountains National Park." In light of these findings, the GAO recommended that the TVA should provide Congress "detailed information on the remaining costs and remaining benefits of the Tellico project and its alternatives." Until the TVA provided that information, "Congress should prohibit the Authority from spending any more appropriations" for project work that would "further endanger the snail darter" or that would not be necessary "if the project is not completed or modified."

The TVA objected vehemently to the GAO report. The twenty-six pages of comments that the TVA submitted to the agency were nearly two-thirds as long as the body of the GAO report. Indeed, the length of the TVA comments and the eighteen-page appraisal of those comments by the GAO actually exceeded the length of the main body of the report.

Although the Office of Management and Budget declined to comment on the GAO report, the Department of the Interior responded more favorably. A letter from the department expressed "general agreement with the findings of the report." It also indicated that the National Park Service was willing to assist the TVA "in assessing river-based recreational alternatives along the Little Tennessee."

As the GAO was preparing its report, Congress began to consider a revision of the Endangered Species Act unrelated to the Tellico project. Section 6 of the 1973 act permitted the secretary of the interior to establish cooperative programs with the states and authorized appropriations for those programs through June 1977. During the months following the Sixth Circuit decision, Congress began considering a reauthorization of those appropriations. In December 1977, Congress finally extended the authorization through September 30, 1980.

On May 16, 1977, the Committee on the Environment and Public Works recommended that the Senate extend the Section 6 authorization. The committee report acknowledged "that considerable concern exists with respect to the implementation of the Endangered Species Act." To address these concerns, the committee promised to "conduct comprehensive oversight hearings on the Act during the summer." In light of the plans for those hearings, the committee expressed its hope that the amendments to Section 6 would not be used as a vehicle for addressing these other concerns." After receiving assurances that the committee would hold future hearings on the Endangered Species Act, the Senate approved the Section 6 extension without objection.

The Senate Committee on the Environment and Public Works held the promised oversight hearings in July 1977. In those hearings, the committee heard from a wide variety of witnesses regarding the need for amendments to the Endangered Species Act. Both supporters and opponents of the Tellico project appeared before the committee. Testifying in favor of revisions to the statute were Representative John Duncan from Tennessee, as well as the chairman of the TVA Board of Directors, the Authority's general manager, and the mayor of Tellico Plains. Representing the opponents were Professor Plater, Dr. Etnier, and local landowners.

The Tellico controversy did surface in November 1977, when the House of Representatives considered the conference committee report on the proposal to extend the Section 6 authorization. Representative Whitten of Mississippi called attention to both the snail darter and the sandhill crane as examples of abuses of Section 7. "Down in Tennessee," he asserted, opponents of the Tellico Dam "went down to the bottom of the stream and found a darter, when the citizens who filed an injunction could not identify or separate them from two other darters." The new darter was "what you call a minnow," and nobody had heard of it until opponents "set out to stop the dam." He then asked if the committee had "made an effort to see what damages they are doing to the country's ability to look after itself in the name of protecting something that is worthwhile."

Despite the objections of Representative Whitten (and the related objections of Representative Watkins of Oklahoma), the House of Representatives passed the reauthorization of appropriations for Section 6. The chair of the House Committee on Merchant Marine and Fisheries did, however, advise the House that the committee "had already started working on Section 7." Moreover, he announced that the committee planned "to deal with the critical habitat question early next session."

In 1978, the Senate Committee on the Environment and Public Works acted even before the Supreme Court decided the snail darter case. The principal architects of the Senate proposal were Democrat John Culver of Iowa, the committee chair, and Republican Howard Baker of Tennessee. On April 12, they — along with Senators Wallop, Gravel, and Hodges — offered Senate Bill 2899, which proposed an amendment to the Endangered Species Act to establish a procedure for exempting federal projects from the prohibitions of Section 7. When Senator Culver introduced S.B. 2899, he announced that his committee would hold hearings on April 13 and 14 to determine "whether flexibility should be added to Section 7." As a justification for the hearings, he noted that "at least one major project — the Tellico Dam in Tennessee — has been stopped because of a conflict with the act," and he raised the prospect that similar conflicts might arise in the future. In "the vast majority of cases," he predicted, consultation under Section 7 would succeed in resolving conflicts that jeopardize species. "In those few instances where consultation cannot resolve the problems," he offered the proposed legislation as "a reasonable mechanism of balance."

Senator Baker also made a brief statement in support of S.B. 2899. He emphasized that situations existed "in which a Federal activity, if it is to achieve its stated purpose, cannot avoid a direct impact to a species or its critical habitat." In those cases, "consultation cannot resolve the impasse." The existing act permitted "no flexibility to balance other legitimate national goals and priorities," but the proposed amendment offered a reasonable procedure to resolve the conflict. It permitted "a balancing of interests" that would allow a federal action to proceed "if it is decided that the Federal activity is of more importance than the protection of a particular species."

Two other sponsors of the proposed amendment made brief statements in support of the Senate bill. Senator Randolph noted that the Sixth Circuit decision in the Tellico case had "caused considerable concern among some who fear that some environmentalists, armed with Section 7 will be able to literally shut down Federal construction programs by finding a remote species of mussel, snail, or fish at any project site." Although these concerns seemed to be "an over-reaction," he supported the amendment because it provided "needed flexibility where conflicts develop between two Federal objectives." Senator Wallop supported the proposed amendment because he believed Congress needed "to act now to avert a wave of amendments designed to weaken the act." The proposal was, he emphasized, "a tough amendment with tough criteria for any exemption."

At the hearings on April 13 and 14, the Senate committee heard from a number of witnesses and received a number of written statements. This round of hearings had less of a Tellico focus. The only protagonist in the Tellico fight to appear was Professor Plater, and he appeared as the representative of the American Rivers Conservation Council. The breakdown of the witnesses revealed the growing ideological division over the Endangered Species Act. Business and development groups supported revision of the act, while the national environmental organizations led the opposition to amending the statute.

The Senate committee submitted its report recommending favorable action on S.B. 2899 in May, approximately a month before the Supreme Court decision in *TVA v. Hill.* The report described the Tellico Dam project as "the most visible case in which the Committee found a seemingly irresolvable conflict between project objectives and the requirements of section 7 of the Endangered Species Act." According to the report, the April hearing indicated that "a substantial number of Federal actions currently underway appear to have all the elements of an irresolvable conflict" and that the number of such conflicts might well "increase significantly in the future as the Fish and Wildlife Service continues to list additional species and critical habitat." Moreover, some evidence suggested that the Fish and Wildlife Service had "refrained from listing species which may pose a conflict with a federal action, for fear of provoking Congress into weakening the protective provisions of section 7." In light of these circumstances, the committee urged its proposal as an amendment that would provide "flexibility" in the administration of the act "while maintaining protection for threatened and endangered species."

The Senate did not consider S.B. 2899 until after the Supreme Court had affirmed the injunction against completion of the Tellico Dam. Eventually, the Senate overwhelmingly approved the committee proposal. Before taking that final vote, it decisively defeated efforts to

{ *Chapter 6* }

weaken Section 7 further, as well as a proposal to eliminate the proposed exemption procedure.

Senator Culver, the floor manager of the bill, acknowledged the importance of the Supreme Court decision in *TVA v. Hill* for the Endangered Species Act, and he secured permission to have the syllabus of the Court's opinion printed in the *Congressional Record*. "Strictly speaking," he declared, the Supreme Court decision was a good one. It "correctly interpreted the purposes of the law and the intent of Congress, which was to give priority to the important value of endangered species." However, oversight hearings had revealed "that there are now many other projects where consultative resolution may not be possible under the existing arrangement." Moreover, some evidence suggested that the Fish and Wildlife Service had "refrained from listing species which may pose a conflict with a Federal action for fear of provoking Congress into weakening the protective provisions of section 7." In light of this evidence, the committee had endorsed S.B. 2899. It amended the Endangered Species Act "to establish a rational and responsible mechanism for resolving future conflicts and at the same time assure maximum protection for all endangered species."

Senator Stennis offered the primary attempt to introduce additional flexibility into the act. He proposed an amendment that would have modified the protections afforded by Section 7 in three respects. First, it would have added the phrase "insofar as practicable and consistent with their primary responsibilities" to qualify the duties of federal agencies to ensure that their actions did not jeopardize endangered species or destroy critical habitat. Second, the Stennis Amendment would have given an agency head authority to proceed with an action after balancing "the social, cultural, economic and other benefits to the public which would occur if [the] action is carried out as planned against the esthetic, ecological, educational, historical, recreational, or scientific loss which would occur if such species were to" become extinct. Third, the Stennis Amendment would have exempted any project from the prohibitions of Section 7 if the project was "at least 50 per centum completed based upon the amount expended." After a debate of an hour and a half, the Senate rejected the amendment by a vote of 22 to 76.

The Senate rejected more extreme amendments by Senator Scott of Virginia by even larger majorities. On a vote of 10 to 86, the Senate refused to limit the conservation purpose of the Endangered Species Act by adding the phrase "consistent with the welfare and national goals of the United States." By a vote of 2 to 87, the Senate defeated an amendment that would have limited the protections of the act to species that "are of substantial benefit to mankind."

Senator Nelson fared no better with an attempt to eliminate the proposed exemption procedure altogether. His amendment would have deleted everything from the committee bill except the reauthorization of appropriations. The Senate rejected the Nelson Amendment by a vote of 25 to 70.

The controversy over the Tellico Dam surfaced at several points during the Senate debate. The most heated exchange came between Senator Nelson and Senator Baker during the debate over the amendment to delete the exemption procedure.

"At this time," Senator Nelson argued, "no justification" existed for modifying the Endangered Species Act. "The panic being expressed" by some was a "smokescreen" to hide the fact that "the law has worked very well." In his view, "all the emotional upset around the country is not justified by the facts."

In response, Senator Baker claimed that the committee bill reflected "no panic, no emotion." To the contrary, "the people of Tennessee and the Tennessee Valley region have been very unemotional." In "political terms," the simplest solution would be to exempt the Tellico Dam, but he did "not believe exemption for particular projects is a legitimate function of Congress." Thus, he had worked to adjust the act "to take care of situations where the act clearly did not work."

The House of Representatives produced the specific exemption that Senator Baker had argued was not a legitimate function of Congress. Following the Sixth Circuit decision enjoining completion of the dam, dam supporters in the Tennessee congressional delegation immediately introduced bills to exempt the dam from the Endangered Species Act. Representative Robin Beard introduced two versions of his proposal, House Resolution (H.R.) 4167 and H.R. 7392. Representative John Duncan introduced an alternative proposal in H.R. 4557.

The Beard proposal would have created a general exemption for federal public works projects that were located on or affected a navigable water. The exemption applied to projects that were commenced before the secretary of the interior published the notice that the addition of a species to the list of endangered or threatened species was being contemplated. Paragraph 1 of the exemption provided that no such public works project "shall be deemed" either "to jeopardize the continued existence" of the species or "to result in the destruction or modification" of the critical habitat of the species. Paragraph 2, however, authorized the secretary to "prescribe such requirements regarding . . . such project as may be necessary and appropriate to minimize the averse effects" on any endangered or threatened species and to "implement such protective measures (including, but not limited to, transplantation) with respect to" the endangered or threatened species as the secretary "deems necessary and appropriate." Paragraph 3 of the proposed exemption provided that harm to any endangered or threatened species would "not be deemed a taking of any endangered species" under Section 9 of the act if the harm was "directly attributable to" the project and did not violate "any requirement imposed by the Secretary."

H.R. 4557 was a specific exemption for the Tellico project. It provided that the provisions of the Endangered Species Act "shall not apply with respect to the construction and operation of the Tellico Dam and Reservoir Project." In addition, it declared that any "harassment, harm, killing, or wounding" of an endangered species from the operation or construction of the dam would "not be deemed to be a taking" under Section 9 of the act.

The House of Representatives never considered either the Duncan or the Beard proposal. Nonetheless, the House did enact a special provision exempting the Tellico Dam from the prohibitions of the Endangered Species Act.

A subcommittee of the House Committee on Merchant Marine and Fisheries held extensive hearings on the Endangered Species Act in 1978. The hearings began while the snail darter case was pending before the Supreme Court and concluded ten days after the Supreme Court rendered its decision. Following these hearings, the House committee considered various alternatives in a series of meetings during August. On September 18, Representative Leggett of California introduced H.R. 14104, a clean bill that reflected the committee deliberations.

Like the bill passed by the Senate, H.R. 14104 proposed a procedure for exempting actions from the absolute prohibitions of Section 7, but it included no specific exemption for the Tellico project. A week after Leggett introduced the bill, the House committee reported it favorably with a few additional amendments. The House of Representatives passed the Leggett bill on October 14, 1978, but only after adopting a floor amendment that specifically exempted the Tellico Dam project from the prohibitions of the Endangered Species Act.

The House report on H.R. 1414 noted that "the celebrated snail darter case" demonstrated that Section 7 "can potentially have an enormous impact on Federal activities." As a result of the decisions of the Sixth Circuit and the Supreme Court, the TVA had "not conducted any further work on the Tellico Project" since January 1977. Through February 1977, the TVA "had obligated about $103 million" for the project. The GAO estimated that "about $53 million of the $103 million invested in the project could provide some benefit if the project is not completed." However, the report noted that "the amount of benefit to be derived from the investment . . . probably will not be proportionate with the original cost."

As reported by the committee, H.R. 14104 did not contain any special exemptions. Floor amendments added two. One excused the Grayrocks Dam on the Platte River in Wyoming from the prohibitions of Section 7; the other exempted the Tellico Dam from those provisions.

The central debate on the House floor concerned the amendment by Representative John Duncan of Tennessee to exempt "the construction and operation of the Tellico Dam and Reservoir project in Tennessee" from the provisions of the Endangered Species Act. Duncan gave three principal reasons why the Tellico project deserved a special exemption. First, the TVA had begun the project long before the Endangered Species Act of 1973 was enacted, and the project was now 99 percent complete. Second, Congress and the TVA had invested the money in the project in good faith. Third, the TVA had recently been successful in transplanting the snail darter to other rivers in the area. Representatives Beard, Quillen, and Roncalio also spoke briefly in favor of the amendment.

Representative Dingell of Michigan led the debate for opponents of the exemption for the Tellico Dam. He denounced the project as the product of "an outlaw agency which arrogantly, flagrantly, and vigorously disregarded what they knew to be the clear thrust of the law."

Representatives Forsythe and Studds also made brief statements opposing the Tellico exemption.

Following this brief debate, the House approved the exemption for the Tellico project by a vote of 231 to 157. After disposing of various other amendments, the House overwhelmingly approved H.R. 14104 by a vote of 384 to 12. By unanimous consent, the House then substituted the text of H.R. 14104 for the text of S.B. 2899, adopted the Senate bill as amended, and requested a conference with the Senate.

The day after the House vote, the conference committee submitted its report. The conference report recommended elimination of the special exemptions for both Grayrocks and Tellico. However, the conference bill directed the Endangered Species Committee to consider exemptions for these projects and provided an accelerated schedule for considering them. At the same time, the report expressed the committee's "strong sense" that the special provisions for Grayrocks and Tellico were "the last instances when any project should receive special consideration in the exemption process." After brief debates, both the House and the Senate approved the conference report by voice votes.

The Endangered Species Act Amendments of 1978 preserved the basic structure of the 1973 statute but addressed several issues that had proved controversial in the snail darter litigation. Congress formalized the consultation process required by Section 7 and created a committee with authority to grant exemptions from the prohibition against any federal action that jeopardized the existence of an endangered species or destroyed its critical habitat. It also specifically required the committee to consider whether an exemption should be granted for the Tellico project.

As originally enacted in 1973, Section 7 consisted of a single paragraph entitled "Interagency Consultation." The 1978 amendments expanded the section into seventeen subsections that consume nine pages in the *Statutes at Large*.

The first new subsections, b and c, established a formal process for consultation between the secretary of the interior and other federal agencies. Basically, the new subsections codified the consultation procedures that the Department of the Interior had established by regulation. The procedures obligate the secretary of the interior to prepare a written opinion regarding the impact of the proposed action on the endangered species and its critical habitat. In addition, they require the consulting agency to assess the impact of its proposed action on any endangered species that might be affected by the action.

Subsection b requires that the consultation process be completed within ninety days unless some other period is "mutually agreeable" to the federal agency and to the secretary. "Promptly after the conclusion of consultation," the secretary must prepare a "written statement" that sets forth "the Secretary's opinion, and a summary of the information on which the opinion is based, detailing how the agency action affects the species or its critical habitat." In addition, the secretary has to suggest "reasonable and prudent alternatives" which he believes would avoid jeopardizing the species or modifying its habitat adversely.

"To facilitate compliance" with the consultation requirement, Subsection c directs federal agencies "to request of the Secretary information whether any species which is listed or proposed to be listed may be present in the area of [a] proposed action." If the secretary reports "that such species may be present," the agency proposing the action must prepare a "biological assessment" to identify any endangered or threatened species that "is likely to be affected by such action." Moreover, the agency must complete the assessment "before construction is begun with respect to such action."

More important for the TVA, the 1978 amendments established a process for exempting a federal agency from the prohibitions of Sections 7 and 9 of the Endangered Species Act. They created a new Endangered Species Committee, which was promptly called the God Squad because of its power to authorize federal actions that could result in the extinction of a species. In addition to creating the God Squad, the amendments also established the substantive standards for granting an exemption and the procedures for considering requests for exemptions. For the Tellico project, however, the 1978 amendments short-circuited the new process. They expressly directed the Endangered Species Committee to consider whether an exemption was appropriate for the Tellico Dam.

The 1978 amendments made the secretary of the interior the chair of the newly created Endangered Species Committee. They also designated the following individuals as the other members of the committee: the secretary of agriculture, the secretary of the army, the chairman of the Council of Economic Advisors, the administrator of the Environmental Protection Agency, the administrator of the National Oceanic and Atmospheric Administration, and a presidentially appointed representative for each state affected by the project for which an exemption was sought. Supporters of the amendments argued that they created a balanced committee to resolve intractable issues. Three of the federal agencies represented (the Department of Agriculture, the Department of the Army, and the Council of Economic Advisors) were sympathetic to development, and the other three (the Environmental Protection Agency, the Department of the Interior, and the National Oceanic and Atmospheric Administration) focused on environmental issues. To grant an exemption required the committee to reach a consensus because an exemption required a positive "vote of not less than five . . . [committee] members voting in person."

The 1978 amendments gave the committee substantial powers to help it resolve the issues referred to it. Specifically, the committee can hold hearings and issue subpoenas to obtain any "information necessary for the consideration of an application for an exemption." It can also "promulgate . . . such rules, regulations, and procedures, and issue . . . such orders as it deems necessary."

Under the 1978 amendments, the Endangered Species Committee has to "make a final determination whether to grant an exemption" from the prohibitions of Section 7. Before the committee can do so, a five-member majority has to make the following three determinations "on the record":

- "there are no reasonable and prudent alternatives to the agency action";
- the benefits of the action "clearly outweigh the benefits of alternative courses of action consistent with conserving the species, and such action is in the public interest"; and
- the proposed action is one "of regional or national significance."

When the committee grants an exemption, it has to establish "such reasonable mitigation and enhancement measures . . . as are necessary and appropriate to minimize the adverse effects of the agency action upon the endangered species." The statute specifically lists "transplantation" as one of the mitigation measures the agency may consider.

If an exemption is granted, it applies to Section 9's prohibition against "taking" an endangered species, as well as to Section 7's requirement that the federal agency avoid any action that will jeopardize the continued existence of the species or destroy or modify its critical habitat. Once the Endangered Species Committee grants an exemption allowing a federal action to proceed, no "activity which is necessary to carry out such action" will "be considered a taking of any endangered or threatened species."

For most actions, the 1978 amendments established a complicated screening procedure. The agency seeking the exemption had to submit a written application for an exemption to the secretary. The secretary then referred the application to a three-member review board. Before the Endangered Species Committee considered the application, the review board had to make a series of affirmative determinations. First, the review board had to decide whether an "irresolvable conflict" existed. The board then had to determine that the agency had

- carried out its consultation responsibilities in good faith and "made a reasonable and responsible effort to develop and fairly consider modifications or reasonable and prudent alternatives to the proposed agency action";
- conducted the biological assessment required by the 1978 amendments; and
- avoided "any irreversible or irretrievable commitment of resources" during the consultation process.

If the review board made an affirmative determination with respect to each of these factors, it prepared a report referring the matter to the Endangered Species Committee. A negative decision with respect to any of the factors resulted in a denial of the exemption application.

The 1978 amendments excused the TVA from the application process with respect to the Tellico project. Instead, a separate section of the 1978 amendments required the Endangered Species Committee to "proceed to consider an exemption" for the project within thirty days after enactment of the amendments. The Tellico provision directed the committee to grant an exemption if two conditions were satisfied: the agency had "no feasible and prudent alternatives" to the proposed action, and the benefits of the proposed action "clearly outweigh[ed] the benefits of alternative courses of action consistent with conserving the species or its critical habitat, and such action is in the public interest." The 1978 amendments also required that the Endangered Species Committee make its final decision on the Tellico project within ninety days of the enactment of the amendments. If the committee failed to reach a decision within ninety days, the project would "be deemed to be exempted" from the prohibitions of Section 7.

These special provisions for Tellico did more than simply speed the decisional process for a project on which the construction had been substantially completed before the 1978 amendments were enacted. They exempted the project from the preliminary review that established conditions the TVA could not easily satisfy, and they qualified the normal requirement that five members of the Endangered Species Committee vote in favor of an exemption.

The elimination of the review board process was crucial. A review board might well have found the existence of an "irresolvable conflict" between the TVA and the secretary. However, a review board would have been far less likely to find that the agency had established the other three prerequisites to review by the Endangered Species Committee: the lack of alternatives to the project, the preparation of a biological assessment by the agency, and the avoidance of all irreversible and irretrievable commitments of resources during the consultation process.

Until the TVA began work on a joint report with the Department of the Interior in the summer of 1978, the Authority had always rejected the idea that any alternatives existed for the Tellico project. However, the 1978 amendments broadly defined the term "alternative courses of action" to mean "all alternatives" and specifically declared that the term was "not limited to original project objectives and agency jurisdiction." At a minimum, this language appeared to require consideration of the river-based development that the opponents of the dam had proposed and that the Park Service had endorsed.

The directive that the agency had to prepare a "biological assessment" during the consultation process with the secretary was a new requirement of the 1978 amendments. If it had applied to the Tellico project, it would have delayed consideration of the exemption request for at least several months while the assessment was being prepared.

The TVA would also have had great difficulty establishing a third factor on which the review board had to make a finding. Section 7(d), another addition of the 1978 amendments, limits an agency's authority to make "irreversible and irretrievable" commitments of resources to a project "after initiation of consultation" with the secretary. Once consultation is initiated, the agency has to avoid any such commitments that would "have the effect of foreclosing . . . any reasonable and prudent alternative measures" that might avoid jeopardizing a species or destroying its critical habitat. The review board could only forward a request for an exemption to the Endangered Species Committee if it finds that the agency had "refrained from making any irreversible or irretrievable commitment of resources prohibited by [Section 7(d)]."

The TVA had never delayed the Tellico project in response to the jeopardy and critical-habitat determinations by the secretary because the agency took the position that it — not the secretary — was ultimately responsible for deciding whether a project should proceed. Indeed, the TVA worked continuously to complete the project from the time the NEPA injunction was lifted in October 1973 until the Sixth Circuit issued its injunction in *TVA v. Hill* in January 1977. As Professor Plater noted in his oral argument before the Supreme Court, the agency tripled its rate of expenditure and doubled the amount spent after the lifting of the NEPA injunction. When Judge Taylor dissolved the NEPA injunction, the TVA had spent slightly more than half of the project costs, which was then estimated at $60 million. When the Sixth Circuit issued its injunction, the TVA had obligated $103 million and estimated that another $13 million would be required to complete the project.

Finally, the Tellico provision in the 1978 amendments reversed the usual requirement for an affirmative vote by five of the seven members of the Endangered Species Committee to grant an exemption. Instead, the Tellico provision provided that the project would receive an exemption if the board failed to make a decision within ninety days after the enactment of the statute. Presumably, a four-member majority of the committee could have effectively granted an exemption for the Tellico project by delaying a final decision until after the ninety days had passed.

President Carter signed the 1978 amendments into law on November 10, 1978. At that time, he issued a statement indicating that he regarded the new provision for the Endangered Species Committee as unnecessary. "In the past," he asserted, "the act has worked well without this exemption process because all agencies have made efforts to resolve conflicts and, where necessary, to pursue alternate courses of action." He asked, therefore, "that the Committee members be exceedingly cautious in considering exemptions."

As the 1978 amendments were working their way through Congress, the TVA gave some indications that it might be willing to compromise on the Tellico project. The new chairman of the TVA Board of Directors indicated a willingness to consider the alternative of a river-based development, and he authorized the TVA staff to work with the Department of the Interior to prepare a report analyzing alternatives. The TVA board never, however, abandoned the dam project, and Congress ultimately made the decision to proceed with the dam and reservoir.

The first signs of change at the TVA came while *TVA v. Hill* was pending before the Supreme Court. In August 1977, the Senate confirmed S. David Freeman as the third TVA director. Although Freeman privately opposed the Tellico project, he publicly maintained that he had not yet made up his mind and that he would have to study the problem further. He even insisted that the following sentence be included on all correspondence relating to Tellico: "Our new board member, S. David Freeman, has not yet formed an opinion on the Tellico project."

After the Supreme Court granted the certiorari petition in the snail darter case, President Carter asked Cecil Andrus, the secretary of the interior, to contact the TVA to inquire about the possibility of a joint study of alternatives to the Tellico reservoir. On March 31, 1978, Aubrey Wagner, who was still the TVA chairman, responded that the Authority was "unwilling to discuss the alternatives mentioned." Six days later, Freeman released a letter to Andrus in which he indicated his belief that compromise was possible. Freeman also insisted that this letter be attached to the reply brief the TVA filed in the Supreme Court in *TVA v. Hill*.

Freeman's influence at the TVA increased in 1978. Director William Jenkins suddenly resigned in May, and Wagner retired on May 18. Thus, when the Supreme Court announced its decision in *TVA v. Hill*, Freeman was the lone director of the TVA. The day after the Supreme Court decision, Freeman met with Robert Herbst, assistant secretary of the Department of the Interior in charge of the Fish and Wildlife Service. At the end of the meeting, they announced that employees of the TVA and the Interior Department would begin weekly meetings to seek a solution that "both respects the law and benefits the economy." A joint statement issued by the two men optimistically indicated "that preliminary information suggests that an alternative may be fashioned that can provide benefits for people equal to or hopefully superior to those which would have been provided by completion of the dam."

Congressional supporters of the Tellico project tried to apply pressure to discourage Freeman's enthusiasm for alternatives. On June 19, Representative John Duncan of Tennessee sent Freeman a letter; it reported poll results indicating that 80 percent of respondents favored completion of the dam. Ten days later, Senator Howard Baker asked Freeman to delay "final action" on any changes until Congress confirmed a new board member for "at least one of the vacancies . . . on the Board and until Congress has had a reasonable opportunity to act on the reauthorization of the Endangered Species Act."

The congressional pressure did not dissuade Freeman. On June 24, he testified before a subcommittee of the House Merchant Marine Committee. "It may turn out to be a good thing for the taxpayer," he told the subcommittee, "that legal constraints on completing the dam will cause us to take a harder look at how to make the best use of the government's investment in the land." He also directed TVA employees to continue working with the Department of the Interior to develop alternatives.

On August 10, the TVA–Interior Department study group issued a preliminary report with a cover sheet signed by Freeman and Herbst. The cover sheet invited "any concerned citizen" to submit public comments within the next thirty days. It indicated that the study group would then make available a final report "so that an informed and wise decision can be made."

In the preliminary report, the representatives of the TVA and the Department of the Interior considered four alternatives: the original dam; a dam on the Tellico River, a tributary of the Little Tennessee; and two proposals for river development. One of the river-based development proposals would retain the Tellico Dam but operate it only when needed for flood control. The other would remove the earthen portion of the dam and reopen the east channel of the river.

The preliminary report evaluated the four proposals without providing a recommendation. It did not endorse either of the river-development alternatives or advocate the abandonment of the reservoir project. Indeed, the report emphasized at several points that the Supreme Court decision did not completely forbid completion of the dam and reservoir if the snail darter were successfully transplanted to other locations.

Despite the lack of a specific recommendation, the general tenor of the preliminary report differed significantly from prior analyses by the TVA. Most important, it acknowledged the existence of "several feasible and beneficial alternative ways to develop the 38,000 acres of Tellico Project lands in the Little Tennessee River Valley." The preliminary report also recognized the uncertainties of benefit-cost analyses, and it explained in some detail the difficulty of quantifying "the nonmonetary or intangible values of certain resources." In addition, the report noted that the reservoir would inundate "33 miles of flowing river with exceptionally high water quality and sport fishing value," as well as an area of "considerable archaeological and historical value." Thus, the report concluded: "Even if current legal constraints were not present, it is by no means clear whether a reservoir development option or a river development option would benefit society most."

By mid-October 1978, Congress had included an exemption procedure in the 1978 amendments to the Endangered Species Act. The new legislation specifically directed the Endangered Species Committee to consider whether an exemption for the Tellico Dam was appropriate. Because of the Interior Department's responsibility to provide staff support to the committee, the department employees did not participate in the preparation of the final report analyzing alternatives to the dam and reservoir project. Thus, the TVA alone issued the final report in December 1978.

The final report differed from the draft in several respects. The biggest change between the preliminary and final drafts was the reduction of alternatives. According to the final report, only two of the four options considered in the draft were "worthy of further consideration, the reservoir as planned and the developed river with earth dam removed." The final report also excluded cost-benefit tables used in the draft because comments and new staff work had resulted in such a wide range of projected benefits for each option that the tables would have "little meaning without a narrative explaining the basis of the differences." In addition, the final report was substantially longer than the draft because it included nearly fifty pages of public comments and responses.

Like the preliminary report, the final version avoided definitive recommendations. Moreover, even though the report had "been prepared by TVA staff and reviewed by the TVA Board of Directors," the final version emphasized that the report did not "reflect a decision by the Board or the Secretary of the Department of the Interior on any option."

The summary portion of the final report acknowledged that "tangible benefits that can be quantified without dispute cover only a small proportion of the project." As a result, the report asserted, "the assumptions and value judgments and the weights given by the final decision makers to the numerous intangible benefits and costs associated with each option" were likely to control the choice of a particular option. The difficulty of quantifying all these costs and benefits made the final decision "difficult and controversial."

After withdrawing from the joint study group analyzing the Tellico project, the Interior Department focused its efforts on implementing the 1978 amendments to the Endangered Species Act. Following enactment of the amendments, the secretary of the interior scheduled a public meeting of the Endangered Species Committee for January 23, 1979. He also directed the staff assigned to assist the committee to prepare yet another analysis of the Tellico project. Finally, he scheduled two public hearings for January 8, one in Knoxville, Tennessee, and the other in Washington, D.C.

A story in the *Knoxville News-Sentinel* for January 7 reported charges that S. David Freeman, the new TVA chairman, had ordered TVA employees not to make any statements at the public hearing. Responding to the alleged "gag order," Representative John Duncan sent Freeman a letter declaring that "such an order has no place in our open society, and I am deeply distressed by it." After receiving the letter, Freeman clarified the TVA position in a telephone call to Representative Duncan's office. Because the TVA "was not taking a position" in the exemption proceedings, Freeman "felt that the appearance of TVA personnel at the hearing would 'give the wrong impression.'" However, Freeman also said "that 'any TVA employee who wants to testify as a private citizen . . . is welcome to do so.'"

The public hearing in Knoxville largely repeated the arguments of opponents and supporters of the Tellico project. According to reports in the *Knoxville News-Sentinel*, "the only significant new argument" came from two University of Tennessee scientists, David Etnier and Clifford Amundson, who claimed that the reservoir would not remain clean enough for recreation forever. Other opponents who spoke against the dam included Zygmunt Plater and Hiram Hill, two of the named plaintiffs in the Supreme Court litigation. In addition, the opponents also picked up new support from Dr. John Gibbons, director of the University of Tennessee Environmental Center.

Representative Duncan led the dam supporters at the public hearing. "Speaking on behalf of the entire Tennessee [congressional] delegation," he declared "the Tellico project is as valid today as it was in 1936 when it was conceived." He also read a statement from Senator Baker urging an exemption, and he arranged for an appearance by Charles Wagner III, the former associate general counsel who had represented the TVA in the snail darter litigation.

On the same day as the public hearing, the Fish and Wildlife Service submitted its views and recommendations to the Endangered Species Committee. In a letter to the committee chair, David Hales—assistant secretary of the Department of the Interior for Fish, Wildlife, and Parks—endorsed efforts to "provide for the long-term welfare of the endangered species." The Hales letter criticized the development scenario presented in the TVA analysis and suggested that the navigation benefits from the reservoir developments would be zero. More important, Hales challenged the TVA assumption that the land costs were sunk costs that should be ignored. Instead, he claimed the current value of the land was "an opportunity cost which must be counted against any benefits attributed to public development." In addition, the Hales letter suggested that the TVA should be required to implement a series of mitigation measures even if an exemption were granted. These measures included delaying closure of the dam for one to three years, selecting additional rivers for transplanting the snail darter, rescuing the snail darters from the Little Tennessee River, preserving populations that had already been transplanted, and expanding research efforts to preserve the snail darter.

On Friday, January 19, the Interior Department employees assigned to assist the Endangered Species Committee issued a staff report. Although the staff report emphasized that "only the committee can decide whether one quantity or fact clearly outweighs another," the executive summary of the report seemed to suggest an exemption should not be granted. It described "development of the Little Tennessee Valley without the reservoir" as the "principal alternative to completing the Tellico reservoir." Moreover, the evidence established that "the river development alternative is feasible and commensurate with the reservoir in economic value." Because the river development alternative would maintain the critical habitat of the snail darter, it was also "consistent with conserving the snail darter" as a species.

Interestingly, the staff report was "unable to justify assigning positive net economic benefits for either of TVA's proposed alternatives." The reason the staff concluded that the costs for each alternative exceeded its economic benefits was the inclusion in its report of land value as a cost of either alternative. Accepting the argument advanced in the Hales letter, the staff treated the value of the land as an "opportunity cost." Moreover, the staff assessed the annualized value of the land at $4 million. When this value was added to the other costs and benefits, the staff analysis produced the following results: "Measured benefits of the reservoir option are $6.5 million compared to capital and land costs of $7.2 million; river development benefits are $5.1 million compared to capital and land costs of $6.2 million." The staff report emphasized that the unfavorable benefit-cost analyses included only "measured benefits." With river development, the primary "unmeasured benefits" were "the existence of the snail darter" plus "the cultural, historical, and archaeological values" of the river valley. On the other hand, the reservoir development alternative would include "the uncompensated costs inherent in the loss of customary fish and wildlife values," as well as the unmeasured benefit of "the reservoir . . . as an amenity." In addition, for both alternatives, "creation of jobs and wages income in the region" was "important," even though it was "not counted as a national benefit."

The Endangered Species Committee convened on Tuesday, January 23, 1979, at 9:00 A.M. In addition to the prescribed federal officials, the committee included William R. Willis Jr. of Nashville, who had been nominated by Governor Ray Blanton and appointed by President Carter to represent the state of Tennessee. Willis, a Nashville attorney, was a member of the Tennessee Wildlife Resources Commission at the time of his appointment. Curiously, the furious political maneuvering over the snail darter seems never to have reached Willis. In a June 2005 interview, he said that no state or federal officials lobbied him regarding the committee's decisions, nor did any of them contact him to complain after the committee made its decision. He indicated that he simply used the information supplied by the committee staff to reach a decision in accordance with the criteria established by the 1978 amendments.

The committee began its consideration of the Tellico exemption by listening to a summary of the staff report by Dr. Robert K. Davis, the project director. In response to a question by Secretary of the Army Clifford Alexander, Dr. Davis clarified that the TVA had not made a recommendation to the committee. Next, Charles Schultze, the chairman of the Council of Economic Advisors, noted the TVA report indicated that the river development alternative would likely include "some purchases or leases of the land by private individuals." He then asked "whether or not the proceeds from purchase or lease are explicitly or implicitly already included in the benefits of the project, or would they be in some sense additive." Dr. Davis responded that "no purchase or lease of land has been included in the benefits of the river development alternative." He went on to suggest, however, that the question raised the point that river development has "other alternatives" than the ones explored in the staff report. "The extreme case," he said, would involve the TVA selling "all of the land back to the private market." Moreover, he indicated "the value for the opportunity costs of the land" made that possibility "a very difficult alternative to ignore."

At that point, Mr. Willis — the representative from Tennessee — asked whether the committee could "infer from the TVA report December '78 that TVA itself feels that river development is a viable alternative." Dr. Davis responded that he would "leave the committee's inferences to the committee." However, "speaking as a staff member," he characterized the river development alternative as "a surprisingly well developed alternative relative to the reservoir which TVA has been analyzing and proposing building for two decades."

In response to a question, Mr. Willis indicated his inability to articulate the single "position of the state of Tennessee," but he offered a summary of "the positions of various and sundry segments." The Tennessee Wildlife Resources Commission had "consistently deplored the completion of the Tellico Dam" and claimed "much more than the snail darter was at stake in the controversy." On the other hand, the "entire Tennessee congressional delegation" favored completion of the dam. Finally, he indicated that the term of the "new governor" Lamar Alexander had begun less than forty-eight hours earlier. Willis said he was not aware that the new governor had taken a position on the Tellico project.

Willis then offered his own opinion. Congress, he suggested, "had made life relatively simple for us." The committee should deny an exemption if it found "any reasonable and prudent alternative," and "the TVA report of December 1978 itself presents a reasonable alternative to the completion of the dam."

At that point, Chairman Andrus recognized Schultze again. Schultze said that the staff report, which he described as "excellently done," made it "very difficult . . . to say there are no reasonable or prudent alternatives to the project." In his view, "the interesting phenomenon" was that the project "is 95 percent complete, and if one takes just the cost of finishing it against the benefits and does it properly, it doesn't pay." That analysis, he added, "says something about the original design." Although the particular river development plan posed by the TVA as an alternative "had slightly larger negative net benefits," the staff report suggested that those negative benefits could be reduced if the TVA looked "very carefully at what mix of private and public ownership, lease and purchase would maximize the total value."

The foregoing analysis led Schultze to oppose an exemption. He said it was impossible "to find that there is no reasonable and prudent alternative" to the reservoir project when a development alternative exists that preserves "some archaeological sites and some scenic value" with negative benefits "only slightly larger" than the reservoir. Nor could he conclude in light of that evidence "that the benefits of completing the project clearly outweigh the benefits of alternatives consistent with conserving the species."

After offering this analysis, Schultze moved that the committee deny an exemption. Richard Frank, administrator of the National

Oceanic and Atmospheric Administration, seconded the motion, and the committee passed it unanimously.

The denial of the exemption did not end the controversy over the Tellico Dam. On the day the exemption was denied, Senator Howard Baker, one of the sponsors of the 1978 amendments to the Endangered Species Act, blasted the committee's decision: "If that's all the good the committee process can do, to put us back where we started from, we might as well save the time and expense. I will introduce legislation to abolish the committee and exempt the Tellico Dam from the provisions of the [Endangered Species Act]." Although Congress refused to abolish the Endangered Species Committee, it did eventually grant an exemption for the Tellico Dam. However, it did so only after a protracted legislative struggle, the outcome of which remained in doubt until the very last moment.

The 1978 amendments to the Endangered Species Act had only authorized appropriations for the act through the middle of the 1980 fiscal year. When the Senate considered bills authorizing appropriations through fiscal year 1982, supporters of the Tellico Dam offered amendments exempting the dam from the protections of the Endangered Species Act. Those amendments were, however, defeated in committee and on the Senate floor.

In the House of Representatives, the dam supporters took a different approach. When the committee responsible for the Endangered Species Act proved unreceptive to an exemption for the Tellico project, the dam supporters attached the exemption to the TVA appropriation bill.

The bill reported by the appropriations committee contained no exemption, but a carefully orchestrated performance on the floor of the House of Representatives added one. On June 18, 1979— exactly one year after the Supreme Court decision in *TVA v. Hill*, the House floor was nearly empty when Representative Duncan proposed an amendment to the Energy and Water Development Appropriation Act of 1980. The amendment directed the TVA to impound the Tellico Reservoir "notwithstanding the provisions of [the Endangered Species Act] or any other law." Although the amendment violated the House rule against changing substantive law by appropriation act, no opponent of the dam raised a point of order. When both the chair of the appropriations committee and the ranking minority member agreed to accept the amendment, the House approved it without a formal vote. Opponents later tried to delete the amendment, but they lacked sufficient political support in the House of Representatives, so the appropriation bill contained the Tellico exemption when it reached the Senate.

The Senate remained less willing than the House of Representatives to grant a specific exemption for the Tellico project. On July 17, Senator Culver offered an amendment deleting the Tellico exemption from the appropriation bill. The next day, the Senate adopted the amendment by a vote of 53 to 45. The Senate then passed the bill without the Tellico exemption. When the House refused to agree to the Senate version of the bill, the bill was referred to a conference committee.

The conference committee was unable to resolve the disagreement over the Tellico exemption, so it referred the matter back to the House and the Senate for further consideration. On August 2, Representative John Breaux of Louisiana moved that the House accept the Senate's deletion of the Tellico exemption, but the House of Representatives rejected the motion by a vote of 156 to 258. Eight days later, however, the Senate reversed its position. By a vote of 48 to 44, the Senate accepted the Tellico exemption. The biggest change from the previous vote involved six senators — Bayh, Durenberger, Inouye, Muskie, Pell, and Pressler — who had previously voted for deleting the exemption but who did not vote on the motion to accept the House position. In addition, five senators who had voted against the exemption on the earlier vote — Cannon, Dole, Gravel, Mathias, and Ribicoff — now voted in favor of accepting it.

Dam opponents still hoped for victory. Cecil Andrus, the secretary of the interior, had indicated he would recommend that the president veto the appropriation bill unless the Tellico exemption was removed. Moreover, White House sources had promised dam opponents that the president would veto the bill if it included an exemption for Tellico. The opponents were, however, destined for yet another disappointment. After calling the dam opponents from Air Force One to tell them that he had decided not to veto the bill, President Carter signed the Energy and Water Development Appropriation Act of 1980 on September 25, 1979.

When President Carter signed the appropriation act, he issued a statement deploring the Tellico exemption. The statement said the president was "satisfied" that the Congress had "clearly confronted this issue and settled on its action with clear majority votes in both Houses." "With regret," he accepted "this action as expressing the will of the Congress." If the bill were vetoed, the statement declared, the president was "convinced" that "Tellico exemptions would be proposed repeatedly in the future." Moreover, the statement predicted, "this resolution of the Tellico matter will help assure the passage of the Endangered Species Act reauthorization without weakening amendments or further exemptions."

According to the *Washington Post*, other political considerations also influenced President Carter's decision to sign the appropriation act. He feared that a veto would prompt congressional retaliation on two important initiatives of the administration, ratification of the Panama Canal Treaty and establishment of a separate Department of Education.

Although dam opponents tried a few more legal maneuvers, the signing of the appropriation act with the Tellico exemption effectively determined the fate of the Little Tennessee River. When the TVA started to close the dam without obtaining a judicial dissolution of the injunction, Peter Alliman filed a motion to hold the Authority in contempt. Judge Taylor summarily dismissed the motion, ruling that the injunction was no longer effective after the president signed the appropriation act. The parties also fought over court costs and attorney fees, although they ultimately settled on an award that Professor Plater donated to an environmental organization.

The Eastern Band of the Cherokee Indians launched a final effort to stop the Tellico Dam project in the courts, but the challenge was unsuccessful. The Cherokees argued that the reservoir's flooding of the sacred sites of the Cherokees would violate the rights of Native Americans under various federal statutes and the Free Exercise Clause of the First Amendment. Both the Eastern District of Tennessee and the Sixth Circuit rejected these claims. They ruled that the appropriation act overrode the other statutory provisions and that the Cherokees had failed to establish a constitutional violation.

The TVA began filling the reservoir even before the Sixth Circuit issued its decision rejecting the claims of the Cherokees. On November

29, 1979, the TVA began closing the dam, and the reservoir was filled to its normal level approximately a month later. The TVA did, however, receive one last bit of adverse publicity over the project. On November 13, federal marshals physically removed Thomas Burel Moser and Nellie McCall, the last two holdouts among the landowners. A television film crew from CBS was present to record the removals, and the *Washington Post* ran a short story on the incident. According to the newspaper, Nellie McCall was crying as she left her home. As she walked away with her daughter, the seventy-five-year-old widow "said she did not know where she would move" now that she had lost "the 91-acre farm her husband had purchased in 1939."

Although the closing of the Tellico Dam flooded the Little Tennessee River, it did not make the snail darter extinct. The fish did disappear from the Tellico Reservoir, but the snail darter remains in the Hiwassee River, the river to which it was transplanted by the TVA. Moreover, Dr. Etnier and others have discovered additional population groups in other streams in the Tennessee River valley. As a result, the Snail Darter Recovery Team recommended that the species be classified as threatened rather than endangered, and the secretary of the interior accepted the recommendation in 1984.

Closing the dam did have the other environmental consequences that had inspired opposition to the project. The farms that had operated in the valley for more than 200 years are gone, and the reservoir eliminated what many believed was the best trout stream east of the Mississippi. Fort Loudoun is located on a reservoir rather than on a river's edge. The Cherokees lost access to their sacred sites, and archaeologists lost a valuable source of data about Native American culture.

On the other hand, the Tellico Dam never produced the economic benefits the TVA predicted. Recreational use has never approached the projections in the TVA's calculation. Nor did the TVA realize the amount it projected from shore land development. No one ever built the proposed model industrial city that would stimulate economic development in the area. The 5,300 jobs that the Tellico Reservoir Development Agency claimed the Tellico project had produced by 2001 amount to less than a quarter of the 25,000 jobs that the TVA had forecast.

The Tellico Dam and its reservoir remain part of the eastern Tennessee environment today. The reservoir is a quiet lake not far from

Knoxville or several other lakes created by TVA dams. The TVA donated much of the excess land it condemned to the local development agency, which sold a substantial portion to real estate developers. Today, the west side of the lake includes several upscale residential developments and golf courses. Boaters and fishers use the reservoir, albeit in much smaller numbers than the TVA projected. Water is diverted to help run the turbines at the Fort Loudon Dam, and the dam has undoubtedly produced some flood control benefits in the Chattanooga area. But not even the TVA ever claimed that the dam's power and flood control benefits exceeded its costs.

CHAPTER 7

The Snail Darter and the Tellico Dam

A Complicated Legacy

The story of the struggle over the Tellico Dam is a complicated one. The dispute consumed fifteen years, and both supporters and opponents of the dam experienced moments of victory and moments of defeat. Moreover, the outcome remained in doubt until the very end.

One can assess this story from a variety of perspectives, but none of them provide simple answers. The outcomes are themselves complicated. The snail darter has survived, but opponents of the dam failed in their effort to preserve the Little Tennessee River. On the other hand, the TVA's victory was a costly one, and completion of the Tellico Dam effectively ended the "new mission" of projects designed to promote economic development. From the standpoint of environmental law, the fight to stop the dam established some important legal principles, but subsequent application of those principles has not always supported environmental protection. Finally, the struggle over the dam demonstrates both the possibilities and the limits of legal protections for the environment.

In some respects, the story of the snail darter is a complicated version of a common tale in federal environmental law. It begins with a federal development agency. For many years, the agency pursued its primary mission with little regard for the impact of its development activities on the environment. The rules began to change, however, in the 1960s as courts became more sympathetic to environmental claims and in the 1970s when Congress enacted new environmental statutes, including NEPA and the Endangered Species Act.

Even after NEPA required all federal agencies to consider the environmental effects of their actions, the agency resisted its new environmental responsibilities, particularly with respect to projects already begun. The courts did force the agency to comply with NEPA's mandate to prepare a statement analyzing the environmental impacts of the proposed action, but they allowed the agency to proceed once the statement was prepared.

The unusual aspect of the Tellico Dam story is, of course, the discovery of a new species, but even that aspect is a NEPA by-product. The professor who served as the expert ichthyologist for the plaintiffs in the NEPA litigation discovered the species as he was preparing for possible testimony in the NEPA litigation. Dam supporters in Congress and elsewhere protested that dam opponents had sought out an insignificant species to take advantage of the Endangered Species Act, but the facts do not support that charge. David Etnier discovered the snail darter four months before Congress enacted the Endangered Species Act of 1973. He actually explored the site to strengthen the testimony he offered in the first NEPA hearing. On that occasion, Etnier had testified that the Little Tennessee River was a possible home to several previously identified rare or endangered species of fish.

New litigation to enforce the Endangered Species Act followed the discovery of the snail darter. Fortunately for dam opponents, the protections of the Endangered Species Act were more substantive than those of NEPA. The Endangered Species Act required the agency to do more than simply assess the impact of its proposed action on the species. The agency also had to avoid any action that would jeopardize the continued existence of the species or destroy its critical habitat. The Endangered Species Act litigation consumed more than two years, but ultimately the U.S. Supreme Court ordered an injunction that precluded completion of the dam.

At that point, the dam supporters exerted their political muscle to complete the project. First, Congress established an exemption process to allow a project to proceed when its benefits exceed the cost of losing the species jeopardized by the project. When an exemption was denied under that standard, the House of Representatives ignored its own rules and approved an appropriation rider that created a substantive exception to the Endangered Species Act. Ultimately, the Senate and the president acquiesced in the decision of the House of Representatives.

As the preceding chapters have demonstrated, the story of the TVA, the Tellico Dam, and the snail darter is considerably more complex than can be captured in the foregoing summary. Moreover, the complexity is rich in irony. The paragraphs that follow explore some of that complexity and some of those ironies in terms of result, legal process, and substantive law.

The most obvious complexities involve results. The fight over the Tellico Dam took place in many forums, and the outcome was frequently uncertain. Indeed, the fate of the dam was not settled until President Carter signed the Energy and Water Development Appropriation Act of 1980.

When Congress began appropriating funds for the Tellico project in 1966, opponents of the dam had little hope of victory. Their prospects improved considerably with the enactment of NEPA, and in January 1972 they secured an injunction halting the project until an environmental impact statement was prepared. At that point, the dam opponents did not regard the NEPA litigation as a mere delaying strategy. Documenting the environmental impacts of the project might, they believed, force the TVA or Congress to abandon the project. If the Authority persisted with the project despite the documentation of its environmental impacts, the opponents hoped to prevail in court by showing that the decision to proceed was arbitrary and capricious.

In fact, NEPA proved to be a procedural rather than a substantive obstacle to completion of the dam. The TVA never considered abandoning the project, and Congress continued to appropriate funds for it. Moreover, the courts remained unwilling to review the merits of the project despite professional criticism of the benefit-cost analysis prepared by the TVA.

The NEPA delay was crucial for the next challenge lodged by dam opponents. Just two months before Judge Taylor dissolved his NEPA injunction in October 1973, David Etnier discovered the snail darter in a section of the Little Tennessee River that would be inundated by the Tellico Reservoir. Four months after Etnier made his discovery, Congress enacted the Endangered Species Act of 1973. Without the delays occasioned by the NEPA litigation, the reservoir might have been flooded before the snail darter was discovered or before opponents could have obtained relief under the Endangered Species Act.

Once Etnier's identification of the snail darter had been accepted for publication, the dam opponents petitioned to have the fish listed as an endangered species. In October 1975, the Fish and Wildlife Service added the snail darter to the list of endangered species. Hank Hill, Zygmunt Plater, and Donald Cohen then filed a suit that sought to enjoin completion of the dam. Just before the trial began in April 1976, the Fish and Wildlife Service also designated the last eighteen miles of the Little Tennessee River as the critical habitat of the snail darter.

Despite finding that completion of the dam would jeopardize the snail darter and destroy its critical habitat, the district court refused to grant an injunction. After granting an injunction pending appeal, the Sixth Circuit reversed the decision of the trial court. The court of appeals ruled that an injunction was mandatory once a violation of Section 7 of the Endangered Species Act was established.

The dam opponents also prevailed in the Supreme Court, but the papers of Justice Marshall and Justice Blackmun reveal how close they came to losing. Although five members of the Court favored a summary reversal of the Sixth Circuit, the Court agreed to hear oral argument when the majority was unable to agree on a single opinion. Fortunately for the opponents, the Court also rejected Justice Blackmun's suggestion that the injunction be lifted until the Supreme Court rendered its opinion. If the Supreme Court had taken that approach, the dam would probably have been completed and the reservoir filled before the Court issued its decision.

Despite the Supreme Court decision, the congressional supporters remained determined to complete the dam. In 1978, Congress amended the Endangered Species Act to create the Endangered Species Committee with power to exempt federal projects from the prohibitions of the act. To the surprise of dam supporters, the committee unanimously denied the request for an exemption for the Tellico project.

The decision of the Endangered Species Committee sent dam supporters back to Congress, where they prevailed by legislative sleight of hand and political arm-twisting. Acting when the House of Representatives was nearly vacant, Representative Duncan managed to secure unanimous consent to amend the TVA appropriation act to exempt the Tellico project from the Endangered Species Act and any other laws that might bar its completion. Although the amendment was a clear violation of House rules, representatives supporting the dam defeated efforts to delete the rider and then persuaded the House of Representatives to insist on the rider after the Senate removed it. Ultimately, the Senate relented and passed the appropriation act with the Tellico exemption.

Opponents of the dam still hoped for victory. President Carter had threatened to veto the appropriation bill if it contained an exemption for the Tellico Dam, and supporters of the dam had no realistic hope of securing the two-thirds vote necessary to override the veto in the Senate. Ultimately, however, President Carter reneged on his threat to veto the bill if the Tellico exemption were not eliminated. Shortly after he signed the appropriation act, the TVA closed the dam and created the Tellico Reservoir.

Final winners and losers are difficult to identify in the snail darter case. Although the environmentalists prevailed in the Supreme Court, the TVA won the congressional battle. As a result of the legislative victory, the Tellico Dam went into operation, but it never stimulated the economic development that the TVA had predicted. Moreover, the project marked the end, not the beginning, of the TVA's "new mission" of multiuse projects to promote economic development; and it exposed raw political power rather than rational analysis as the basis for the agency's agenda. On the other hand, the snail darter survives, but the final section of the Little Tennessee River is now a reservoir, not a trout stream. The restored Fort Loudoun now sits near one edge of the reservoir rather than on the river's edge. The reservoir covers thousands of acres of some of the best farmland in eastern Tennessee, acres that also included the remains of several ancient Cherokee villages.

Unfortunately for dam opponents, the Supreme Court decision in the snail darter case did not provide the final word on the Tellico project. Mobilizing their supporters in Congress, the dam proponents reversed the outcome produced by the Supreme Court judgment and achieved the goal to which they had so tenaciously adhered from the time the Tellico Dam was first publicly proposed in 1963. Despite the snail darter litigation and the refusal of the Endangered Species Act to grant an exemption, the Authority completed the Tellico project and closed the floodgates to the dam on November 29, 1979. By then, the costs had nearly doubled since Congress first appropriated funds for the project in 1966, and its completion had been delayed by several years from the original projections. Nonetheless, the TVA had demonstrated that it did not have to alter its plans because of opposition from environmental groups and some portions of the local community.

For the TVA and its allies, the victory in the Tellico Dam battle was a costly one. The Authority succeeded in completing the dam, and the snail darter survived. The dam has, however, never produced the benefits that the TVA claimed would result from its construction. Moreover, the snail darter contributed to the demise of the Authority's "new mission" and helped to diminish the TVA image as an impartial agency of experts.

The TVA might well claim credit for both the discovery and the survival of the snail darter. Had the TVA never resurrected the Tellico project, Etnier might never have surveyed Coytee Springs and discovered the snail darter. Once the snail darter was discovered, the TVA certainly spent large sums to try to transplant the fish. Most observers have concluded that at least the transplant to the Hiwassee River was successful, but Etnier remains unconvinced. In an interview, he speculated that the snail darters in the Hiwassee might be a distinct population, citing physical differences from the Little Tennessee snail darters and the location of the Hiwassee population several miles from the transplant site. Perhaps, he suggested, a new generation of ichthyologists will use DNA samples to determine the origin of the Hiwassee population.

The results of the Tellico project differ greatly from the predictions the TVA offered to Congress and in its environmental impact statement. The project has produced the power generation and flood control benefits that the TVA envisioned, but those benefits were always a minor portion of the justification for the project. Some recreational use and economic development has followed the construction of the Tellico Dam, but the dam has never fulfilled the TVA predictions. The TVA estimates for navigational benefits were particularly wide of the mark, and the opponents were correct in warning that the dam would adversely affect water quality and that the TVA had overestimated the fishing benefits.

The disparity between the TVA's projections and the current landscape is striking. The dam and the reservoir exist pretty much as expected, but the land uses are not at all what the TVA promised. A quarter century after the completion of the dam, no substantial industrial development has occurred on the property that the TVA obtained as part of its "large take" policy; and no new city of 50,000 has emerged around the reservoir. Instead, the TVA conveyed the land to the Tellico Reservoir Development Authority, which assumed responsibility for economic development of the reservoir area. A few new industries have located in the industrial park at the south end of the reservoir, but the reservoir does not seem essential for most of the development that has occurred. In 2001, the development authority's annual report claimed that the Tellico project had resulted in the creation of approximately one-fifth the number of jobs the TVA projected. On the west side of the reservoir, the development authority sold the land to a developer who constructed Tellico Village, an upscale golf and lakefront development. The east side remains much more rural, probably because it has less convenient access to any significant population area or the interstate highway.

In some ways, the results in the Tellico Dam fight parallel those of the Norris Dam, the TVA's first attempt at area planning in the 1930s. The TVA also adopted a "large take" policy for the Norris Dam, and it built the planned community of Norris, Tennessee. Originally projected as the ideal home for rural poor who were displaced by the dam and reservoir, it eventually survived as a white-collar suburb for professionals who worked for the TVA or in Knoxville. Because dam workers occupied the first temporary homes, the displaced residents of the Norris valley had to find other accommodations and never populated Norris. Moreover, the TVA excluded black families from the "model city." As more affluent residents replaced the dam workers, the cooperative activities the TVA had established gradually disappeared. In 1948, the TVA sold the town to a private corporation, which then resold the individual lots to residents.

In the case of the Tellico Dam, the TVA never even built the new city. Once the Boeing Corporation pulled out of the project, the model city proposal died a quiet death. After the dam was completed, the TVA transferred the property to the local development district, and the district in turn sold much of the property to private developers. According to a developer's Web site, lakefront lots in the subdivisions on the west side of the reservoir are available for $150,000. One suspects that few of the low-income families whose lives the TVA said would be benefited by the Tellico Dam have taken advantage of the lake and golf communities that have been established in the area. These results seem at odds with the original planning purposes of the

TVA Act. The justification for giving the TVA power to promote economic development was to improve the lives of the people living in an economically deprived area. Instead, the TVA took the land of local residents, built a reservoir, and eventually reconveyed the land to a group whose median income is likely much larger than that of the group whose property was taken.

Of course, the TVA and local officials might assert that the legal struggle doomed subsequent efforts to stimulate economic development. However, all independent evaluations concluded that the TVA projections were unrealistically optimistic from the beginning. The more natural conclusion is to understand the TVA projections as the consequences of an agency needing to provide a positive benefit-cost ratio for a project to which it was already committed.

The TVA was also overly optimistic in predicting the main direct benefits for the project: recreational use and navigation. The reservoir does attract boats for recreation uses of the reservoir, but in numbers far below the 1,750,000 annual visitors that the TVA projected. In addition, the navigation benefits the TVA promised are largely nonexistent, unless one wishes to include the wealthy supporters of football at the University of Tennessee. They now have a navigable waterway all the way from their lakefront homes on the Tellico Reservoir to Neyland Stadium in Knoxville. Or perhaps that opportunity qualifies as a recreational benefit.

By contrast, the TVA underestimated the environmental costs of the Tellico project. The water quality and fishing reputation have certainly deteriorated. According to the latest information on the TVA Web site for the Tellico Reservoir, the Authority has assigned the reservoir an ecological health rating of "poor," and the state advises against eating catfish from the reservoir because of PCB contamination. As compared with other reservoirs, fishing is average to below average for most species.

The fight over the Tellico Dam also had a negative impact on the image of the TVA. To achieve victory, the TVA had to abandon its image as an agency guided by the rational analysis of experts and to rely on raw political power. Use of political power was not a new strategy for the TVA. It had received substantial congressional appropriations since the 1930s, and it had used those appropriations to develop its political support. When seeking appropriations, the TVA offered rational defenses of its proposals before friendly committees, thus preserving the facade that impartial rationality guided its decisions. In reality, of course, the TVA relied on its political supporters to win the appropriations. Over the years, the Authority had expanded its support from the original Democratic base to include the entire Tennessee congressional delegation, Republican and Democratic. Not even Albert Gore Jr., who was elected in 1976 to represent the Fourth Congressional District in the House of Representatives, would aid the opponents of the dam in their legislative battles. In an interview, Hank Hill still remembered his keen disappointment on learning that Representative Gore would not assist the dam opponents despite appearing sympathetic in an initial meeting.

The Authority always offered rational defenses of the Tellico project, but opponents challenged the decisions in forums that were less sympathetic than the congressional appropriation committees. In all those forums, the TVA lost. The District Court for the Eastern District of Tennessee and the Sixth Circuit ruled that the original analysis of environmental issues was inadequate to satisfy NEPA. The Supreme Court held that completion of the dam violated the plain language of the Endangered Species Act. The TVA protested that these decisions failed to consider the economic realities of the Tellico project, but the TVA was the only entity that ever studied the Tellico project and concluded that it had a positive benefit-cost ratio.

The benefit-cost issue was unreviewable in court, so opponents never got a judicial determination of that question. Other evaluations did review the economic analysis, and they consistently rejected the TVA position. As early as 1971, the Phillips Report challenged the benefit-cost analysis prepared by the TVA. In 1977, the GAO recommended that Congress should order the TVA to prepare a new benefit-cost analysis before appropriating additional funds to complete the Tellico project. Two years later, the Endangered Species Committee unanimously rejected the TVA proposal even though by that time the TVA had already spent many millions more than the project was originally projected to cost. The committee unanimously rejected the claim that the benefits of the proposed action "clearly outweigh[ed]" alternative courses of action or that the TVA had no "reasonable and prudent alternatives." Charles Schultze, chairman of the Council of Economic Advisors and a member of the committee, offered the following observation: "The interesting phenomenon is that here is a project that is 95 percent complete, and if one takes just the cost of finishing it against the total benefits and does it properly, it doesn't pay, which says something about the original design." Cecil Andrus, secretary of the Department of the Interior and chair of the Endangered Species Committee, said he "hate[d] to see the snail darter get the credit for stopping a project that was ill-conceived and uneconomical in the first place."

In part, the Tellico dispute involved a change in forum; in part it involved a change in the TVA opponents. The preceding paragraph highlights the forum change. Opponents now had legal arguments to which they could force the TVA to respond in forums that were less hospitable than appropriation committees, and the rationale the Authority offered was substantially less successful in those venues. The change in the nature of the opposition may be less obvious.

Opponents had challenged the TVA from its creation, but they could generally be divided into two classes: power companies and individuals displaced from their communities by TVA projects. The TVA could dismiss the opposition of the power companies as motivated by self-interest and fear of competition from the new federal agency. As for the individuals who had to be relocated, the TVA treated them as too poor and too poorly educated to realize that the rational experts of the federal government were acting in their best interests.

The TVA could dismiss the new opponents less easily. Certainly, the core of the opposition still came from individuals who were concerned about loss of the traditional amenities of the Little Tennessee River. They were, however, not only landowners and residents but also trout fishers and individuals interested in ecology, archaeology, and history. Moreover, they were economists, biologists, archaeologists, lawyers, and other professionals who regarded themselves as the intellectual equals of the TVA employees and experts.

The Tellico litigation was not the only arena in which this rise in professional opposition presented itself. In the 1960s, the TVA resisted efforts by environmental organizations to force the Authority to ensure that the mines providing the coal it was purchasing were following federal environmental standards. Later, the TVA also fought the attempts of state and federal regulators and environmental groups to force the Authority to comply with new environmental regulations. For a time, the TVA defeated the efforts of the states to require permits for stationary source pollution, and it fought the EPA's orders to install scrubbers on the Authority's coal-fired power facilities until David Freeman negotiated a settlement between the two federal agencies in the late 1970s. During the 1970s, the TVA also faced substantial opposition from ratepayers because by then low-cost, hydroelectric power provided only a fraction of the power generated by the TVA. The cost of TVA coal purchases and the spiraling costs of nuclear facilities prompted new complaints about rising energy rates and about imposing construction costs for future nuclear facilities on current ratepayers.

By the 1980s, a professionally trained economist was even willing to challenge the conventional wisdom that the TVA had contributed significantly to the economic growth of the Tennessee River Valley. William Chandler's critique of the Authority identified lack of accountability to markets or the political process as the crucial defect of the TVA. That critique led him to propose that the TVA's power operations should be regulated by state utility commissions in the areas in which the Authority furnishes electricity.

When the TVA failed to prevail against its new opponents in the new judicial forums available to opponents of the Tellico Dam, dam supporters turned to political hardball. At a time when the House of Representatives was almost empty, Representative Duncan secured unanimous consent for an amendment to the public works appropriation act; and he later persuaded his colleagues to retain the amendment even though it violated House rules. The Tennessee delegation — Republican Baker and Democrat Sasser — then secured just enough votes to have the Senate accept the action of the House of Representatives. Finally, dam supporters persuaded the president to abandon his promise to veto the appropriation bill if the Tellico exemption were included.

These political machinations prevailed, but they exposed the Authority as a political animal that could no longer claim its actions should be immune from political scrutiny. One ironic cost of victory was the loss of the very justification for creating the TVA: the desire to create an agency of impartial experts who could rationally pursue the public good free from political pressure.

Perhaps nothing illustrates the vehemence of the snail darter struggle better than the attacks on the lawyers representing the dam. Both Zygmunt Plater and Peter Alliman faced professional attacks for their participation in the snail darter litigation.

Zygmunt Plater was the chief legal strategist for the snail darter litigation. Plater came to the University of Tennessee Law School as an associate professor in 1973 and became involved in the fight to preserve the snail darter and the Little Tennessee River near the end of 1974. While the snail darter litigation was proceeding, members of the Tennessee bar filed a barratry complaint against him for his work on the case. The bar association dismissed the complaint after Plater wrote a letter explaining why his actions were permissible under the canons of ethics.

More significantly, the faculty at the law school voted to deny tenure to Plater as *TVA v. Hill* was pending in the Sixth Circuit in 1976. Members of the faculty emphatically rejected the charge that the tenure denial was politically motivated because of his involvement with the snail darter case, although some did claim his involvement with the case distracted him from his law school duties. The no-impact explanation for the faculty's actions rings hollow, however. Plater was already a productive young scholar at Tennessee, and the students who joined his campaign to stop the Tellico Dam still remember him as an excellent teacher. In a 2005 interview, the former dean of the law faculty told the author he was surprised by the faculty decision, and one senior colleague told Plater that the young professor never understood the "moderation" expected of a member of the Tennessee law faculty. Presumably, the moderation Plater lacked was avoiding an adversarial relationship with an important local institution like the TVA.

Ultimately, this portion of the story has a happy ending. Plater went from Tennessee to teach in the law school at Wayne State University. While teaching there, he successfully argued *TVA v. Hill* in the U.S. Supreme Court and led opponents in the unsuccessful legislative battle in Congress. Subsequently, Plater moved on to the Boston College Law School, where he still teaches. He is coauthor of a casebook in environmental law, the one, not surprisingly, with the most complete discussion of the snail darter litigation. Moreover, he is widely regarded as one of the nation's leading experts on the Endangered Species Act.

Peter Alliman was a law student when he became involved in the Endangered Species Act case, and he continued to work on it after graduation. After Congress passed the Tellico exemption in 1979, the TVA resumed work to complete the project. Because the TVA had not asked the district court to dissolve its injunction, Alliman filed a motion to hold the Authority in contempt. Judge Taylor promptly dismissed the motion, but the TVA was not satisfied. It filed a motion for sanctions against the recent graduate.

Fortunately, the TVA also failed to derail the legal career of Peter Alliman. Judge Taylor refused to impose sanctions. In an interview, Alliman recalled that when Judge Taylor denied the request for sanctions, he told the TVA attorneys: "But he is so young." Today, Alliman has a successful legal practice in Knoxville and Madisonville, a small town in Monroe County.

Now that the political struggle over the Tellico Dam is over, no one appears to have reexamined the benefit-cost issue. The TVA reluctance is understandable; few would credit a new analysis that found the benefit ratio positive, and a negative conclusion would contradict the position to which the Authority tenaciously adhered for more than a decade and a half. As for the opponents, they probably see little to gain. The river they sought to protect is gone, and a new analysis will not restore it. In any event, both the opponents and most scholars probably lack the resources to prepare a credible analysis.

If an impartial post-dam analysis were done, it would almost certainly document a negative benefit-cost ratio for the Tellico project. In the first place, various technical critiques of the TVA analysis have documented a number of errors, such as assuming that all economic benefits occurring in the area were products of the project, counting all benefits as accruing immediately when the reservoir was filled, and using an unrealistically low discount rate. Second, the economic costs nearly doubled between the last time the TVA evaluated the project and the completion of the dam. Third, the TVA substantially overestimated the major benefits it used to justify the project. As explained earlier, these errors involve recreation and navigation, the principal direct benefits, as well as the TVA's major justification for the project, the economic development that it would stimulate. Fourth, the TVA also substantially underestimated the adverse environmental impacts on areas such as water quality and fishing.

One striking aspect of the snail darter litigation is the political division that it produced. Opponents of the dam were fighting wasteful appropriations and supporting property owners. Nonetheless, most conservatives enthusiastically supported completion of the dam. To some extent, this conservative support represented a traditional pattern in which southern politicians support public works projects for their region even as they complain about the overreaching power of the federal government. But the support for the dam clearly went beyond the traditional political support for the TVA. At least two factors seem to have contributed to the political divide over the dam. First, the TVA and its supporters maintained a successful publicity campaign that convinced many that the Tellico project was a sensible project that was being stalled by environmental extremists, and the list of those who were convinced is surprisingly diverse. It includes Ronald Reagan, Griffin Bell, Lewis Powell, and Ronald Dworkin. Second, the political division over the snail darter litigation was a sign of the increasing polarization of the environmental debate in the late 1970s, especially the debate over the Endangered Species Act. For many conservatives, environmentalists had become a group they were determined to fight at every opportunity.

In addition to its negative impact on the TVA image, the Tellico "victory" contributed to the demise of the Authority's "new mission" of economic development projects. The Endangered Species Act stopped at least one other project, and the TVA has refocused its activities on power generation.

In 1977, the Fish and Wildlife Service determined that construction of the Columbia Dam on the Duck River would jeopardize two species of mussels that had been listed as endangered. The TVA stopped construction as it awaited the resolution of the snail darter case. Following the Supreme Court decision and extensive studies, the Authority eventually abandoned the project and demolished the nearly completed dam structure. In 2001, the TVA donated the lands it had condemned for the dam to the state, and the state designated a portion of the Duck River as a scenic river.

The Tellico Dam and the aborted Columbia Dam marked the end of the TVA's "new mission." In the 1980s, the TVA increasingly returned to its roots as a federally owned power company. As a result, it focused its attention on solving the environmental problems of its generating plants and controlling the costs of the power it generated. Today, the TVA totally funds its operations from self-generated funds; it receives no congressional funding. Ironically, some environmental critics of the TVA now claim that the Authority is abandoning its commitment to preservation of the natural resources around its reservoirs.

The fight over the Tellico Dam also provides a complicated legacy for dam opponents. At a superficial level, one can claim that the Tellico Dam litigation achieved the specific objective of Section 7 of the Endangered Species Act: to prevent federal action that destroys a species. Notwithstanding the construction of the dam, the snail darter is not extinct. Moreover, part of the reason for the survival of the snail darter may be the colony that the TVA transplanted to the Hiwassee River; and the transplantation effort was a direct response to the threat that the project might be enjoined because the TVA was violating Section 7 of the Endangered Species Act.

In 1984, the Department of the Interior upgraded the status of the snail darter from endangered to threatened. Dr. Etnier and others have discovered small colonies of snail darters in other rivers of the region, and a substantial population (either the result of successful transplantation or a separate population) exists in the Hiwassee River. As a result, the snail darter's long-term prospects for survival are much stronger today than they were when the Little Tennessee River was impounded. The Snail Darter Recovery Team has recommended that at least five viable populations of snail darters should be identified to eliminate the threat of extinction. A 1992 Internet posting suggested that the current populations "may be sufficient enough to eventually achieve this objective and provide a basis for removing the snail darter from the Federal List of Endangered and Threatened Wildlife," but the Service has not yet taken that step. In interviews in 2005, both Dr. Etnier and a Fish and Wildlife Service biologist said that the snail darter would probably be removed from the threatened list today if the Service had the resources to assemble current data on the species. Because the current listing is not adversely affecting the plans of any federal agency or private entity, the Service is understandably focusing its resources on species facing greater threats.

On a more fundamental level, of course, the fight to protect the snail darter was simply one part of a long struggle that the opponents of the Tellico Dam ultimately lost. In the mid-1970s, the snail darter provided a useful legal handle for opposing the Tellico Dam and its destruction of the Little Tennessee River Valley, but it marked neither the beginning nor the end of the political and legal opposition to the Tellico project. Opponents began their fight against the dam years before Congress enacted the Endangered Species Act of 1973. In the 1970s, NEPA — the first statute signed in the so-called decade of the environment — enabled opponents to delay the project for approximately twenty months. Moreover, after Congress specifically authorized construction of the dam notwithstanding violations of the Endangered Species Act, they even tried additional constitutional arguments.

Some observers have criticized the dam opponents for using the Endangered Species Act to stop the dam. They contend the argument about the need to save the snail darter was simply a sham. That contention is wrong for several reasons. First, many of the dam opponents saw the policy expressed in Section 7 of the Endangered Species Act as a pragmatic decision to preclude the federal government from making the extinction problem worse. For them, the question was not one of comparing the economic value of one species against the economic value of one project; instead, it was a commitment to minimizing the extinction crisis that threatens the globe. Second, few — if any — of those fighting to stop the dam ever claimed that the Tellico struggle was just about the snail darter. Instead, they repeatedly argued that the disappearance of the snail darter was the result of the larger disappearance from the Tennessee River basin of the habitat that supported the species. Protection of the snail darter thus served as a surrogate for protecting all the environmental values of the Little Tennessee River Valley because those values would also be preserved if the snail darter were saved. Third, those who have criticized the dam opponents for seizing the Endangered Species Act argument to stop the dam have not made similar criticisms of the dam supporters. They have not, for example, criticized the TVA for relying on precedents to immunize its benefit-cost analysis from judicial scrutiny, even though every independent evaluation concluded that the analysis was flawed, or from accelerating its construction efforts while the Fish and Wildlife Service was considering whether the snail darter should be listed as an endangered species. Litigants rely on arguments that give them a chance of winning the litigation. For forty years, the law provided no effective judicial remedy for unwise decisions of the TVA. Surely, it is unrealistic to suggest that the dam opponents would ignore the one effective legal claim Congress established in 1973.

If the environmentalists won the snail darter battle, they clearly lost the Tellico Dam war. Ultimately, those who wanted to preserve the Little Tennessee River lost. The dam began to operate in 1979, and its reservoir quickly flooded the Little Tennessee River.

The loss demonstrated the limits of the Endangered Species Act as a litigation tool. The goal of the Endangered Species Act litigation was not simply to preserve the snail darter. The plaintiffs in *TVA v. Hill* were trying to preserve the snail darter by stopping the construction of the dam that would destroy the last segment of the darter's natural habitat, and the lawsuit failed to achieve that goal. Because the basis for the Supreme Court decision was a statute, Congress had the ultimate authority to decide whether the dam should be built.

For almost all opponents of the dam, the snail darter was only one basis for opposing the dam; for many, it was not even the most important reason. Thus, opponents uniformly regard the completion of the dam as a crushing defeat because it destroyed other resources that animated opposition. The flooding of the Little Tennessee River not only destroyed the snail darters in its waters; it also eliminated trout fishing on a stream that was rated one of the best east of the Rockies. In addition, the Tellico project removed thousands of acres of the most valuable farmland in eastern Tennessee from agricultural production. The loss was much greater than the 12,500 acres the reservoir flooded; even more farmland was lost to the TVA's "large take" policy that converted the land to lakeshore homes. Yet another loss from the completion of the dam was the historical setting of Fort Loudoun, the westernmost outpost in the French and Indian War, and the Tellico Blockhouse, which was constructed in 1794 just across the river from the fort. The reconstructed fort and the ruins of the blockhouse remain, but in a strange setting. The fort now sits on the edge of the huge reservoir, and the blockhouse lies across a narrow bit of reservoir water rather than on the other side of a small river. Finally, several important Cherokee sites now lie under the reservoir waters, although the TVA did eventually agree to build a levee to keep the village of Chota from being submerged.

Finally, the completion of the Tellico Dam almost certainly reflects a permanent defeat for the opponents. In many areas, environmentalists have campaigned for removing dams with harmful environmental effects; they have even succeeded in a few cases. One finds it hard to imagine that such an effort will eliminate the Tellico Dam. The upscale developments on the west side of the reservoir have created enormous economic interests that would oppose such an effort and would almost certainly doom it to political failure.

To be sure, the Tellico project was not the most wasteful public works project of the 1960s and 1970s, and others were at least as environmentally harmful. The $116 million appropriated for the Tellico Dam pales in comparison to more than $1 billion spent on the Tennessee-Tombigbee waterway. Moreover, the environmental damage of the Tennessee-Tombigbee was also extensive, as was the damage from other projects. For example, the opponents of the Gilham Dam might regard the loss of one of the last free-flowing streams in the Ouachita Mountains as just as serious as the loss of the last section of the Little Tennessee River. Nonetheless, the environmental loss from the Tellico project was substantial, and former users of the river and valley still miss the environmental amenities of earlier days.

The Tellico Dam controversy shows the inherent bias of the traditional federal approach of authorizing federal expenditures for a single type of development project. Local boosters understandably wanted to stimulate the economy of the Little Tennessee River valley. If they agreed to support the TVA's proposal to dam the river, a large sum of money — eventually more than $100 million — would flow into the area; if they opposed the project, the local economy would receive no stimulus. The TVA's support for the project was equally understandable. Congress was willing to give the Authority substantial annual appropriations for construction of the dam. If the Authority concluded that the costs of the dam exceeded its benefits, the agency would get nothing.

During the fight over the Tellico Dam, opponents proposed alternate plans for the development of the valley without a reservoir. By that time, however, the battle lines were drawn, and the TVA could only support them by admitting it had been wrong for fifteen years and by abandoning those who had supported it politically in the long struggle over construction of the dam. A far better solution would allow consideration of federally funded alternatives to agency proposals from the beginning of the authorization process. Such an approach would make political fights over federal funding of development less of a zero-sum game. The original supporters of NEPA envisioned that it would perform this role, but the courts were never willing to make that statute's substantive provisions judicially enforceable. Unfortunately, the current demands for reform of NEPA call for weakening even its procedural protections.

The story of the Tellico litigation also contains complicated twists regarding legal proceedings. The first of these twists involves the TVA appeal of the first NEPA litigation. That appeal may have made possible the discovery of the snail darter and the subsequent litigation under the Endangered Species Act. Second, the decision of the attorney general to embrace the TVA position helped to contribute to the inaccurate portrayal of the case as a straightforward choice between literalism and purposive jurisprudence. Finally, the proceedings in the Supreme Court were unusual in several respects.

The TVA filed its final environmental impact statement the month following the issuance of Judge Taylor's injunction in the first NEPA case. Unlike the Corps of Engineers in the Gilham Dam litigation, the TVA continued its appeal rather than returning to ask Judge Taylor to lift the injunction once the Authority completed the impact statement. Because the Sixth Circuit upheld the injunction on appeal, more than twenty months elapsed before the injunction was lifted in October 1973. Had the TVA abandoned its appeal once the final impact statement was completed in February 1972, the Authority might have been free of the injunction even before the fall of 1972 when Dr. Etnier first identified Coytee Springs as the likely home of rare and unusual fish. Moreover, even if the snail darter had been discovered, the dam might have been operational before the Endangered Species Act case reached the Sixth Circuit.

As noted in chapter 1, a leading casebook designed to introduce law students to the Anglo-American legal system provides a typical description of the snail darter case, emphasizing Chief Justice Burger's assertion that "this language admits of no exception." Certainly, this description mirrors the one offered by the Supreme Court; but it ignores the position of the Department of the Interior, the agency charged with administering the Endangered Species Act. The department agreed with the plaintiffs; both the interim and final versions of the guidelines declared that the prohibition in Section 7 against any federal action that would jeopardize an endangered species or destroy its critical habitat applied to projects initiated prior to the listing of a species as endangered. Neither the majority nor the dissenting opinions in the Supreme Court relied on the interpretation of the Department of the Interior. Federal courts have long deferred to the interpretation of an ambiguous statute by the agency charged with administering it, and the Supreme Court itself was deferential to the secretary of the interior in subsequent Endangered Species Act litigation involving private parties. In 1995, the Court upheld the secretary's interpretation that destruction of the habitat of an endangered species on private property could violate Section 9's prohibition against "taking" any member of an endangered species.

The failure of the Supreme Court to rely on the position of the Department of the Interior was not the result of ignorance. Instead, the Court appears to have been reluctant to defer to the secretary's interpretation because his position was inconsistent with the official position of the United States. In effect, the attorney general eliminated the deference ordinarily due the Department of the Interior, the agency charged with administering the Endangered Species Act, by supporting the position of the TVA.

Procedurally, *TVA v. Hill* is a very unusual case because the United States actually filed two briefs in the Supreme Court. Even though the attorney general argued the case for the TVA, he secured the Court's permission to file a second brief on behalf of the United States, a procedure that the Court had allowed previously in a few cases. The solicitor general of the Department of the Interior signed the second brief. In it, he articulated the department's interpretation, which directly contradicted the position of the attorney general. According to the department's interpretation of the Endangered Species Act, Section 7 precluded the TVA from completing the dam because the dam would jeopardize the snail darter and destroy its critical habitat.

The snail darter case also provides a surprising confirmation that briefing and oral argument can be important in the Supreme Court. When the TVA applied for certiorari, the U.S. Supreme Court voted five to four to reverse the case summarily, without further briefing or oral argument. The majority was, however, unable to agree on a single opinion, and so the Court accepted Justice Brennan's suggestion that full briefing and oral argument might be appropriate. Following oral argument, the Supreme Court majority shifted when Justice White and the chief justice switched their votes. The five-four majority for reversing the Sixth Circuit shifted to a six-three majority for affirming the court of appeals.

The shift in the decision of the Supreme Court following oral argument confirms the wisdom of the custom that apparently limits summary dispositions to cases in which a six-member majority favors that result. The justices will have a more complete understanding of the case after briefing and oral argument. Respect for the decision of the lower court seems to caution against a summary decision on the merits when the Court is nearly evenly divided. As the snail darter case illustrates, initial positions may change on further reflection.

The legal legacy of the snail darter is also complicated. *TVA v. Hill* was an important legal victory for environmentalists, but it did not represent a sharp greening of the law of the United States. The Supreme Court has declined to extend the mandatory injunction rule of *TVA v. Hill* as a general principle applicable to all environmental statutes. The distinction drawn between appropriation acts and substantive legislation in *TVA v. Hill* has not stopped Congress from using appropriation acts to override substantive rules of the Endangered Species Act. On the other hand, the struggle over Tellico Dam foreshadowed the limited protection that would be afforded to sacred sites of Native Americans, and the snail darter case failed to open new legal challenges to the substantive merits of public works projects.

On the issue of remedies, *TVA v. Hill* was a tremendous victory for environmentalists, but the victory has been limited to the Endangered Species Act. In the snail darter litigation, the Supreme Court ruled that an injunction was mandatory once a violation of Section 7 was proved. The Court has not, however, used this mandatory injunction rule when construing other environmental statutes. The retreat began just four years after the snail darter decision. In a case involving the U.S. Navy's failure to obtain a permit under the Clean Water Act, an eight-to-one majority declined to require an immediate cession of the statutory violation. Instead, the majority held that the district court had the discretion to allow the violator a reasonable time to apply for a permit before granting an injunction.

TVA v. Hill emphatically rejected the argument that appropriation acts can amend the requirements of substantive law by implication, but subsequent cases have demonstrated the limited nature of this protection. Congressional rules forbid using appropriation acts to amend substantive laws, but those rules are not judicially enforceable. Thus, the courts will apply substantive provisions when Congress expressly includes them in appropriation acts.

The Tellico Dam struggle itself shows the limited nature of the protection of the implied-repeal rule. In the Energy and Water Development Appropriation Act of 1980, Congress expressly overrode Section 7 of the Endangered Species Act, as well as the restrictions in all other federal statutes, and the TVA closed the dam on November 29, 1979.

Legislators concerned about the impact of the substantive rules of the Endangered Species Act have not forgotten the lesson of the Tellico Dam litigation. In the nearly three decades since the Supreme Court's decision in *TVA v. Hill*, Congress has modified substantive rules through appropriation acts on several occasions. Although the congressional opponents of the Endangered Species Act have thus far been unable to secure repeal of the listing obligations imposed by Section 4, they have managed to make performance of many of those obligations impossible by denying the agency funds to perform them. Similarly, supporters of the timber industry remembered the snail darter lesson fifteen years later during the spotted owl controversy. When the Endangered Species Committee allowed a very limited harvest in the areas of the owls' habitat, Congress regularly expanded the harvest for several years by including substantive provisions in various appropriation acts. So long as the appropriation riders were explicit in permitting the harvests, the courts allowed them to change substantive law.

The distinction between substantive laws and appropriations is important because amending substantive statutes and securing congressional appropriations are very different processes. Representatives and senators unhappy with particular decisions generally have great difficulty amending substantive laws to dictate particular results. The congressional committees responsible for a substantive law will ordinarily resist changes designed to overturn particular decisions. On the other hand, the committees responsible for appropriations regularly include sums for particular purposes. Moreover, opponents of a particular appropriation often find it difficult to delete a line item once it has been added to an appropriation act. If the line item is not deleted, the only way one can vote against it is to vote against the entire appropriation act, and the act may include many projects the legislator favors.

The fight over the snail darter illustrates the differences described in the preceding paragraph. Following the Supreme Court decision in *TVA v. Hill*, the committees responsible for the Endangered Species Act produced not a specific exemption but a process for deciding when exemptions were appropriate. When that process denied an exemption for the Tellico Dam, the substantive committees still refused to support a special exemption for the Tellico project. By contrast, the alleged appropriations "for" the Tellico Dam prior to 1979 were actually appropriations to the TVA with no restriction to a particular project. The appropriation committees did establish the restrictions in the legislative history, but members of Congress who were not members of the committees had no say in the preparation of the committee reports. Moreover, when Representative Duncan added a Tellico exemption to the annual appropriation act in 1979, he did it when the House floor was largely empty. Then he succeeded in defeating subsequent efforts to delete the exemption in the House of Representatives and persuaded the House to insist on the exemption. At that point, the Senate accepted the exemption to avoid jeopardizing the entire appropriation act, and President Carter retreated from his veto threat.

The Tellico Dam struggle also foreshadowed the limited protection provided to the sacred sites of Native Americans. The final litigation over the Tellico Dam involved claims by the Eastern Band of the Cherokee Indians; the tribe argued that the reservoir would interfere with the First Amendment rights of its members by denying them access to sacred sites that would be flooded. Both the U.S. District Court for the Eastern District of Tennessee and the Sixth Circuit summarily rejected the constitutional claims of the Cherokees. In the 1990s, the Supreme Court adopted a similarly restrictive view of the free exercise rights of Native Americans, rejecting the claim that the First Amendment forbade federal actions that would deny Native Americans access to sacred sites on public lands.

Perhaps most fundamentally, the legal battles over the Tellico Dam provided no significant changes in the limited judicial review available for federal public works projects. The crucial questions are all still immune from meaningful judicial review. The Supreme Court remains extraordinarily deferential to governmental decisions regarding the validity of the public use of a project, having reaffirmed the deference principle as recently as 2005. The government's benefit-cost analysis remains a political document prepared for public relations and congressional consideration, not a legal document whose compliance with statutory or regulatory norms can be challenged in court. Likewise, the necessity for the taking of an individual's property and the scope of the property taken remain subject only to the minimal scrutiny of the arbitrary and capricious rule. Without NEPA, the Endangered Species Act, and other environmental statutes enacted during the 1970s, opponents of public works projects would have no meaningful legal challenges.

The snail darter litigation has also impacted the Endangered Species Act. The Supreme Court decision produced statutory changes in the Endangered Species Act, but those changes did not gut the statute. Moreover, the Supreme Court has generally continued its sympathetic interpretation of the Endangered Species Act. However, in doing so, it has relied not on textual clarity but on administrative deference.

Congress amended the Endangered Species Act immediately following the Supreme Court's 1978 decision in the snail darter case. The result was a revision of the act, not a destruction of its protections. The 1978 amendments clarified the requirement that federal agencies consult with the Fish and Wildlife Service whenever a project might jeopardize an endangered species and created the Endangered Species Committee with power to grant exemptions from Section 7. The changes converted the absolute prohibition of Section 7 into one with an administrative safety valve, but the standard to receive an exemption was a high one. Equally important, the amendments focused attention on the search for reasonable alternatives that would avoid jeopardizing the species. Even when the new procedures failed to produce the result that the Tellico Dam supporters desired and expected, Congress retained them. Although Congress eventually authorized the building of the dam, it did so without a permanent change in the substance of the Endangered Species Act.

In 1995, the Supreme Court again interpreted the Endangered Species Act broadly to protect endangered species. Section 7 of the act is the only provision that includes an explicit prohibition against destruction of the critical habitat or an endangered species, and its prohibition applies to actions of the federal government. However, Section 9 makes it illegal for any person to "take" an individual member of an endangered species. In 1975, the secretary of the interior defined the word "take" to include the destruction of the critical habitat of a species in some circumstances, thus extending the ban on destruction of habitat to private parties as well as government agencies. Nearly two decades after the snail darter case, a divided Supreme Court upheld the regulatory definition. Justice Scalia's dissent argued that the text clearly limited the prohibition against habitat destruction to federal actions, but the majority found the text ambiguous. It therefore deferred to the interpretation of the Department of the Interior, the agency whose views it had completely ignored in the snail darter litigation.

The snail darter case remains an important one in the environmental law of the United States. As noted in the introduction, a 2001 survey of environmental law professors rated *TVA v. Hill* one of the five most important judicial decisions in environmental law, and the rating seems a fair one. A contrary decision would have made the Endangered Species Act a far less potent statute. Moreover, the general impact of the statutory revisions that the decision induced has been positive.

The prohibitions that Section 7 places on federal actions remain among the most absolute prohibitions found in U.S. environmental law. A determination that a project will jeopardize the existence of an endangered species or destroy its critical habitat is a potential killer for the projects of federal agencies, and agencies go to great links to avoid such determinations. Like the TVA, other federal agencies frequently spend significant amounts to mitigate the harm to endangered species so the Fish and Wildlife Service will agree that the project can proceed.

Two aspects of the statutory requirement are important. First, the requirement is substantive, not procedural. Comparing Section 7 with the NEPA requirement to prepare an environmental impact statement is instructive. Although the NEPA requirement may delay a project, it will not stop any agency from completing a project with adverse environmental consequences. When an agency proposal will jeopardize an endangered species or destroy its critical habitat, the project cannot proceed unless the agency either develops an alternative that will not jeopardize the species or secures an exemption from the God Squad. Second, the agency cannot decide for itself what the consequences of its actions will be. The agency must consult with the Department of the Interior, and that agency must make a finding with respect to whether the proposed action will jeopardize the species or destroy its critical habitat.

If the Supreme Court had reversed the Sixth Circuit in the snail darter case, it would have substantially reduced the impact of the Endangered Species Act. The dissents in *TVA v. Hill* and the Marshall and Blackmun papers document that the Court considered three different rationales. If any of the approaches had prevailed, the protections of the Endangered Species Act would be much weaker.

Justice Powell's exemption for existing projects might have been the least objectionable, but it would surely have encouraged federal agencies to search for other exemptions that would make the seemingly clear language of the text less "unreasonable." For example, one would have needed only a modest expansion of Justice Powell's rationale to extend the exemption to projects initiated after the Endangered Species Act was enacted when the endangered species was discovered in the project area as the project was nearing completion.

The approach of Justice Rehnquist would have been even more troubling. His deference to the discretion of the district court would have encouraged federal agencies to ignore the pesky biologists in the Fish and Wildlife Service, at least when an agency thought that the local district judge might take a less absolutist view of the need to protect endangered species. In many cases, a balancing process would likely favor the project. The cost of losing most endangered species, especially newly discovered ones, is extremely difficult to quantify; by contrast, the immediate benefits of a massive federal appropriation are apparent, especially since the benefit-cost analysis prepared by the agency is largely immune from judicial review. At least some federal judges might have been tempted to accept the agency's denigration of the loss of an "insignificant" species so that the local area could receive the influx of federal funds.

Finally, allowing appropriation acts to amend substantive legislation by implication, as Chief Justice Burger suggested when the Court was considering summary reversal, would have been most unfortunate. That rationale would have encouraged legislators to hide substantive exemptions in the legislative history of large appropriation acts to shield them from normal legislative scrutiny. Although the requirement for an express repeal provision has not stopped Congress from using appropriation acts to change legislation, the process would be far simpler if implied amendments were allowed.

The exemption process added to the Endangered Species Act following the Supreme Court decision in the snail darter litigation has not significantly qualified the absolute prohibitions of Section 7. Only a few cases have been referred to the God Squad, and the committee's decisions have tended to reinforce the statutory goal of protecting endangered species. The committee denied an exemption in the snail darter case, and the contemporaneous exemption for the Grayrocks Dam essentially ratified an agreement reached by the parties to the dispute. Fifteen years later, the committee did allow the Forest Service to complete a limited timber harvest in the spotted owl case, but environmentalists were generally happier with that decision than the timber industry was.

The 1978 revisions have altered the focus of the Endangered Species Act. Although Section 7 still prohibits federal actions that jeopardize an endangered species or modify its critical habitat, the section no longer creates a zero-sum game of destructive action or no action. Instead, the consultation and exemption process now encourages a constructive focus on reasonable alternatives that can allow agencies to perform their missions without jeopardizing endangered species or destroying their critical habitats. Indeed, an agency that acted as the TVA did with Tellico Dam — accelerating its project when the endangered species was discovered — would no longer qualify for an exemption. To have an exemption considered by the Endangered Species Committee, an agency must demonstrate that it has avoided irretrievable and irreversible resource commitments during the consultation process.

Of course, one might ask why endangered species should receive strong legal protections. Advocates for endangered species have advanced a variety of answers. Endangered species may have medicinal and other economic values that will be lost if they are destroyed. As temporary residents of the planet, current citizens have a duty to protect the world for future generations. However, the reason that most resonates with the current version of the Endangered Species Act sees endangered species as a surrogate for fragile ecosystems. Once so much habitat has been destroyed that a species is endangered, prudence counsels stopping governmental destruction of the habitat so long as reasonable alternatives exist or the benefits of the proposed action do not "clearly outweigh" the benefits of preserving the species.

Finally, one must remember that the snail darter litigation may be only one chapter in broader stories of both the Little Tennessee River and the Endangered Species Act. Efforts to preserve the sections of the river not yet in reservoirs continue, as do efforts to lessen the protections of the Endangered Species Act.

In the West and in the Northeast, new challenges have arisen to some existing dams, and a few dams have even been removed. Given the strong economic interests in the homes and resort developments on the shore of Tellico Reservoir, the loss of this segment of the Little Tennessee River is probably permanent. Since the Tellico Dam was completed, however, organized efforts have made some progress in protecting upstream stretches that remain free-flowing. Those portions of the river also house several rare species of fish, at least one of which has been listed by the Fish and Wildlife Service as threatened.

Likewise, the final chapter of the Endangered Species Act remains to be written. Today, the statute remains an important limitation on development projects, but the effort to stop the Tellico Dam serves as a reminder that protecting environmental values requires winning politically as well as judicially.

Perhaps, then, the ultimate lesson of the snail darter litigation is to emphasize the importance as well as the limits of the judicial process. Because of the Supreme Court's decision, the Endangered Species Act has been and remains a valuable tool for securing injunctions to stop projects that jeopardize endangered species or their critical habitat. But judicial victories are not necessarily permanent. Congress can — and has — sidestepped those limits by adding riders to appropriation bills. In recent years, both private developers and governmental agencies have claimed that the substantive limits of the statute itself are overly restrictive. The Bush administration has responded to those complaints by proposing changes to make the statutory prohibitions less absolute and to exempt training activities of the Department of

Defense. As this chapter was being written, the House of Representatives passed a bill that would substantially weaken the protections of the Endangered Species Act. Whether these efforts will prove successful remains uncertain because environmental groups are strongly committed to the statute. What is clear, however, is that legislative as well as judicial victories will be necessary to provide continued protection for endangered species.

May 18, 1933	President Roosevelt signs into law the Tennessee Valley Authority Act of 1933 (TVA Act), the federal statute creating the TVA.
August 31, 1935	President Roosevelt signs into law an amendment of the TVA Act that authorizes the TVA to provide for the generation of electricity at its dams and to create a nine-foot navigation channel from Knoxville to the mouth of the Tennessee River.
1936	The TVA identifies the mouth of the Little Tennessee River as a potential dam site in the Tennessee River watershed.
February 17, 1936	The Supreme Court decides *Ashwander v. TVA*, the case upholding the authority of the TVA to distribute and sell electric power produced at the Wilson Dam.
January 3, 1938	The Supreme Court decides *Alabama Power Co. v. Ickes*, the case holding that power companies lacked standing to challenge the constitutionality of federal loans and grants to assist municipalities in constructing electricity-distribution systems.
January 30, 1939	The Supreme Court decides *Tennessee Electric Power Co. v. TVA*, the case holding that power companies lacked standing to restrain the TVA from generating and selling electric power from hydroelectric dams other than the Wilson Dam.
August 3, 1942	The TVA Board of Directors withdraws its application for a project rating on the Fort Loudon Extension Project, which included building a dam near the mouth of the Little Tennessee River, after the War Department refused preference ratings that would allow new generating units to be added to the Fort Loudon facility.
March 25, 1946	The Supreme Court decides *United States ex rel. TVA v. Welch*, the case that broadly construed the

	Authority's discretion as to whether particular land was needed for a hydroelectric project.
May 29, 1962	The Senate publishes the standards prepared by the President's Water Resources Council for evaluating water resources projects as Senate Document 97.
April 15, 1963	The TVA Board of Directors approves the Tellico Dam project.
October 19, 1966	President Johnson signs into law the 1967 Public Works Appropriation Act, which included the initial $3.2 million appropriation to begin work on the Tellico Dam.
November 8, 1966	The TVA Board of Directors adopts a resolution authorizing construction of the Tellico Dam.
March 7, 1967	The TVA begins construction on the concrete portion of the Tellico Dam.
February 28, 1969	The TVA completes construction of the concrete portion of the Tellico Dam.
January 1, 1970	President Nixon signs into law the National Environmental Policy Act (NEPA).
April 30, 1970	The Council on Environmental Quality (CEQ) issues interim NEPA guidelines.
April 23, 1971	The CEQ issues final NEPA guidelines.
June 18, 1971	The TVA files its draft environmental impact statement for the Tellico Dam with the CEQ.
August 1971	An economics class taught by Professor Keith Phillips at the University of Tennessee completes a report critical of the TVA's benefit-cost analysis for the Tellico Dam.
August 11, 1971	The Environmental Defense Fund and others file a suit based on NEPA in the U.S. District Court for the District of Columbia.
October 13, 1971	The U.S. District Court for the District of Columbia dismisses the NEPA suit for improper venue.
December 2, 1971	The plaintiffs refile the NEPA suit in the U.S. District Court for the Northern District of Alabama.

December 7, 1971	Governor Winnfield Dunn sends a letter opposing construction of the Tellico Dam to the TVA.
December 27, 1971	The U.S. District Court for the Northern District of Alabama transfers the NEPA suit to the U.S. District Court for the Eastern District of Tennessee.
January 3, 1972	Plaintiffs in the NEPA suit file a motion for preliminary injunction.
January 7 and 10, 1972	Judge Robert Taylor of the Eastern District of Tennessee holds a hearing on the motion for a preliminary injunction hearing in the NEPA suit.
January 11, 1972	Judge Taylor issues a preliminary injunction in the NEPA suit, *Environmental Defense Fund, Inc. v. TVA (EDF I);* the injunction halts most work on the Tellico Dam.
February 10, 1972	The TVA files its final environmental impact statement on the Tellico Dam with the CEQ.
June 19, 1972	The House Appropriations Committee report on the 1973 Public Works Appropriation Act recommends a $7.5 million appropriation for the Tellico project.
June 27, 1972	The Senate Appropriations Committee report on the 1973 Public Works Appropriation Act recommends that the appropriation for the Tellico project in fiscal year 1973 be raised to $11.25 million.
August 7, 1972	The conference committee report on the 1973 Public Works Appropriation Act recommends the Senate's $11.25 million appropriation for the Tellico project.
August 25, 1972	President Nixon signs into law the 1973 Public Works Appropriation Act, which included the $11.25 million figure that the conference committee recommended for the Tellico Dam.
December 13, 1972	The Sixth Circuit decision in *EDF I* affirms Judge Taylor's grant of a preliminary injunction.
June 27, 1973	The House Appropriations Committee report on the 1974 Public Works Appropriation Act

	recommends a $7.5 million appropriation for the Tellico Dam.
July 20, 1973	The Senate Appropriations Committee report on the 1974 Public Works Appropriation Act also recommends an appropriation of $7.5 million for the Tellico project in fiscal year 1974.
August 12, 1973	Dr. David Etnier discovers the snail darter, *Percina (Imostoma) tanasi*, in the Little Tennessee River.
August 16, 1973	President Nixon signs into law the 1974 Public Works Appropriation Act, which included the $7.5 million figure that the Senate and House Appropriations Committees recommended for the Tellico Dam.
September 17–20, 1973	Judge Taylor holds a hearing on the TVA motion to dissolve the injunction in the NEPA litigation.
October 25, 1973	Judge Taylor dissolves the preliminary injunction in *Environmental Defense Fund v. TVA (EDF II)* and dismisses the NEPA suit.
December 28, 1973	President Nixon signs into law the Endangered Species Act of 1973.
February 22, 1974	The Sixth Circuit decides *EDF II*, affirming Judge Taylor's dissolution of the preliminary injunction and dismissal of the NEPA suit.
June 27, 1974	The House Appropriations Committee report on the 1975 Public Works Appropriation Act recommends a $16.9 million appropriation for the Tellico Dam.
July 20, 1974	The Senate Appropriations Committee report on the 1975 Public Works Appropriation Act also recommends a $16.9 million appropriation for the Tellico Dam.
August 28, 1974	President Ford signs into law the 1975 Public Works Appropriation Act, which included the $16.9 million figure that the Senate and House Appropriations Committees recommended for the Tellico Dam.
January 20, 1975	Joseph Congleton, Zygmunt Plater, and Hiram Hill petition the Fish and Wildlife Service to list the snail darter as endangered.

March 7, 1975	The Fish and Wildlife Service sends a letter to the TVA advising the Authority of the Service's determination that the snail darter petition contained "substantial evidence" to warrant further investigation of the need for listing and of the possible consequences of listing the snail darter as endangered.
March 12, 1975	The Fish and Wildlife Service publishes in the *Federal Register* its finding that the snail darter petition contained "substantial evidence" to warrant further investigation of the need for listing the snail darter as endangered.
March 12, 1975	The TVA general manager sends a response to the March 7 letter rejecting the Fish and Wildlife Service interpretation of the Endangered Species Act.
June 17, 1975	The Fish and Wildlife Service publishes in the *Federal Register* a proposed rule listing the snail darter as endangered.
June 20, 1975	The House Appropriations Committee report on the 1976 Public Works Appropriation Act recommends a $23.742 million appropriation for the Tellico Dam and completion of the dam as soon as possible.
October 2, 1975	Zygmunt Plater, Donald Cohen, and Hank Hill send letters notifying the TVA and the Department of the Interior that the activities of the TVA with respect to the Tellico Dam violate the Endangered Species Act.
October 9, 1975	The Fish and Wildlife Service publishes in the *Federal Register* the final rule listing the snail darter as endangered.
December 4, 1975	The Senate Appropriations Committee report on the 1976 Public Works Appropriation Act also recommends a $23.742 million appropriation for the Tellico Dam.
December 15, 1975	The Fish and Wildlife Service publishes in the *Federal Register* a proposed rule designating mile .5 to mile 17 of the Little Tennessee River as critical habitat of the snail darter.

December 26, 1975	President Ford signs into law the 1976 Public Works Appropriation Act, which included the $23.742 million that the House and Senate Appropriations Committees recommended for the Tellico Dam.
February 28, 1976	Hiram Hill, Zygmunt Plater, Donald Cohen, the Audubon Council of Tennessee, and the Association of Southeastern Biologists file an Endangered Species Act citizen suit in the District Court for the Eastern District of Tennessee; they seek an injunction forbidding completion of the Tellico Dam.
April 1, 1976	The Fish and Wildlife Service publishes in the *Federal Register* the final rule designating mile .5 to mile 17 of the Little Tennessee River as critical habitat of the snail darter.
April 22, 1976	The Fish and Wildlife Service circulates guidelines to assist federal agencies in complying with § 7 of the Endangered Species Act.
April 29–30, 1976	Judge Taylor presides in the trial of the Endangered Species Act suit.
May 25, 1976	Judge Taylor issues his decision in the Endangered Species Act suit, *Hill v. TVA;* he refuses to enjoin completion of the Tellico Dam.
June 8, 1976	The House Appropriations Committee report on the 1977 Public Works Appropriation Act recommends a $9.7 million appropriation for the Tellico Dam.
June 17, 1976	The Senate Appropriations Committee report on the 1977 Public Works Appropriation Act also recommends a $9.7 million appropriation for the Tellico Dam, and the report directs that the dam "be completed as promptly as possible in the public interest."
July 12, 1976	President Ford signs into law the 1977 Public Works Appropriation Act, which included the $9.7 million that the House and Senate Appropriations Committees recommended for the Tellico Dam.

July 26, 1976	The Sixth Circuit issues an injunction forbidding completion of the Tellico Dam pending a decision on the appeal in *Hill v. TVA*.
August 2, 1976	The Sixth Circuit modifies the July 26 injunction, but the injunction still prohibits closure of the dam until the appeal is decided.
October 14, 1976	The Sixth Circuit hears oral argument in *Hill v. TVA*.
January 31, 1977	The Sixth Circuit decides *Hill v. TVA*, ordering an injunction that forbids completion of the Tellico Dam.
February 28, 1977	The TVA petitions the Fish and Wildlife Service to remove the snail darter from the endangered species list and to eliminate the designation of the Little Tennessee River as the critical habitat of the snail darter.
May 31, 1977	The TVA files a petition for a writ of certiorari from the U.S. Supreme Court in the Endangered Species Act suit, which is now known as *TVA v. Hill*.
June 2, 1977	The House Appropriations Committee report on the 1978 Public Works Appropriation Act declares the committee's view that the Endangered Species Act was not intended to halt the Tellico Dam project.
June 25, 1977	The Senate Appropriations Committee report of the 1978 Public Works Appropriation Act indicates the committee's disagreement with the Sixth Circuit's interpretation of the Endangered Species Act.
October 14, 1977	The General Accounting Office releases its report reviewing the benefit-cost analysis that the TVA prepared for the Tellico Dam.
November 14, 1977	The U.S. Supreme Court grants the petition for a writ of certiorari in *TVA v. Hill*.
December 5, 1977	The Fish and Wildlife Service denies the TVA petition to remove the snail darter from the endangered species list and to eliminate the

	designation of the Little Tennessee River as the critical habitat of the snail darter.
April 13–14, 1978	The Senate Committee on Environment and Public Works conducts hearings on § 7 of the Endangered Species Act.
April 18, 1978	The U.S. Supreme Court hears oral arguments in *Hill v. TVA*.
May 15, 1978	The Senate Committee on Environment and Public Works issues a report recommending addition of an exemption procedure for § 7 of the Endangered Species Act.
June 18, 1978	The Supreme Court decides *TVA v. Hill*, affirming the Sixth Circuit judgment that ordered an injunction against completion of the Tellico Dam.
August 10, 1978	A joint study group of the TVA and the Department of the Interior publishes a preliminary report on alternatives to completion of the Tellico Dam.
November 10, 1978	President Carter signs into law the Endangered Species Act Amendments of 1978, which added an exemption procedure to § 7.
December 1978	The TVA publishes the final report analyzing alternatives to completion of the Tellico Dam.
January 19, 1979	The staff of the Endangered Species Committee submits its report analyzing whether the Tellico Dam satisfied the statutory requirements for an exemption under the Endangered Species Act Amendments of 1978.
January 23, 1979	The Endangered Species Committee unanimously refuses to grant the Tellico Dam an exemption from § 7 of the Endangered Species Act.
June 18, 1979	Representative John Duncan inserts into the Energy and Water Development Appropriation Act of 1980 a rider allowing the Tellico Dam to be completed notwithstanding the Endangered Species Act "or any other law."

September 25, 1979   President Jimmy Carter signs into law the
Energy and Water Development Appropriation
Act of 1980 (with the rider allowing completion
of the Tellico Dam).

November 29, 1979   The TVA closes the Tellico Dam and begins to
fill the Tellico Reservoir.

BIBLIOGRAPHIC ESSAY

Note from the Series Editors: The following bibliographical essay contains the major primary and secondary sources the author consulted for this volume. We have asked all authors in the series to omit formal citations in order to make our volumes more readable, inexpensive, and appealing for students and general readers. In adopting this format, Landmark Law Cases and American Society follows the precedent of a number of highly regarded and widely consulted series.

The Supreme Court opinion, *TVA v. Hill*, 437 U.S. 153 (1978), is the obvious starting place for any evaluation of the snail darter case. For recent analyses of the decision, see Holly Doremus, "The Story of *TVA v. Hill*: A Narrow Escape for a Broad New Law," in Richard J. Lazarus and Oliver A. Houck, eds., *Environmental Stories* (New York: Foundation Press, 2005), 109; and Oliver A. Houck, "Unfinished Stories," *University of Colorado Law Review* 73 (2002): 921–942. Zygmunt Plater, the driving force behind the snail darter litigation, has written several articles about the Endangered Species Act and the snail darter case. See Zygmunt Plater, "Endangered Species Act Lessons over 30 Years, and the Legacy of the Snail Darter, a Small Fish in a Pork Barrel," *Environmental Law* 34 (2004): 289–308; "The Embattled Social Utilities of the Endangered Species Act — A Noah Presumption and Caution against Putting Gasmasks on the Canaries in the Coal Mine," *Environmental Law* 27 (1997): 845–876; "In the Wake of the Snail Darter: An Environmental Law Paradigm and Its Consequences," *University of Michigan Journal of Law Reform* 19 (1986): 805–862; "Reflected in a River: Agency Accountability and the TVA Tellico Dam Case," *Tennessee Law Review* 49 (1982): 747–787; "Statutory Violations and Equitable Discretion," *California Law Review* 70 (1982): 524–594; and "The Snail Darter: It's More Than a Little Fish," *Frontiers* 41 (Summer 1977): 15–19.

Books on the TVA abound. The discussion in chapter 1 draws heavily on William Bruce Wheeler and Michael J. McDonald, *TVA and the Tellico Dam, 1936–1979: A Bureaucratic Crisis in Post-industrial America* (Knoxville: University of Tennessee Press, 1986), an excellent study of the Tellico project. McDonald was also the coauthor of a separate study of the Norris Dam. See Michael J. McDonald and John Muldowny, *TVA and the Dispossessed: The Resettlement of Population in the Norris Dam Area* (Knoxville: University of Tennessee Press, 1982). Also helpful were collections of essays on the TVA prepared shortly after the Tellico Dam was completed: Edwin C. Hargrove and Paul Conklin, eds., *TVA: Fifty Years of Grass Roots Bureaucracy* (Urbana: University of Illinois Press, 1983), and "Symposium on the TVA," *Tennessee Law Review* 49 (1982): 679–918. Other general monographs on the TVA include North Callahan, *TVA: Bridge over Troubled Waters* (South Brunswick, N.J.: A. C. Barnes, 1980); Walter L. Creese, *TVA's Public Planning: The Vision, the Reality* (Knoxville: University of Tennessee Press, 1990); and Preston J. Hubbard, *Origins of the TVA: The Muscle Shoals Controversy, 1920–1932* (Nashville: Vanderbilt University Press, 1961). The TVA's official history of its early years is Roscoe C. Martin, ed., *TVA: The First Twenty Years: A Staff Report* (University: University of Alabama Press; Knoxville: University of Tennessee Press, 1956).

The references in chapter 1 to legal and other commentary on the Supreme Court decision come from a variety of sources. James Salzman, then a member of the law faculty at American University, conducted the Internet survey of law professors who subscribed to the environmental law professors listserv. Kiron K. Skinner, Annelise Anderson, and Martin Anderson, eds., *Reagan in His Own Hand: The Writings of Ronald Reagan That Reveal His Revolutionary Vision for America* (New York: Free Press, 2001), 30, contains a printed version of Ronald Reagan's radio address. Ronald Dworkin set forth his analysis of the snail darter case in *Law's Empire* (Cambridge, Mass.: Belknap Press, 1986). The casebook reference is to Edgar Bodenheimer, John B. Oakley, and Joan C. Love, *An Introduction to the Anglo-American Legal System: Readings and Cases*, 4th ed. (St. Paul, Minn.: West, 2004), 180–181.

The TVA Act is Public Law No. 17, 73d Cong., 1st sess., *U.S. Statutes at Large* 48 (1933): 58. The 1935 Amendment is Public Law No. 74-412, *U.S. Statutes at Large* 49 (1935): 1075. The modern codification of the act is *U.S. Code*, title 16, §§ 831–831ee (2000).

The struggle over the constitutionality of the TVA power program merits no more than a brief note in contemporary constitutional law casebooks, usually in conjunction with the development of the law of standing. The cases, however, remain an important part of the story of the New Deal development of constitutional law pertaining to federal power. The Supreme Court decisions discussed in the text are *Ashwander v. TVA*, 297 U.S. 288 (1936); *Alabama Power Co. v. Ickes*, 302 U.S. 464 (1938); *Tennessee Electric Power Co. v. TVA*, 306 U.S. 118 U.S. (1939); *United States v. Appalachian Electric Power Co.*, 311 U.S. 777 (1940); *Oklahoma v. Atkinson Co.*, 313 U.S. 508 (1941); and *United States ex rel. TVA v. Welch*, 327 U.S. 546 (1946). TVA attorneys provided a good overview of the decisions in Joseph C. Swidler, "Legal Foundations," in *TVA: The First Twenty Years*, 16–34, and Joseph C. Swidler and Robert H. Marquis, "TVA in Court: A Study of TVA's Constitutional Litigation," *Iowa Law Review* 32 (1947): 296–326. For a more recent analysis of the Supreme Court decisions, see George D. Haimbaugh Jr., "The TVA Cases: A Quarter Century Later," *Indiana Law Journal* 41 (1966): 197–227. Richard Wirtz provides a more comprehensive explanation of the legal authority of the TVA in "The Legal Framework of the Tennessee Valley Authority," *Tennessee Law Review* 43 (1976): 573–612.

Chapter 2 summarizes several cases that are significant in the development of judicial review of environmental issues. *Scenic Hudson Preservation Council v. Federal Power Commission*, 354 F.2d 608 (2d Cir. 1965), cert. denied, 384 U.S. 941 (1966), is the case that set aside the administrative decision to allow a generating station on Storm King Mountain. The Supreme Court cases halting the dam on the Snake River and the extension of Interstate 40 in Memphis are *Udall v. Federal Power Commission*, 387 U.S. 428 (1967), and *Citizens to Preserve Overton Park, Inc. v. Volpe*, 401 U.S. 402 (1971). Oliver Houck analyzes the *Scenic Hudson* and *Overton Park* cases in "Unfinished Stories," *University of Colorado Law Review* 73 (2002): 869–880 and 893–921; and Michael Blumm discusses the significance of the *Udall* case in "Saving Idaho's Salmon: A History of Failure and a Dubious Future," *Idaho Law Review* 28 (1992): 675–678.

The Supreme Court's standing cases that are described in chapter 2 are *Association of Data Processing Service Organizations, Inc. v. Camp*, 397 U.S. 150 (1970); *Barlow v. Collins*, 397 U.S. 159 (1970); and *Sierra Club v. Morton*, 405 U.S. 727 (1972). For a contemporary critique of the *Sierra Club* decision, see Joseph Sax, "Standing to Sue: A Critical Review of the Mineral King Decision," *Natural Resources Journal* 13 (1973): 76–88.

The original version of the Administrative Procedure Act is Public Law No. 79-404, *U.S. Statutes at Large* 60 (1946): 237; its modern codification with amendments is *U.S. Code*, title 5, §§ 551 et seq. (2000).

Chapter 2 also explains the inability to obtain judicial review of benefit-cost analyses that were mandated for public works projects by statutes and administrative directives. The Flood Control Act of 1936 is Public Law No. 74-738, *U.S. Statutes at Large* 49 (1936): 1570; the Senate printed the administrative directive establishing the methodology for benefit-cost analysis as Senate Document 97, 87th Cong., 2d sess. (1962). The text also discusses two appellate decisions construing the Flood Control Act of 1936: *United States v. West Virginia Power Co.*, 122 F.2d 733 (4th Cir.), cert. denied, 314 U.S. 683 (1941), and *Yalobusha County v. Crawford*, 165 F.2d 867 (5th Cir. 1947). For a general explanation of how benefit-cost analyses have been used for public works projects, see Deborah Lee Williams, "Benefit-Cost Analysis in Natural Resources Decisionmaking: An Economic and Legal Overview," *Natural Resources Lawyer* 11 (1979): 761–794.

The Supreme Court decision broadly defining what constitutes a public use in a condemnation action is *Berman v. Parker*, 348 U.S. 26 (1954). On several occasions, the Court has reaffirmed that broad definition. See *Hawaii Housing Authority v. Midkiff*, 467 U.S. 229 (1984); *National Passenger Railroad Corp. v. Boston & Maine Corp.*, 503 U.S. 407 (1992); and *Kelo v. City of New London*, 545 U.S. 469 (2005).

The statute that repealed the jury-trial exemption for TVA condemnations is Public Law No. 90-536, *U.S. Statutes at Large* 82 (1968): 885. The only Tellico case that produced reported opinions on condemnation issues is *United States v. Two Tracts of Land*, 387 F. Supp. 319 (E.D. Tenn. 1974), aff'd, 32 F.2d 1083 (6th Cir. 1976).

The original version of the National Environmental Policy Act (NEPA) is Public Law No. 91-190, *U.S. Statutes at Large* 83 (1970): 852; its modern codification with amendments is *U.S. Code* 42 §§ 4321 et seq. (2000). The citation for the interim NEPA Council on Environmental Quality Guidelines is *Federal Register* 35 (1970): 7390; for the final guidelines, it is *Federal Register* 36 (1971): 7224. Judge Wright's opinion in the *Calvert Cliffs'* case is reported at *Calvert Cliffs' Coordinating Committee, Inc. v. Atomic Energy Commission*, 449 F.2d 1109 (D.C. Cir. 1971). The district court decision that halted the Cross-Florida Barge Canal is *Environmental Defense Fund, Inc. v. Corps of Engineers*, 324 F. Supp. 878 (D.C.D.C. 1971). The reported decisions in the *Gilham Dam* case discussed in the text are *Environmental Defense Fund v. Corps of Engineers*, 325 F. Supp. 728 (E.D. Ark. 1971), and *Environmental Defense Fund v. Corps of Engineers*, 342 F. Supp. 1211 (E.D. Ark. 1972), aff'd, 470 F.2d 289 (8th Cir. 1972).

The amount of scholarly writing on NEPA is enormous. For recent analyses of the *Calvert Cliffs'* decision, see Oliver Houck, "Unfinished Stories," *University of Colorado Law Review* 73 (2002): 880–893; and A. Dan Tarlock, "The Story of *Calvert Cliffs'*: A Court Construes the National Environmental Policy Act to Create a Powerful Cause of Action," in Richard J. Lazarus and Oliver A. Houck, eds., *Environmental Stories* (New York: Foundation Press, 2005), 77. For the author's analysis of the NEPA cases from the perspective of the early 1980s, see Kenneth M. Murchison, "Does NEPA Matter? — An Analysis of the Historical Development and Contemporary Significance of the National Environmental Policy Act," *University of Richmond Law Review* 18 (1984): 557–614. One of the first articles to suggest that confining NEPA to procedural protections would severely limit its effectiveness was Joseph L. Sax, "The (Unhappy) Truth about NEPA," *Oklahoma Law Review* 26 (1973): 239–248.

The official source of the Endangered Species Act of 1973 is Public Law No. 93-205, *U.S. Statutes at Large* 87 (1973): 884. For the current version (with amendments), see *U.S. Code* 16, §§ 1531 et seq. (2000). The text discusses two early decisions construing the Endangered Species Act: *National Wildlife Federation v. Coleman*, 400 F. Supp. 705 (S.D. Miss. 1975), rev'd, 529 F.2d 359 (5th Cir. 1976), and *Sierra Club v. Froehlke*, 392 F. Supp. 130 (E.D. Mo. 1975), aff'd, 534 F.2d 1289 (8th Cir. 1976). Shannon Peterson, *Acting for Endangered Species: The Statutory Ark* (Lawrence: University Press of Kansas, 2002), offers a useful summary of the development of federal law protecting endangered species. For a broader overview of U.S. laws regarding wildlife, see Michael J. Bean and Melanie J. Rowland, *The Evolution of National Wildlife Law*, 3d ed. (Westport, Conn.: Praeger, 1997).

The NEPA challenge to the Tellico Dam project produced four reported decisions, two by Judge Taylor of the U.S. District Court for the Eastern District of Tennessee and two by the U.S. Court of Appeals for the Sixth Circuit. The citation for the first round of litigation is *Environmental Defense Fund v. TVA*, 339 F. Supp. 807 (E.D. Tenn.), aff'd, 468 F.2d 1164 (6th Cir. 1972). For the second round of litigation, the citation is *Environmental Defense Fund v. TVA*, 371 F. Supp. 1004 (E.D. Tenn. 1973), aff'd, 492 F.2d 466 (6th Cir. 1974). The Eastern District of Tennessee has transferred the court record for these cases to the National Archives in Morrow, Georgia, where it is cataloged as accession number 02-180-094, boxes 9 and 10. The court record contains the various unpublished documents described in the text, including the draft and final environmental impact statement, the Phillips Report, and the exchange of letters between Governor Dunn and TVA chairman Wagner. The 1973 congressional documents discussed in chapter 3 are U.S. Congress, House Committee on Appropriations, 1972, 92d Cong., 2d sess., H. Rep. 1151; Senate Committee on Appropriations, 1972, 92d Cong., 2d sess., S. Rep. 923; Conference Committee, 1972, 92d Cong., 2d sess., Conf. Rep. 1310; Senate Committee on Appropriations, 1972, 92d Cong., 2d sess., *Hearings on Public Works for Water, Pollution Control, and Power Development and Atomic Energy Commission Appropriation for Fiscal Year 1973*; House Committee on Appropriations, 1973, 93d Cong., 1st sess., H. Rep. 327; Senate Committee on Appropriations, 1973, 93d Cong., 1st sess., S. Rep. 338; and House Committee on Appropriations, 1973, 93d Cong., 1st. sess., *Hearings on Public Works for Water, Pollution Control, and Power Development and Atomic Energy Commission Appropriation for Fiscal Year 1974*.

The description in chapter 4 of the events preceding the filing of the Endangered Species Act litigation comes principally from interviews with David Etnier, Hank Hill, and Zygmunt Plater. Dr. Etnier's article describing the snail darter was published as "*Percina (Imostoma) Tanasi*, A New Percid Fish from the Little Tennessee River, Tennessee," *Proceedings of the Biological Society of Washington* 88 (1976): 469–488. A picture and short description of the snail darter appears in Daniel C. Eager and Robert H. Hatcher, eds., *Tennessee's Rare Wildlife*, vol. 1, *The Vertebrates* (Nashville: Tennessee Wildlife Resources Agency, 1980), B-1.

The citation for the reported decisions of the lower courts in the snail darter litigation is *Hill v. TVA*, 419 F. Supp. 753 (E.D. Tenn. 1976), rev'd, 549 F.2d 1064 (6th Cir. 1977). The court record for this case is also available in the National Archives center at Morrow, Georgia; it is cataloged as accession number 021-00-003, boxes 6 and 7. The court record contains the various unpublished documents discussed in the text.

Most of the Fish and Wildlife Service materials discussed in chapter 4 are available in printed sources. The various Fish and Wildlife Service documents pertaining to the snail darter appear in the *Federal Register* 40 (1975): 11,618 (preliminary notice regarding possible listing of snail darter), 25,597 (proposed listing decision), 47,505 (final listing decision), 58,308 (proposed designation of critical habitat), and 41 (1976): 13,926 (final designation of critical habitat). Unfortunately, the Fish and Wildlife Service was unable — despite a diligent search at local, regional, and national offices — to locate the file containing the original comments on the listing and critical-habitat decisions. As a result, the descriptions in the text come from the summaries of the comments found in the preambles to the final rules.

Two of the Fish and Wildlife documents do not appear in print. I obtained a copy of the letter rejecting the TVA petition to delist the snail darter from the files of the Cookesville, Tennessee, office of the Fish and Wildlife Service. In addition, the Fish and Wildlife Service summary of the characteristics of the snail darter and its current status appear on a Fish and Wildlife Web site, http://www.fws.gov/endangered/i/e/sae15.html (last viewed on Jan. 10, 2006).

Chapters 4 and 5 discuss legislative materials for 1974 to 1977. For the 1975 fiscal year, the TVA testimony in the text comes from U.S. Congress, House Committee on Appropriations, 1974, 93d Cong., 2d sess., *Hearings on Public Works for Water and Power Development and Atomic Energy Commission Appropriation Bill, 1975 (Part 6)*; the committee reports are U.S. Congress, House Committee on Appropriations, 1974, 93d Cong., 2d sess., H. Rep. 1077, and Senate Committee on Appropriations, 1974, 93d Cong., 2d sess., S. Rep. 1032. For the testimony on the appropriation for fiscal year 1976, see U.S. Congress, House Committee on Appropriations, 1975, 94th Cong., 1st sess., *Hearings on Public Works for Water and Power Development and Atomic Energy Commission Appropriation Bill, 1976 (Part 7)*; the committee reports are U.S. Congress, House Committee on Appropriations, 1975, 94th Cong., 1st sess., H. Rep. 319, and Senate Committee on Appropriations, 1975, 94th Cong., 1st sess., S. Rep. 505. The fiscal year 1977 hearings are U.S. Congress, House Committee on Appropriations, 1976, 94th Cong., 2d sess., *Hearings on Public Works for Water and Power Development and Atomic Energy Commission Appropriation Bill, 1976 (Part 5)*, and Senate Committee on Appropriations, 1976, 94th Cong., 2d sess., *Hearings on Public Works for Water and Power Development and Atomic Energy Commission Appropriation Bill, 1976 (Part 4)*. The committee reports are U.S. Congress, House Committee on Appropriations, 1976, 94th Cong., 2d sess., H. Rep. 1223, and Senate Committee on Appropriations, 1976, 94th Cong., 2d sess., S. Rep. 960. For fiscal year 1978, the hearings are U.S. Congress, House Committee on Appropriations, 1977, 95th Cong., 1st sess., *Hearings on Public Works for Water and Power Develop-*

ment and Atomic Energy Commission Appropriation Bill, 1977 (Part 4). The committee reports are U.S. Congress, House Committee on Appropriations, 1976, 95th Cong., 1st sess., H. Rep. 379, and Senate Committee on Appropriations, 1976, 95th Cong., 1st sess., S. Rep. 301.

The Supreme Court rules pertaining to the considerations governing review on writ of certiorari and summary dispositions are Rule 10 and Rule 16. The book that reports the "convention" of requiring six votes for a summary disposition is H. W. Perry Jr., *Deciding to Decide: Agenda Setting in the United States Supreme Court* (Cambridge, Mass.: Harvard University Press, 1991), 100.

Chapter 5 also analyzes the briefs filed in the Supreme Court, the oral arguments, and the Court's opinion. The Supreme Court briefs are available on microfiche in the government documents collection of the law library at Louisiana State University. The basis for the text's summary of the oral argument before the Supreme Court is a transcript supplied by Zygmunt Plater. *Hecht Co. v. Bowles,* 321 U.S. 321 (1944) is the 1944 case on the scope of a district court's discretion to grant an injunction; Chief Justice Burger and Justice Rehnquist disagreed as to its applicability to the Endangered Species Act.

The Library of Congress houses the Marshall, Blackmun, and Brennan papers. In the Marshall papers, the *TVA v. Hill* records are filed in boxes 195–199 and 211; in the Blackmun papers, they are located in boxes 255, 256, and 268. Robert Percival has made the most complete analyses of the significance of the Marshall and Blackmun sets of papers for environmental law cases; see Robert Percival, "Environmental Law in the Supreme Court: Highlights from the Marshall Papers," *Environmental Law Reporter* 23 (1993): 10,606–10,626; and "Environmental Law in the Supreme Court: Highlights from the Blackmun Papers," *Environmental Law Reporter* 35 (2005): 10,637–10,665. Percival's 1993 article was the first to call attention to the switch in voting positions after oral argument in the snail darter case. The Brennan papers still require special permission to access materials from the 1977 Term; the Library of Congress granted access to selected folders pertaining to *TVA v. Hill.* The material in the text comes from Part I, boxes 428, 429, 431, and 453.

Griffin Bell, the attorney general who argued the snail darter case in the Supreme Court, discusses his role in the case in Griffin B. Bell and Ronald J. Ostrow, *Taking Care of Law* (New York: William Morrow, 1982), 42–44. See also Brian C. Kalt, "Wade H. McCree, Jr., and the Office of the Solicitor General, 1977–1981," *Detroit College of Law Michigan State Law Review* (1998): 720–724; *Brigham Young University Law Review* (2003): 27–28 (remarks of Daniel Friedman at the Rex E. Lee Conference on the Office of the Solicitor General of the United States). Both Bell and Kalt claim that the Justice Department of the Ford administration made the initial decision to support the TVA's application for a writ of certiorari. However, the TVA's own lawyers had represented the Authority in the lower courts, and the Sixth Circuit did not issue its decision until after Jimmy Carter was inaugurated as president. Of course, the Office of the Solicitor General made the decision to support the position of the TVA at the very beginning of the Carter administration. Daniel Friedman, the acting solicitor general, said that the Interior Department in the new administration had not yet adopted a position regarding the case when he had to make a decision to support the TVA application for a writ of certiorari.

The Congressional Research Service has prepared a research aid that is invaluable in tracing the congressional action that followed the Supreme Court decision. *The Legislative History of the Endangered Species Act* (Washington, D.C.: U.S. Government Printing Office, 1982) includes the text of bills introduced and the laws passed by Congress, as well as the committee reports, floor debates, and lists of those who appeared at committee hearings. The citation for the 1978 act is Public Law No. 95-632, *U.S. Statutes at Large* 92 (1978): 3751. For contemporaneous evaluations of the 1978 amendments, see "The 1978 Amendments to the Endangered Species Act: Evaluating the New Exemption Process under § 7," *Environmental Law Reporter* 9 (1979): 10,031; Stromberg, "The Endangered Species Act Amendments of 1978: A Step Backwards," *Boston College Environmental Affairs Law Review* 7 (1978): 33; and Nancy M. Ganong, "Endangered Species Act Amendments of 1978: A Congressional Response to *TVA v. Hill*," *Columbia Journal of Environmental Law* 5 (1979): 283.

The other government documents discussed in the text came from a variety of sources. Charlene Cain, the government documents librarian at the Louisiana State University Law Center, obtained the Government Accounting Office Report, *The Tennessee Valley Authority's Tellico Dam Project — Costs, Alternatives, and Benefits* (Oct. 14, 1977); the interim joint report of the TVA and the Department of the Interior on possible alternatives to the dam (Aug. 10, 1978); the final TVA report, *Alternatives for Completing the Tellico Project* (Oct. 1978); and the staff report of the Endangered Species Committee, *Tellico Dam and Reservoir* (Jan. 19, 1979), from government document collections at various libraries. In addition, the Department of the Interior supplied a compact disc containing other documents of the Endangered Species Committee; and Zygmunt Plater provided a transcript of the meeting of the Endangered Species Committee. President Carter's statement on signing the 1978 Amendments appears in *Public Papers of the Presidents of the United States: Jimmy Carter, 1978* (Washington, D.C.: U.S. Government Printing Office, 1979), 2002. The statement on signing the 1980 appropriation act is available at *Public Papers of the Presidents of the United States: Jimmy Carter, 1979* (Washington, D.C.: U.S. Government Printing Office, 1980), 1566. Professor Plater offered a contemporaneous critique of the passage of the Duncan amendment in the *Los Angeles Times* for Sept. 2, 1979; it was entitled "Those Who Care about Laws or Sausages Shouldn't Watch Them Being Made."

News stories in the *New York Times*, the *Washington Post*, and the *Knoxville News-Sentinel* provided additional background on the political maneuvering and the public hearing that was held prior to the Endangered Species Committee meeting. Specific issues used directly in the text are *New York Times*, June 17, 1978, p. 1, col. 2; *Washington Post*, June 24, 1978, p. A2, col. 3; June 24, 1979, p. A12, col. 5; Sept. 26, 1979, p. A2, col. 1; and Nov. 14, 1979, p. A6, col. 1; and *Knoxville News-Sentinel*, Jan. 7, 1979, p. 1, col. 3; Jan. 8, 1979, p. 1, col. 3; and Jan. 9, 1979, p. 1, col. 2. On November 30, 1979, the *New York Times* included a one-paragraph report of the closing of the dam.

The final, unsuccessful challenge to the Tellico Dam filed by the Eastern Band of the Cherokee Indians produced two reported opinions. The citation for these opinions is *Sequoyah v. TVA*, 480 F. Supp. 608 (E.D. Tenn. 1979), aff'd, 620 F.2d 1159 (6th Cir. 1980).

Sources cited in the preceding paragraphs provided the basis for most of the analysis in chapter 7, but a few additional sources deserve to be mentioned. The observations regarding the Tellico Reservoir landscape come from a personal visit to the area in the summer of 2004. The TVA Web site for the Tellico Reservoir is http://tva.com/environment/ecohealth/tellico.htm (last viewed Dec. 13, 2005). The citation for the Fish and Wildlife Service decision reclassifying the snail darter as threatened rather than endangered is *Federal Register* 49 (1984): 27,510. Jason M. Patlis, "The Endangered Species Act: Thirty Years of Politics, Money, and Science — Riders on the Storm, or Navigating the Cross Winds of Appropriations and Administration of the Endangered Species Act: A Play in Five Acts," *Tulane Environmental Law Journal* 16 (2003): 257–329, discusses the continued use of appropriation acts to effect changes in the Endangered Species Act. For criticism of the TVA for its allegedly reduced protection of natural resources, see Joe W. McCaleb, "Stewardship of Public Lands and Cultural Resources in the Tennessee Valley: A Critique of the Tennessee Valley Authority's New Deal," *Res Communes: Vermont Journal of Environmental Law* 1 (1998–1999) (online publication). William U. Chandler is the economist who offered his challenge to the traditional analysis of the economic impact of the TVA in *The Myth of the TVA: Conservation and Development in the Tennessee Valley, 1933–1983* (Cambridge, Mass.: Ballinger, 1984).

For an analysis of the impact that the Tellico controversy had on the TVA, see Michael Fitzgerald and Stephen Rechichar, *The Consequences of Administrative Decision: TVA's Economic Development Mission and Intragovernmental Relations* (Knoxville: University of Tennessee Knoxville, Bureau of Public Administration, 1983); and Erwin C. Hargrove, *Prisoners of Myth: The Leadership of the Tennessee Valley Authority* (Princeton, N.J.: Princeton University

Press, 1994). Jack Neely, "Tellico Dam Revisited," Metro Pulse Online http://www.metropulse.com/dir_zine/dir_2004/1450/t_cover.html (last viewed Sept. 26, 2005), provides a recent journalistic assessment of the Tellico project. The snail darter case was one of several efforts during the 1970s to try to preserve natural waterways. A study of the much more expensive program to construct the Tennessee-Tombigbee Waterway is Jeffrey K. Stine, *Mixing the Waters: Environment, Politics, and the Building of the Tennessee-Tombigbee Waterway* (Akron, Ohio: University of Akron Press, 1993). Brief descriptions of the TVA decision to abandon the Columbia Dam are available at http://www.state.tn.us/environment/tn_consv/duckriver, htm (last viewed Dec. 13, 2005), and http://www.oakridger.com/stories/071999/stt_0719990038.html (last viewed March 24, 2004). The contemporary efforts to protect the undammed sections of the Little Tennessee River are documented at http://www.ltlt.org/needmore.html.

The Supreme Court decisions mentioned in chapter 7 of the text are *Weinberger v. Romero-Barcello*, 456 U.S. 305 (1982) (denial of injunction for Clean Water Act violation); *Lyng v. Northwest Indian Cemetery Protective Association*, 485 U.S. 439 (1988) (rejection of freedom of religion claim of Native Americans); and *Babbitt v. Sweet Home Chapter of Communities for a Great Oregon*, 515 U.S. 687 (1995) (acceptance of Fish and Wildlife Service definition of the word "harm" in the Endangered Species Act). One other Endangered Species Act case, *Bennett v. Spears*, 520 U.S. 154 (1997), has also reached the Supreme Court: in *Bennett*, the Court allowed two irrigation districts to challenge a biological opinion of the Fish and Wildlife Service.

The Stanford Environmental Law Society has published a summary of current law relating to the Endangered Species Act. See *The Endangered Species Act* (Stanford, Calif.: Stanford University Press, 2001). For recent proposals to improve the Endangered Species Act by one who is sympathetic to its provisions, see J. B. Ruhl, "Who Needs Congress? An Agenda for Administrative Reform of the Endangered Species Act," *New York University Environmental Law Journal* 6 (1998): 367–410; "Past, Present, and Future Trends of the Endangered Species Act," *Public Land and Resources Law Review* 25 (2004): 15–38; "Prescribing the Right Dose of Peer Review for the Endangered Species Act," *Nebraska Law Review* 83 (2004): 398–431; and "Taking Adaptive Management Seriously: A Case Study of the Endangered Species Act," *University of Kansas Law Review* 52 (2004): 1249–1284.

Administrative Procedure Act,
33–34
Agricultural Adjustment Act, 26
Alabama Power Company, 8, 24–25
Alabama Power Co. v. Ickes, 27
ALCOA. *See* Aluminum Company
of America
Alexander, Clifford, 163
Alexander, Lamar, 164
Allender, Allen, 21
Alliman, Peter, 167, 181–82
Aluminum Company of America
(ALCOA), 14, 19
A Man for All Seasons (Boalt), 134
American Rivers Conservation
Council, 146
Amundson, Clifford, 161
Andrus, Cecil, 157, 164, 166, 179
appropriations for the Tellico Dam
project
during the 1960s, 21
environmental impact statements
and, 70–71
for fiscal year 1973, 65–66
for fiscal year 1974, 71–72
for fiscal year 1976, 83–86, 90
for fiscal year 1977, 101–102
for fiscal year 1978, 108–11
as an implied exception to the
Endangered Species Act, 1,
131–33
reliance on in district court
decision, 99–100, 105
archaeological sites. *See* historical
and archaeological sites
Army Corps of Engineers, U.S.
Gilham Dam, litigation and
completion of, 42–44 (*see also*
Gilham Dam)

Meramec Park Lake Dam,
litigation regarding, 49
navigability of the Tennessee
River, report on, 26
recreational use as benefit
justifying projects of, 13, 17
review of the TVA's benefit-cost
analysis by, 21
Wilson Dam, completion of, 8
Ashwander v. TVA, 24–27, 33
Association for the Preservation of
the Little Tennessee River, 19,
50
Association of Southeastern
Biologists, 91
Audubon Council of Tennessee,
91

Baker, Howard, 145, 148, 158, 161,
165, 180
Baker, Newton D., 8, 24
bats, Indiana, 48–49
Bayh, Birch, 166
Beard, Robin, 148–50
Beck, James M., 24
Bell, Griffin, 119, 121–23, 183
benefit-cost analyses
court review of, 42, 77, 193
criticism of the TVA's, 18, 21, 55,
142–43, 178–79, 182
difficulties of, 159–60
Endangered Species Com-
mittee, considered by, 164,
178–79
land value as opportunity cost,
implications of weighing,
161–62
public works projects,
requirement for, 12–13, 35

benefit-cost analyses, *continued*
  Tellico project results contrasted
    with the TVA's, 175–76
  by the TVA, 16–18, 52, 63, 110
Bevill, Tom, 110
Biological Society of Washington,
    D.C., 82
Black, Hugo, 26, 29–31, 35
Blackmun, Harry, 1, 114, 117–18,
    123–26, 134, 173
Blanton, Ray, 162
Boalt, Robert, 134
Boeing Corporation, 17, 176
Boschung, Herbert, Jr., 95
Bowman House, 53
Brandeis, Louis D., 25–27, 33
Breaux, John, 166
Brennan, William J., Jr., 114, 116,
    118–19, 123, 125–26, 189
Burger, Warren
  appropriation acts as amendments
    to substantive legislation,
    argument for, 195–96
  majority opinion, 1, 3, 123–34,
    188
  writ of certiorari, position on
    petition for, 114, 117–18
Butler, Pierce, 27

*Calvert Cliffs' Coordinating
    Committee v. Atomic Energy
    Commission*, 40, 44, 67
Cannon, Howard, 166
Cardozo, Benjamin, 25
Carroll, Joseph, 73
Carter, Jimmy
  appointment to the Endangered
    Species Committee made by,
    162
  election of, position of solicitor
    general temporarily vacant
    following, 113

signing of the appropriation act
    including the Tellico
    exemption, 142, 156, 166–67,
    172, 174, 192
TVA-Interior joint study, inquiry
    initiating, 157
TVA v. Hill, the government's
    position in, 119
Celebrezze, Anthony, 102–7
Chandler, William, 180
Cherokees
  limited protection available for
    sacred sites of, 192
  removal of by Andrew Jackson,
    14, 20
  village sites in the valley of the
    lower Little Tennessee River,
    14, 20, 186
  See also Eastern Band of the
    Cherokee Indians
Chilhowee Dam, 14, 19, 63
Churchill, Milo A., 74
Clean Air Act of 1970, 36
Clebsch, Edward, 57, 73
Clinch River, 11
Cohen, Donald S., 90–91, 120,
    172
Cole, William E., 74
Columbia Dam, 183
condemnation power. *See* eminent
    domain; "large take" policy
Congleton, Joseph P., 82
Congress, U.S.
  appropriations for the Tellico
    Dam project (*see*
    appropriations for the Tellico
    Dam project)
  authorization and appropriation
    procedures, the TVA and,
    9–10
  environmental legislation of the
    1970s, 36–37 (*see also*

Endangered SpeciesAct of
1973; National Environmental
Policy Act of 1970)
hydroelectric development in the
Muscle Shoals area,
authorization of, 7–8
power of over navigable
waterways, 28
Tellico Dam project, initial
support for, 20–21
Tellico Dam project, overriding
the court's injunction
regarding (*see*congressional
action to complete the Tellico
project)
See also House of Representatives,
U.S.; Senate, U.S.
congressional action to complete
the Tellico project, 5, 141–42,
173–74
Endangered Species Committee,
consideration of exemption for
Tellico,160–65
exemptions from Section 7,
amendment authorizing, 141,
145–57
the GAO review of the project,
142–43
Sixth Circuit injunction,
TVA request following,
108–11
specific exemption for the Tellico
Dam, proposal and enactment
of, 148–51, 165–67
conservatives
environmentalists, opposition to,
183
TVA v. Hill, reaction to, 3–4
Consolidated Edison, 32
Coolidge, Calvin, 8
Council on Environmental Quality,
38–41, 51, 61–62, 68

courts
of appeals (*see* courts of appeals)
condemnation proceedings
initiated by the TVA in, 22
district (*see* district courts)
environmental challenges to
development projects,
changing legal landscape for,
23, 32–34, 36
judicial review of administrative
action, 33–34, 192–93
NEPA requirements, decisions
regarding, 39–44
Supreme Court (*see* Supreme
Court, U.S.)
See also lawsuits/litigation
courts of appeals
District of Columbia Circuit,
*Calvert Cliffs' Coordinating
Committee v. Atomic Energy
Commission,* 40
Second Circuit, decision
supporting environmental
concerns, 32
Fifth Circuit, sandhill crane case,
47–48, 104
Sixth Circuit, appeal of decision
in *EDF I,* 65–71
Sixth Circuit, appeal of decision
in *EDF II,* 78–79
Sixth Circuit, rejection of
Cherokees' claim of
constitutional violation,
167
Sixth Circuit, the snail darter case
appeal and injunction, 1,
101–107, 140
Eighth Circuit, Gilham Dam
case, 43–44
Eighth Circuit, Indiana bat case,
49
Criley, Walter, 73

critical habitat
  administrative definition of, 47
  court decisions regarding in pre-
    Tellico cases, 47–49
  designation of the Little
    Tennessee River as, 82–83,
    91–93
  TVA petition to eliminate
    designation of the Little
    Tennessee River as, 108
Cross-Florida Barge Canal, 41–42,
    69
Culver, John, 145, 147, 166

Davis, Robert K., 163
Defense, U.S. Department of,
    197–98
Dingell, John, 129–30, 150
district courts
  condemnation proceedings in, 22
  *Environmental Defense Fund v.
    TVA (EDF I)*, 56–62
  *Environmental Defense Fund v.
    TVA (EDF II)*, 71, 73–78
  rejection of Cherokees' claim of
    constitutional violation, 167
  the snail darter case (*see* snail
    darter case)
  valuation of property acquired
    through condemnation, 36
Dole, Robert, 166
Dougherty, W. P. Boone, 91, 120
Douglas, William O., 19, 26–27,
    33
Duck River project, 66, 183
Duncan, John
  amendment providing exemption
    for the Tellico Dam, proposal
    of, 148–50, 165, 173, 180,
    192
  consideration of alternatives,
    opposition to, 158

Endangered Species Committee
  public hearing, comments at,
    161
  GAO review of the Tellico
    project, suggestion of, 142
  revision of the Endangered
    Species Act, testimony
    favoring, 144
  TVA "gag order," response to,
    160
Dunn, Winnfield, 56, 60
Durenberger, David, 166
Dworkin, Ronald, 3, 183

Eastern Band of the Cherokee
    Indians, 19–20, 112, 121, 142,
    167. *See also* Cherokees
East Tennessee Development
    District, 60
East Tennessee Valley Landowners
    Association, 121
economic development
  authorization of the TVA to
    promote, 9–10
  benefit-cost ratio of the Tellico
    Dam, as key element of, 16–18
  claims for by the TVA, 51–54,
    62–63, 65, 110
  land enhancement (*see* land
    enhancement)
  "large take" policy and (*see* "large
    take" policy)
  model cities and, 11
  as "new mission" of the TVA,
    13–14, 170, 174, 183–84
  recreational use (*see* recreational
    use)
  results of the Tellico Dam
    project, 175–77
  TVA's contribution to,
    questioning of, 180
  See also benefit-cost analyses

environment, the, *continued*
  implications for described in the
    TVA's final impact statement,
    64–65
  legal protection of, 3 (*see also*
    Endangered Species Act of
    1973)
  political polarization regarding,
    183
  regulatory statutes protecting, 36
  results of the Tellico Dam project
    for, 177, 186–87
Environmental Defense Fund, 36,
    40–41, 50, 55
*Environmental Defense Fund v. TVA
    (EDF I)*, 56–62, 66
*Environmental Defense Fund v. TVA
    (EDF II)*, 71, 73–79
environmental impact statements
  court decisions prior to the Tellico
    litigation regarding, 39–43
  draft statement by the TVA for
    the Tellico Dam project,
    51–55, 59–60
  final statement by the TVA for
    the Tellico Dam project,
    62–65, 73–79
  guidelines for satisfying the
    requirement for, 39, 41
  requirement for in NEPA, 36,
    38–39, 66–67
  Tellico Dam project, TVA denial
    of requirement for, 50–51,
    61–62, 67–69
  See also National Environmental
    Policy Act of 1970; NEPA
    litigation
environmentalists
  conservative opposition to, 183
  environmental impact statement
    requirements, hopes for, 40–42
  TVA v. Hill, reaction to, 3

See also opponents of the Tellico
    Dam project
environmental law
  decisions enforcing NEPA, 39–44
    (*see also* NEPA litigation)
  impact of *TVA v. Hill*, 5–6, 170,
    190–97
  legal landscape for, changes of
    the 1960s and 1970s on, 23,
    32–34, 36
  litigation under the Endangered
    Species Act (*see* Endangered
    Species Act of 1973; snail
    darter case; *TVA v. Hill*)
  polarized debate over, 3–4
Etnier, David
  amendment of the Endangered
    Species Act, participation in
    hearings considering, 144
  discovery of additional
    populations of the snail darter,
    168
  discovery of the snail darter,
    80–81, 85, 171–72, 175
  Endangered Species Committee
    public hearing, comments at,
    161
  *Environmental Defense Fund v.
    TVA (EDF I)*, testimony in, 57,
    171
  the snail darter case, testimony
    in, 94
  snail darters, current status of,
    184
  snail darter transplantation,
    skepticism regarding, 175
  TVA's final impact statement,
    reference to in, 63
Evins, Joe, 21, 71–72

Federal Power Act, 33
Federal Power Commission, 32

Marshall, Thurgood, 114, 116, 123–26, 173
Mathias, Charles McCurdy, Jr., 166
McCall, Nellie, 168
McCree, Wade Hampton, Jr., 67–71, 102, 107, 113, 121, 124
McNutt, Charles, 57
McReynolds, James C., 24, 27
Meramec Park Lake Dam, 48–49
Mineral King Mountain, 34, 41
Mississippi sandhill crane, 47
model cities
    failures of, 175–76
    Norris, Tennessee, 11, 176
    Timberlake, 16–17, 53, 63
Morgan, Arthur E., 5, 10–11
Morgan, Harcourt, 10–11
Moser, Thomas Burel, 50, 168
Muscle Shoals, Alabama, 7–9. *See also* Wilson Dam
Muscle Shoals Corporation, 8
Muskie, Edmund F., 166
Myers, John T., 110

National Defense Act of 1916, 7
National Environmental Policy Act of 1970 (NEPA), 37–39
    enforcement of, federal court rulings regarding, 39–44
    environmental impact statement required of federal agencies, 36, 38–39
    legal landscape for environmental law, part of changing, 23
    litigation opposing the Tellico Dam under (*see* NEPA litigation)
    retroactive enforcement of impact statement requirement, 41–43, 50–51, 61–62, 67–69
National Labor Relations Act, 26
National Park Service, 29, 143

National Resources Defense Council, 112
Navy, U.S., 190
Nelson, Gaylord, 148
NEPA. *See* National Environmental Policy Act of 1970
NEPA litigation
    appeal of decision in *EDF I*, 65–71
    appeal of decision in *EDF II*, 78–79
    dissolution of the injunction, decision supporting (*EDF II*), 75–78
    dissolution of the injunction, lawsuit seeking (*EDF II*), 71, 73–75
    injunction halting work on the dam, issuance of and opinion supporting (*EDF I*), 58–62
    injunction halting work on the dam, lawsuit seeking (*EDF I*), 55–58
Nixon, Richard, 41, 50
Norris, George, 8
Norris, Tennessee, 11, 176
Norris Dam, 11, 24, 176
nuclear power plants, 12

Oakes, James L., 101
Office of Management and Budget, 143
opponents of the Tellico Dam project
    changes in, 179–81
    Cherokees, 19–20 (*see also* Cherokees)
    complexities encountered by, 172–74
    early losses in the political/legislative arena, 20–22